Diverse Pedagogies of Place

Diverse Pedagogies of Place presents eight original place-responsive pedagogies that address a question of paramount importance in today's world: how do we educate the next generation of students to confront the challenges of global climate change and the ongoing degradation of natural environments? Each place-responsive pedagogy is the result of innovative environmental educators' long-term engagement with particular places and demonstrates that personal connectedness is crucial to effective environmental education.

Professional learning and teacher collaboration is an important theme throughout the book, and the editors discuss how teachers could adapt the learning activities and teaching strategies found in the book in order to create their own place-responsive pedagogies. Each case study provides a rich account of how students can learn to be attentive and draws upon a common analytical framework derived from recent theorisation of place that highlights the centrality of stories-in-place, embodiment, and contestation. The authors present detailed and persuasive evidence that place-responsive pedagogies enable students to construct their own identities, as well as develop commitments and a deeper knowledge of the environments that surround them.

A work of international relevance, *Diverse Pedagogies of Place* will appeal to academics, researchers and postgraduate students in the fields of environmental education and sustainability, place-based education, outdoor learning, professional learning and teacher development, as well as policymakers and environmental educators.

Peter Renshaw (PhD) is Professor of Education at the University of Queensland, Australia. His research draws on sociocultural theory to address issues of pedagogy, social justice and inclusion. In the past decade he has collaborated with Ron Tooth to research environmental education and place-responsive pedagogies. He is Senior Editor of the Routledge/AARE book series *Local/Global Issues in Education*.

Ron Tooth (PhD) is Honorary Associate Professor at the University of Queensland, Australia, and founding principal of the Pullenvale Environmental Education Centre, Australia. His experience at the Pullenvale Environmental Education Centre has given him an extended history of professional engagement with teachers and students. He has also worked as a consultant for local councils and schools to lead the design of environmental programs based on a narrative pedagogy called *Storythread*.

Routledge Research in Education

For a complete list of titles in this series, please visit www.routledge.com

This series aims to present the latest research from across the field of education. It is not confined to any particular area or school of thought and seeks to provide coverage of a broad range of topics, theories and issues from around the world.

Recent titles in the series include:

Transnationalism, Education and Empowerment
The Latent Legacies of Empire
Niranjan Casinader

Reflective Practice
Voices from the Field
Edited by Roger Barnard and Jonathon Ryan

Citizenship Education in the United States
A Historical Perspective
Iftikhar Ahmad

Transformative Learning and Teaching in Physical Education
Edited by Malcolm Thorburn

Teaching Young Learners in a Superdiverse World
Multimodal Approaches and Perspectives
Edited by Heather Lotherington and Cheryl Paige

History, Theory and Practice of Philosophy for Children
International Perspectives
Edited by Saeed Naji and Rosnani Hashim

Teacher Professional Knowledge and Development for Reflective and Inclusive Practices
Edited by Ismail Hussein Amzat and Nena P. Valdez

Diverse Pedagogies of Place

Educating Students in and for Local and Global Environments

Edited by Peter Renshaw and Ron Tooth

LONDON AND NEW YORK

First published 2018
by Routledge

2 Park Square, Milton Park, Abingdon, Oxfordshire OX14 4RN
52 Vanderbilt Avenue, New York, NY 10017

Routledge is an imprint of the Taylor & Francis Group, an informa business

First issued in paperback 2018

British Library Cataloguing-in-Publication Data
A catalogue record for this book is available from the British Library

Library of Congress Cataloging-in-Publication Data
A catalog record for this book has been requested

ISBN: 978-1-138-90669-3 (hbk)
ISBN: 978-0-367-19706-3 (pbk)

Typeset in Galliard
by Apex CoVantage, LLC

For our grandchildren and future generations across the globe: Archie Rennie, Ben Tooth, Eamon McCue, Eddie Grist, Eddie Rigney, Eva Rennie, Gabriel McCue, Jonnie Tooth, Sam Tooth, Timothy Tooth, William McCue, and William Tooth.

Contents

Figures

Acknowledgements

We acknowledge the traditional owners and custodians of the land where the research for this volume was conducted. The notion of place-responsiveness is attuned to the cultures and values that characterise Indigenous Australians. A particular Indigenous practice, *dadirri*, was deployed by a number of authors in this volume to educate children about quiet attentiveness and deep respect for place. We acknowledge the generosity of Miriam-Rose Ungunmerr-Baumann and the Ngangikurungkurr people from the Daly River region of the Northern Territory for sharing this practice with us and the wider community. We thank the students and teachers who participated in the research and allowed us to interview them about their experiences during the environmental education programs. We would also like to thank Liz Fynes-Clinton and David Jackson who conducted observations and interviews with the environmental educators as part of our longer-term research into environmental education. We thank the Queensland Department of Education and the staff of each of the state-run Environmental Education Centres for their support and participation. Finally, we thank Ruth Leach for her editorial expertise and enthusiasm for the book, which made the final stages of producing the volume an unexpected joy.

Contributors

Mark Cridland is Principal of the Tallebudgera Outdoor Education School, Queensland, Australia. Mark was also Principal of Barambah Environmental Education Centre for two decades and recently Principal of Moreton Bay Environmental Education Centre for two years.

Belinda Daly was a long-term teacher at Moreton Bay Environmental Education Centre, Queensland, Australia. She recently returned to live in Victoria.

Agatha Gambino is a teacher at Bunyaville Environmental Education Centre, Queensland, Australia.

Sue Gibson is Principal of the Barambah Environmental Education Centre, Queensland, Australia.

Louka Lazaredes was a teacher at the Paluma Environmental Education Centre, Queensland, Australia. In 2017 he enrolled in a postgraduate diploma in theology and religion at Oxford University, UK.

Mary-Ann Pattison is Principal of Nudgee Beach Environmental Education Centre, Queensland, Australia.

Peter Renshaw (PhD) is Professor of Education at The University of Queensland, Queensland, Australia.

Noeleen Rowntree is Principal of the Bunyaville Environmental Education Centre, Queensland, Australia.

Gregory A. Smith (PhD) is Professor at the Lewis and Clark Graduate School of Education and Counseling, Portland, Oregon, USA.

Robert B. Stevenson (PhD) is Adjunct Professor at the James Cook University of North Queensland (JCU), Australia. Until mid-2017 he was Director of the Centre for Research and Innovation in Sustainability Education at JCU.

Ron Tooth (PhD) is Honorary Associate Professor at the University of Queensland and Principal of the Pullenvale Environmental Education Centre, Queensland, Australia.

Linda Venn, before her recent retirement in 2016, was Principal of the Paluma Environmental Education Centre, Queensland, Australia.

1 Diverse place-responsive pedagogies

Historical, professional and theoretical threads

Peter Renshaw and Ron Tooth

Introduction

Diverse Pedagogies of Place is an exploration of the pedagogical possibilities of place. It is the culmination of the creative work of a generation of environmental educators at six of the environmental education centres across Queensland, Australia. The distinctive place-responsive pedagogies designed by these educators drew upon the cultural and material affordances of the environmental education centres at which they worked. In the list below we encapsulate the distinctive pedagogical possibilities in each of the places, and we invite you, the reader, to delve into these chapters to further understand how place can become imbued with "advocacy" or "sacredness" or "slow time":

Ch 2: place as *advocacy*
Ch 3: place as *story*
Ch 4: place as *slow time*
Ch 5: place as *walking*
Ch 6: place as *sacred*
Ch 7: place as *shifting sands*
Ch 8: place as *the edge*

Diverse Pedagogies of Place contributes to the scholarship on pedagogies of place (Gruenewald, 2003; Smith & Sobel, 2010; Somerville, 2010; Wattchow & Brown, 2011; Mannion, Fenwick, & Lynch, 2013; Greenwood, 2014; Stevenson Brody, Dillon & Wals, 2014) by documenting place-responsive pedagogies designed by committed environmental educators who were acutely aware of the material and cultural affordances at each of their centres. The location of the environmental education centres varied from coastal intertidal zones and mangrove forests to a cloud rainforest and urban-fringe forest remnants. The contrasting materiality of the locations is vital to the *diversity* of pedagogies that were created. However, it was through the process of writing this volume in a collaborative co-authoring style that these environmental educators were able to articulate the distinctive aspects of their place-responsive pedagogies and realise how the material affordances of specific places had been crucial. Their journeys into distinctive place-responsive pedagogies are at the heart of this volume.

Our preferred term, *place-responsive pedagogies*, has similarities to place-conscious education as elaborated by Greenwood (2014) and draws on place-responsive pedagogy as defined by Mannion, Fenwick, and Lynch (2013) and Wattchow and Brown (2011). Greenwood (2014) proposed that personal identities and cultural practices derive from a deep consciousness of the land where we live. Like Greenwood we want to contribute to a place-conscious pedagogy that is "committed to care for land and people, locally and globally" (Greenwood, 2014, p. 93). Being place-conscious is to understand the cultural and material complexity of place and the ethical responsibility we share to care for local places in order to address global challenges. There is considerable overlap as well with the model proposed by Wattchow and Brown (2011) who identified four signposts for a place-responsive pedagogy: being attentive in the place, storying place, spending time apprenticed in place, and representing and communicating place experiences (Wattchow & Brown, 2011, p. 182). These signposts are equally applicable to the place-responsive pedagogies that are described in this volume.

Our approach is similar also to place-responsive pedagogy described by Mannion and colleagues (Mannion, Fenwick, & Lynch, 2013; Mannion & Lynch, 2016) who documented the process of teachers becoming sensitive to place as they designed curriculum and taught students by engaging with a particular environment. Teachers who are place-responsive draw upon their own deep knowledge of the place and adapt with spontaneity to the contingencies of events in the place itself. Place-responsive pedagogy relies on a relational ontology of place-making through the intermingling of "learners, places, stories and all kinds of entities" (Mannion & Lynch, 2016, p. 90). Mannion and Lynch (2016) distinguished three levels of place-responsiveness: place ambiguity, where teachers treat the place as simply the staging ground for activities; place sensitivity, where teachers show some awareness of the features of place related to their curriculum and pedagogical goals; and place essential, where the features of place are essential for the activities that are designed to engage students in deep learning about place. Our use of place-responsive pedagogies is similar to the third type of place-responsiveness described by Mannion and Lynch (2016). We decided on the term *place-responsive pedagogies* to foreground the heightened sensitivity and specific responsiveness of the educators to the distinctive pedagogical affordances of their centres. Their responsiveness emerged and flourished through prolonged experience in place as they designed and redesigned environmental education programs for students. It also was heightened through interactions with students and their teachers whose unexpected responses to moments during the excursions revealed new pedagogical possibilities to the educators. *Responsiveness* conveys a heightened consciousness and specific responsiveness to place that captures the pedagogical journeys that are reported in this volume.

The authors in this volume were not always concerned with articulating their responsiveness to place or publishing their pedagogical practices. Much of their energy was devoted to establishing their environmental education centres, dealing with the everyday demands of developing pedagogies and programs, and satisfying the expectations of administrators and clientele. Their engagement in research was instigated initially by an Australian Research Council Linkage project conducted by Ballantyne and Packer (2006–2008) who identified a set of experiential pedagogical practices deployed at the centres, summarised as the *fifth pedagogy*. We describe key aspects of the fifth pedagogy further below. To understand how these environmental education centres became the focus of research interest, it is important to trace the history of the establishment and staffing of the centres. In doing so, we foreground particular writers, theorists and environmental advocates who influenced the pedagogies at the centres.

This chapter begins, therefore, with a brief overview of the origin of the centres – locating them in time and space. We suggest that from the very beginning the environmental education centres were positioned as peripheral rather than central to the education system across Queensland, and that such marginality created an opportunity to experiment and try out ideas that might have been frowned upon within the mainstream. Second, as mentioned, we identify particular theorists and writers who influenced the development of the pedagogies at the centres. These influences were both local, from within the Australian environmental education community, and international. The international scholars and advocates came to Australia to present workshops or to keynote conferences and some of them visited the environmental education centres. Third, we review scholarship regarding the notion of *place* (Tuan, 1979) and propose along with Somerville that place is a productive pedagogical framework because it creates a way of considering simultaneously the materiality of place, its "grounded physical reality" (Somerville, 2010, p. 330), along with the diverse representations of place by people who have given it various meanings through their experiences, aspirations and practices (Tuan, 1979). A deep interest in the local is inherent in the place-responsive pedagogies designed at each of the environmental education centres. But no place is totally isolated, so the pedagogical possibilities of different places must be theorised in terms of relational connectedness across time and space. To construct this connected notion of place we draw upon Massey (2005) and Somerville (2010) to propose that places are not bounded and stable but continually constructed through relational activities between people across time and space. Massey (2005) usefully considers place as an unfolding event with overlapping and intersecting stories. Place is "a simultaneity of stories so far" (Massey, 2005, p. 9). "So far" conveys openness to both the past and the future, and frames place as a site of ongoing negotiation between related unfolding and perhaps incompatible stories. In recognising the contested aspect of place, we move beyond considering environmental education as concerned narrowly with the study of ecology and nature. The relationship between humans and the "more-than-human world" (Abram, 1997) requires consideration of incompatible interests that intersect in place. In this sense the approach adopted here draws upon Gruenewald's (2003) critical place-based pedagogy.

This notion of place as unfinished stories of negotiation and contest has particular relevance to the history of each centre and their location on Indigenous land. We acknowledge the on-going custodianship of Indigenous people to the country described in each chapter. The on-going Indigenous relationship with country provides a rich pedagogical affordance for exploring the meaning and significance of place across time and recognising contested ontologies. Indigenous custodians "belong to country" and take their "being" from country, whereas the majority of the students who come to the environmental education centres bring a western notion of place as a transferable asset (property) that belongs privately to someone. The stories of Indigenous custodianship written across millennia into the land challenge this dominant commodified view of place and open up novel ways for students to understand themselves and others as inherently related to place, rather than just passing through, or using place for instrumentalist goals such as exercise or recreation (Wattchow & Brown, 2011).

In addition to the Indigenous custodianship of the country where the environmental centres were established, the sensitivity of the authors (environmental educators) to their places is crucial to document because they are the key mediators for students of the learning possibilities imbued in each place. It is an interesting fact that many of the authors in this volume spent their childhoods in close proximity to the environmental education centres where they became leaders in adulthood. It's not just that they *know* something about the place. They have developed visceral and embodied relationships to the place that necessarily inform the way they engage with students and teachers who come on excursions to the centres. These embodied ways of knowing place are vividly described by each of the authors in their chapters. However, stories in place are not just human accounts of meaning-making. The rocks and trees and animals and water and soil and sand have stories – stories of materiality also enter into the pedagogies designed at each place. Attentiveness to things "out there", to the material reality of the place, is a key part of the pedagogies described in this volume.

To summarise, the diverse place-responsive pedagogies described in this volume are positioned at the intersection of key aspects of place: first the materiality of the place itself, the unique patterning of living and non-living features of place; second, the cultural meanings that have been storied into the place across time by Indigenous and non-Indigenous people including the educators at each centre; third, the agency of teachers and students, whose purposes and goals selectively foreground and background what can be experienced and learned in place. The pedagogies described here reveal the unique affordances of particular places for learning *in*, *about* and *for* the environment.

Locating the centres in time/place

Surplus to need

The environmental education centres (EEC) are located either in the vicinity of Brisbane (Pullenvale EEC, Bunyaville EEC, Moreton Bay EEC and Nudgee Beach EEC), or in the case of Barambah EEC 160 kilometres north of Brisbane, while Paluma EEC is located in tropical North Queensland, 1200 kilometres north of Brisbane. They are part of a network of environmental education centres (currently 24 centres) that were established across Queensland from the mid-1970s through the mid-1980s by the coincidence of various circumstances in the State bureaucracy, the agency and personal commitments of the environmental educators, and moments of serendipity. A key administrator in the Queensland Department of Education (Agricultural Branch), Jack Althaus, attended a UNESCO conference in 1971 on *Man and the Biosphere*, and he returned with a strong commitment to extending the network of "field studies centres" (later renamed as environmental and outdoor education centres). While scant financial resources were available, Jack had many personal contacts in the bureaucracy, and he gradually pieced together a number of properties and facilities that had been classified as surplus to need. The majority of the centres were established where state schools had closed due to shifts in population. Also, the State Forestry Department closed a number of forest reserves in the 1970s and 1980s where native timber had been logged over many years. These reserves were somewhat remote and had quite good facilities including kitchens, toilets and sleeping quarters that were easily adapted to become environmental education centres. The origin of some centres as recycled and re-used forestry facilities that were "surplus to need" is wonderfully appropriate for the pedagogies of place that were created there in the decades that followed. It is a paradoxical and sobering fact that centres were established in forests only after the natural resources had been fully exploited and the forest remnants were regarded as economically unviable. The centres were never central or particularly important to policymakers, but were initiated and thrived on the margins and with left-overs, supported surreptitiously by administrators such as Jack Althaus. When Jack retired in the early 1990s, Lee Williams maintained the initial enthusiasm and took leadership of the environmental education centres.

Officers in charge

Looking back, it was an advantage that the educators were given the ambiguous designation as "officers in charge of field studies centres" with quite open-ended agendas. The assembled group of environmental educators shared an idealism and enthusiasm that was crucial in the creation of different pedagogies of place. Since there was no blue-print for how a centre should be conducted and no prescribed curriculum or approach, the pedagogies of place that arose in the centres were grass roots efforts by the young educators to devise a set of practices that worked in their local settings. It was a very different era in education where teachers' professional judgements were more highly valued (Biesta, 2015). The marginalized positioning of the centres actually increased the professional discretion of the young educators to experiment and attempt different approaches.

Learn by doing

So, whilst the educators at the centres were still exploring approaches in the mid-1970s and early 1980s, they were given the green light to be adventurous in trying different approaches that might work for them in their setting. There was no expectation that centres would adopt a common pedagogy or set of practices. If there was a directive from above, it was inspired by the phrase "learn by doing" that had resonance with Dewey's progressive approach to experiential education (Dewey, 1938). There was a shared belief that the answers for each centre lay within the individual settings and that ideas should be continually refined in practice. Right from the beginning there was a strong emphasis on action research as the way to forge place-responsive practices. The belief in professional knowledge-making in place through action research was further strengthened at this time by Australian researchers such as Stephen Kemmis (1980; Carr & Kemmis, 1983) and Ian Robottom (1987) whose scholarship had raised the profile and status of collaborative and action-oriented inquiry for educational change.

Professional and personal identities

Personal relationships were implicated in the design of the diverse pedagogies of place. The newly appointed officers in charge formed a close-knit community where the personal and professional were integrated. Each year and sometimes twice a year, they came together across a few days to share their latest practices, insights and challenges. The sharing was direct and practical, its tone summed-up in the focus question, "so, what do *you* do?" There was genuine interest in these sessions because, whilst the pedagogies were developing distinctly in each centre, there was also a strong sense of being part of a common project where learning from each other was important. These meetings forged close friendships and collaborations within the network and created the sense of a tight-knit group unified in the belief that their professional work was critically important for raising consciousness amongst students and the community about ecological thinking and environmental protection and sustainability. In the early years these gatherings were like combined professional and family events. Early mornings could be spent bird watching, bushwalking, investigating the creeks and lakes and enjoying the aesthetic beauty of the particular meeting place at one of the centres. During the day there would presentations, talks and activities where individuals and teams modelled and shared their pedagogy. The nights would be spent singing around a campfire and sharing social time together. The divide between the "the personal" and "the professional" disappeared at these meetings as the group worked, played and lived together in ways that expressed their commitment to environmental education. For many there was a sense of privilege in being able to contribute to a project that was larger than individual careers or personal aspirations and could be seen globally as a broad environmental movement inspired by writers such as Wendell Berry (1970), Rachel Carson (1962) and Henry Thoreau (1906).

Advocacy in the community

Educators interested in deploying a place-responsive pedagogy are inevitably confronted by the political, as Gruenewald (2003) noted in his seminal article on critical place-based pedagogy, "place + people = politics" (p. 3). While the centres were not overtly political, the "officers in charge" enabled local community organisations to use the facilities at the centres for regular meetings. These included organisations related to conservation and farming, and umbrella groups such as the National Council of Women of Queensland, soroptimists and others. Through these associations the "officers in charge" built extensive community networks and close relationships with local citizens. They often became de facto guardians of the natural environments surrounding their centres. At times, they provided expert advice to community groups that were attempting to conserve a local landscape. At other times, they became a conduit for local citizens to share their environmental knowledge and commitments with students. For example, at the Pullenvale Environmental Education Centre, Ron Tooth worked closely with Edith Smith and her son John whose family for three generations had protected the last remaining remnant of the original dry-vine rainforest on the western edge of Brisbane at Brookfield (Moggill Creek Catchment Management Group Inc., 2016). On excursions organised by the Pullenvale Environmental Education centre, students would meet Edith at her farm. She'd walk with them up the mountain to the remnant rainforest, pointing to botanical details that she loved, and she'd tell them why her farming family decided to save the rainforest. She lobbied politicians to establish environmental covenants over the remnant forest on her land and invited children to follow her environmental ethic of caring for land. In various ways, therefore, the centres supported local conservation and education agendas. Again the positioning of the centres on the periphery – both spatially/ geographically and administratively – was important in enabling a degree of civic activism and advocacy that might have been impossible within the mainstream of the schooling system in Queensland.

Locating the centres in networks of influence

When the centres were getting established in the 1970s and 1980s the context for environmental education was vibrant in Australia. The world conservation strategy had been published in 1980, and the Australian conservation strategy was developed in 1983 with input from members of the Australian Association for Environment Education (AAEE). Prominent amongst the members of AAEE were scholars such as Peter Fensham, John Fien, Bob Stevenson, Noel Gough, Ian Robottom and Annette Gough (Greenall). As Annette Gough (2014) noted in a recent reminiscence of the 1980s, environmental issues were on the political agenda and prominent in the media; for example, issues such as the damming of the Franklin River in the Tasmanian wilderness, the commencement of the Ranger Uranium project in the Northern Territory, the declaration of Australia's first UNESCO World Heritage sites (including the tropical rainforests and the Great Barrier Reef), as well as prolonged droughts and land clearing. The growth of public concern for the environment strengthened the resolve of the educators at the centres to promote environmental awareness and action.

A number of international scholars who visited Australia from the 1980s through to the 2000s left a trace on the diverse pedagogies of place at the centres. Foremost among these scholars was Bill Stapp (1930–2001) who was the acknowledged leader of the environmental education movement from the 1960s through the 1980s. He promoted a broad view of environmental education as involving natural and man-made contexts, and encompassing ecological, political, economic, technological, social, legislative, cultural and aesthetic dimensions (Stapp, 1970; Gough, 2001, p. 19). He visited Australia a number of times from the early 1980s through 1990, and in fact visited the centres to provide professional development to the newly appointed principals. He promoted the idea of environmental encounters that placed children in an active role not only to investigate issues in the environment such as water quality and pollution, but also to take action to change the situation. The emphasis on inquiry *and* action remained an important aspect of the pedagogies of place that emerged in the different centres. The broadness of Stapp's vision of environmental education supported the diversity of emphases and approaches that emerged in different centres.

Another influence was Clifford E. Knapp (1972; 1992) who offered to the centres his approach based on humanizing environmental education. First, Knapp foregrounded the notion of *place* per se. *Place* resonated with the principals at the centres because each had walked into a new setting that they needed to appreciate and explore in order to develop their educational programs. Paying attention to place and its affordances became a key part of the diverse pedagogies that emerged in the centres. Second, Knapp had promoted the notion of being in solitude in nature, spending time there alone in silence to develop a new sense of awareness and calmness. This practice of silent awareness in nature and attentiveness to place was taken up by a number of the centres as a key practice in their place-responsive pedagogy. John Cornell, author of *Sharing nature with children: The classic parents' & teachers' nature awareness guidebook* (1979), visited Queensland in the 1990s and presented workshops at the Bunyaville EEC on his experiential and joyful approach to environmental education that was based on listening to and observing children and supporting their love of being in natural places.

Steve Van Matre (1990) who founded the *Earth Education* movement positioned students as "earth keepers" and offered the centres his explicit programmatic approach based on understanding the ecological systems of the planet, cultivating feelings of connection to the natural world and taking action to reduce human impact on ecosystems. Van Matre's approach that combined ecological knowledge, feelings, choices, actions and broader communication resonated with the centres. A key influence on the centres after 2000 was Mitchell Thomashow (1995; 2002) who was the invited keynote at the Australian Association for Environmental Education conference in 2002. Thomashow spoke about the ecological self and the importance of children's early formative experiences in nature and experiential place-based meditations. His approach was guided by notions of praxis and the cultivation of personal responsibility for everyday consumption and ways of living. Rather than detached knowledge of the environment, he emphasised the cultivation of an ecological self as the basis for working more effectively in the community. The influence of Thomashow on the educators at the centres was to strengthen their existing emphases on emotional experiences in place, and the importance of cultivating an ecological self. The focus on "self" reflected a broader shift in educational research to ontological issues (as distinct from issues of epistemology) where students' agency and identity were foregrounded as goals in education (Biesta, 2007; 2015). It wasn't just what one knew (epistemology) and could do (skills) but who one was, and was becoming, that seemed crucial to consider.

Locating the centres pedagogically

The fifth pedagogy

By the early 2000s there was a realisation by the Queensland Department of Education that the centres were sites of innovation and this led to interest from scholars such as Ballantyne and Packer who researched the practices at a number of the environmental education centres in 2005 and 2006 and later published the research in reports and articles (Ballantyne & Packer, 2008; 2009). Their research provides a snapshot of how the pedagogies of place had developed across the decades since the centres were established. The timing of the research project in 2005–2006 coincided with considerable interest in the notion of *Productive Pedagogies* (Lingard, Hayes, & Mills, 2003). *Productive Pedagogies* was an extension of *Authentic Pedagogies* described by Newmann, Marks, and Gamoran (1996) as pedagogies that engaged marginalised students in high quality learning. The four dimensions of *Productive Pedagogies* included: *Intellectual Quality*, such as promoting higher-order thinking and deep knowledge; *Connectedness*, such as making links with events outside the classroom and drawing upon students' existing knowledge; *Social Support*, such as encouraging student input and providing a safe and positive classroom environment; *Valuing Diversity and Active Citizenship*, such as drawing on alternative ways of teaching for example, narrative approaches, and highlighting the implications of classroom learning for civic engagement. Some aspects of *Productive Pedagogies* were relevant to the pedagogies at the centres, for example, civic engagement and linking to events outside the classroom. But Ballantyne and Packer (2009) summarised the distinctive pedagogies at the centres as a *fifth pedagogy* which suggested another whole dimension to teaching that is routinely overlooked in schools – namely teaching and learning through direct experience in places beyond the classroom.

Key aspects of the fifth pedagogy

Ballantyne and Packer (2009), identified five key aspects of the *fifth pedagogy* from their observations at the centres and interviews with students and teachers. First, students *learn by doing* and through active involvement in hands-on exploration and investigation. Second, students *learn by being in the environment* where they are encouraged to experience and appreciate the special characteristics of the natural environment. Third, students *learn by addressing* authentic tasks that are designed in each centre. Fourth, students *learn from sensory engagement* where they are provided with opportunities to use their five senses to explore the environment. Fifth, students *learn in their own context* (backyard) by being encouraged to explore and investigate local problems and issues. Both students and classroom teachers identified these five components as those that had the greatest impact on student learning.

Types of programs

The centres were found to offer three different types of programs (Ballantyne & Packer, 2008). First, programs for short-term experiences at the centres had been developed following the model of *destination excursions*. These short-term programs included prior preparation at the school where teachers promoted students' knowledge and interest in the excursion. These preparatory activities could extend across a number of weeks and included learning about the ecology, flora and fauna of the place and learning something about the history of the place and the people, including Indigenous custodians, who had been significant in that history. Follow-up activities included writing accounts of the excursion based on the artefacts and images they created during the day and sharing the experiences with other classes, parents and community members. Second, longer-term *partnership programs* had been developed between some centres and individual schools or clusters of schools where students were more regularly involved in programs. Third, the centres were also found to have taken on a broader professional development role with teachers in schools by modelling place-responsive pedagogy and sustainable practices and values. The programs provided by the centres were a point of entry for leveraging positive change towards sustainable practices and values within the whole school community.

Teachers' local knowledge

The mediating role of the educators at the centres, particularly their intimate knowledge of specific local environments, was noted by Ballantyne and Packer (2008; 2009) and remains a key aspect of the diverse pedagogies of place documented in this volume. When students and teachers perceived the educators at the centres to have both knowledge of and a passion for the *place*, it increased their engagement and interest in learning more (Ballantyne & Packer, 2008). As the chapters of this volume demonstrate, place-responsive pedagogies require that educators have an intimate knowledge of the ecology and the history of the place, and this includes an acute awareness of the pedagogical affordances of specific sites within the centre (forest or creek or tree or track). A detached scientific and historical knowledge base is insufficient; it is the intricate and intimate knowledge of the teachers and the stories they can tell about "this creek" or "that stand of trees" or "the water in that pond" that engages students more deeply in learning.

Reflective response

Of the different teaching strategies documented by Ballantyne and Packer (2008; 2009), *reflective response* stood out as producing the most memorable learning outcomes as reported by students, influencing their knowledge, attitudes and behaviour. *Reflective response* provided students with opportunities to make new connections between discrete experiences on the excursion and to consider the implications of these experiences for their future. It was particularly important in moving students towards changes in their behaviour after the program had finished. *Reflective response* was emphasised particularly at two centres, Pullenvale (see chapters 2 and 3) and Bunyaville (see chapter 4), where the principals, Ron Tooth and Noeleen Rowntree, deployed quiet attentiveness and reflection on experiences to assist students to transfer their learning from the excursion per se to other contexts in their lives.

Another insight from Ballantyne and Packer's work is that the short-term excursions to the centres were most beneficial for students when teachers connected experiences at the centres with follow-up classroom activities. In particular, teachers mentioned the importance of post-visit activities in reinforcing and deconstructing what students had seen and experienced in the field. Even when the school was some distance from the centre, teachers reported that the skills and approaches learned during the excursion could be applied in the local area, and this enabled students to realise the local relevance of their new understandings and feelings.

In concluding this section on locating the centres in time/space and pedagogically, we recall that the centres began somewhat accidentally and remained peripheral during almost two decades of professional engagement by the network of environmental educators. The research of Ballantyne and Packer brought together key stakeholders – senior officers from the Department of Education, the research team and the principals and staff from the centres. Following the presentation of the final report in 2008 to the assembled stakeholders (Ballantyne & Packer, 2008), recognition grew in the Department of Education that something important and interesting with regard to pedagogy had been happening at the centres. Also, the serendipity of a personal circumstance for one of the Departmental Officers raised the profile of the centres with policymakers. The school-aged son of one Departmental Officer had recently been on an excursion to a centre, and it had profoundly influenced his engagement with learning at school. Prior to the excursion he had struggled with learning at school, but something about his experience during the excursion had changed his relationship with schooling and, according to his mother (the Departmental Officer), he now was progressing well at school. The hidden influence of personal experiences on policy-making cannot be underestimated, and this particular moment certainly reinforced support for the centres within the Department and raised the profile of the innovative pedagogies that had been devised at the centres across time. It was in this context that we began the current research project to articulate in more detail the diverse place-responsive pedagogies that had emerged over time at each centre.

Theorising *place* as profoundly pedagogical

Margaret Somerville's (2010) approach to place pedagogy had a significant influence on the theorising that has informed the writing of this volume. Somerville draws upon insights from Gruenewald's (2003) critical place-based pedagogy and the epistemologies and ontologies of Indigenous Australians (Cohen & Somerville, 1990) to propose a relational understanding of place and pedagogy. As Somerville (2010, p. 329) notes: "place is an enigma and challenge" that exists materially and imaginatively. In our imagination we can see beyond the immediate material features of a place to consider how it was constituted and represented in the past by other dwellers, or how it might be re-inhabited and re-imagined in the present and future through emergent stories. We can imagine how others might see and value the place, and we can tell stories of human and "more-than-human" agency that continually transform the place across time. It is through inhabiting and relating to place that we can uncover and come to know the stories written into the landscape as well as create novel relationships and stories that expand how this place might be inhabited, conceived and valued by others. Like all of the authors in this volume, Somerville (2010) has been concerned with the crucial question of how we might educate children in a globalising world to inhabit and care about their local places. The specific places that children explore on environmental excursions are remnants (like everywhere in the Anthropocene) that have been created by human and natural activity on a global and local scale. Such places cannot be constructed romantically as wilderness or purely natural but they are nonetheless inherently valuable. The pedagogical challenge is to enable students to relate to places knowingly, emotionally and aesthetically. In addressing this challenge, Somerville foregrounds processes of embodiment, storying and contesting within the contact zone.

Embodiment

Embodiment suggests that we learn through the relational activity of the body in place – through walking, touching, shaping, smelling, hearing, sensing in place. Embodiment goes beyond the positivist notion of empirical sensory experiences leading to knowledge of reality. Embodiment suggests that knowing and being are based on a dialogical interpenetration between people and place (Rose, 2002, p. 311). As Somerville notes (2010, p. 338) embodiment requires openness to the materiality of the landscape itself and its agency in shaping what we can come to know. Landscape acts on us and alters our bodies in palpable ways, inscribing a certain particular sense of knowing and being in place. If we accept an embodied notion of knowing and being, the materiality of place becomes a subject (an agent) through which we learn, and as with any dialogue with another, we need to listen and be attentive to what is being communicated. In the space between us and materiality is where dialogue takes place. It is an intimate conversation between the human subject and the more-than-human subject. Following Somerville, therefore, we propose that "place learning gives rise to a different ontology, an ontology of self-becoming-other in the space between self and a natural world, composed of humans and non-human others, animate and inanimate; animals and plants, weather, rocks, trees" (Somerville, 2010, p. 338). Pedagogies based on embodiment turn our faces outwards to the intricate and rich materiality of place (the profoundly pedagogical nature of place), as well as inwards to the necessity to be responsive and attentive to the dialogue with materiality in place. The pedagogies designed by the authors contributing to this volume reveal a practical materialist approach. They have demonstrated a heightened sensitivity to specific sites within their centres where unique kinds of learning are more likely, and they include activities that turn the attention of students outwards to the fine details and particularity of "things out there." They also physically engage students, for example, through walking the land (see chapter 5), or wading in the tidal mudflats (see chapter 7) or handling white crystals (see chapter 2). These forms of physical engagement with the materiality of place create opportunities for embodied learning.

Storying

In addition to embodiment, Somerville proposes that our relationship to place is constituted in stories. Stories create a range of possible relationships to place, for example, as a site for recreation and physical activity ("look at this place – I could ride my bike right through here"), or as a site for contemplation ("look at this place – I could sit quietly here for hours"), or as a site for scientific inquiry ("look at the ecology of this place"), and so on. Narratives in and of places are nested in larger cultural and political narratives that shape how we might come to see and understand places, for example, as an economic resource or a threat or sacred site or comfort zone. A pedagogy of place based on storying opens up a myriad of ways of relating to and understanding place. The history of a place, for example, can be researched to make visible who preceded us here and how the place has been valued, used and transformed across time. Students who come to the environmental education centres for excursions are inducted into modes for representing their experiences that draw upon ecology, biology and history as well as various forms of artistic expression. The stories of place that they create on excursions "embrace the expressions of visual artists, sculptors and poets as well as scientists, policymakers and agriculturalists" (Somerville, 2010, p. 336). In this sense, storying place offers a very open and creative way to consider what students might learn during environmental excursions. Beyond storying as episteme, stories can also be deployed as a pedagogical device to engage students actively and imaginatively in learning. Entering place through the stories of characters, whose lives and values have made a difference, transforms the way students can experience the place. Story laid over the landscape imbues the features of place with emotional significance for the students and opens up imaginative ways for them to make sense of the more-than-human world as well as reflect on the impact of human interests and values on place. This narrative form of pedagogy is explored in particular in chapter 2 and chapter 3.

Contest

Finally Somerville theorises place as a cultural contact zone of difference. Place is inevitably the site of contested stories (Massey, 2005) that arise from different agendas, epistemologies and ontologies that participants bring with them. In Australia the inalienable Indigenous custodianship of land provides an enduring storyline that challenges educators and students alike to confront stories of historical dispossession and cultural marginalisation. Students who come on excursion to different environmental education centres learn something about this Indigenous history and in some cases (see chapter 5) they engage with local elders in learning about Indigenous cultures and practices. These experiences in contested places move the students to reflect on their own cultural assumptions and shift their perspectives and values as documented in chapter 5. In programs at other environmental centres (see chapter 2) students hear stories of the agency of citizens who fought to preserve remnant ecological systems from development as housing estates and shopping centres. The pedagogy at each centre foregrounds the fragility of place if short-term interests are given precedence over longer-term sustainable practices. Students are scaffolded to consider how their personal choices can impact the more-than-human aspects of the places that they have come to know and value through the excursion. In these ways the diverse place-responsive pedagogies described in this volume treat place as a site of ongoing contest and negotiation.

Place-responsive pedagogies

Somerville's notions of embodiment, story and contest enabled us to understand place as profoundly pedagogical in very specific ways. The sensitivity of the educators to these place-specific affordances was revealed through a series of intensive site visits that we organized with the principals of the six centres. During a typical site visit we'd accompany the teachers and students on an excursion, observe the activities and then later talk at length with the educators at the centres about moments we found intriguing. A dialogue followed that explored the centrality of these telling moments for encapsulating the pedagogy at each centre. The way this dialogue flowed and the specific insights that arose is best conveyed by considering each of the place-responsive pedagogies in turn. This section also provides an introduction to each of the chapters in this volume.

Advocacy pedagogy

Karawatha forest (chapter 2) is an ecological hotspot that is rimmed by busy roads and situated in the middle of spreading suburbs that stretch south from the centre of Brisbane. Its conservation in the 1990s is testament to a local citizens' action group led by Bernice Volz who remains part of the environmental education programs at Pullenvale Environmental Education Centre. Many possible pedagogies are associated with Karawatha. As the place where numerous endangered frog species survive, where koalas are still found, and where glossy black parrots still find food, Karawatha could be treated solely as a place for scientific field trips to study these animals. The story of advocacy is not necessary to engage pedagogically with Karawatha. But place-responsive educators, we suggest, cannot ignore the story of advocacy that is inherent in the current existence of Karawatha. The poignancy of the story of Bernice Volz as an advocate and self-educated ecologist and the success of her local action group are powerful pedagogical stories written into the material existence of Karawatha. Ron Tooth and his colleagues at Pullenvale EEC simply became readers and narrators of the stories already written in the place as they designed the advocacy pedagogy.

Pedagogy as story in/of landscape

In Chapter 3 Ron Tooth explores the notion of pedagogy as story in landscape. Pullenvale Environmental Education Centre is situated in an outer suburban area of Brisbane. The nearby creeks, riparian zones and stands of trees are charming, but they are merely remnants of the original ecological systems that thrived prior to colonisation in the early 19th century. One can enter authentically into this place only through story because written into the landscape is a process of habitat transformation and species loss that remains hidden to the contemporary observer. It is only through imagination and story that students can see the present landscape as the outcome of contested interests that intersected at Pullenvale across time. This chapter resonates with Doreen Massey's (2005) notion that *place* is the site of intersecting and unfinished stories, and her insight that places are connected through networks of power that have important consequences locally. This is dramatically revealed to the students on their excursion when they find a display case of preserved birds that a taxidermist made in the 19th century. The birds are extinct in this area primarily because in the late 19th century they were hunted for their colourful feathers that were exported to fashion houses in London and Paris. Story in this landscape is profoundly pedagogical because it reveals the history of the present and heightens students' sense of their own responsibility and agency in place.

Slow pedagogy

At Bunyaville (see chapter 4) we were intrigued by an episode that Noeleen Rowntree and Agatha Gambino reported to us about a group of very young students disembarking from the buses that had transported them from their nearby suburban school. This episode is reported as a portal experience as the students passed from their familiar time/space of fast-paced and noisy everyday life into the Bunyaville time/space that was slower and quieter and opened up opportunities for being attentive to the elements of the forest. As we talked further with Noeleen and Agatha about their pedagogy, we came to understand the centrality of *time* per se in their inquiry-based pedagogy. To connect to the forest and notice its intricacies requires relaxation, slowing down, being attentive and an attitude that each activity can take as long as it requires. From this conversation we realised that slow pedagogy was the distinctive affordance of Bunyaville. Slow pedagogy might inform practices in any context but what Bunyaville offered was a sharp contrast between students' everyday experiences of distracted fast time and the more meditative and attentive sense of time created by the forest and its various niches. Finding the places in the forest that enabled such relaxed concentration was an explicit part of the design process reported by Noeleen and Agatha in chapter 4. For example, a key moment in the excursion is when separate groups of students gather together to share their recent experiences in the forest. After trying many sites in the forest, Noeleen and Agatha discovered a particular place where students were prepared to share more heartfelt and significant comments with each other. This type of site-specific affordance revealed to us that place can indeed be profoundly pedagogical, and in quite concrete and particular ways.

Walking pedagogy

At Barambah, we organised to meet with Sue Gibson (see chapter 5) over two days to consider the types of evidence she had collected on student learning related to the centre programs. We reminisced with Sue about the walking tracks at Barambah and how Mark Cridland (her co-author) had actually constructed many of these tracks during his holidays over a number of years. The importance of the tracks per se was becoming clearer as we talked. At one point Sue reported that she found walking and talking on the tracks a really effective way to engage some reluctant students. It was from this insightful comment that we began to formulate the idea of the distinctive Barambah pedagogy as "walking". Sue had already named her approach of engaging reluctant students as walking-talking pedagogy. She saw it as an inductive strategy of following-in students' casual conversations rather than providing an expert commentary on the forest. From this moment in our conversation, we began to focus intensely on the different tracks at Barambah and the variety of landscapes that were opened up by walking the tracks. Different tracks required students to walk in different ways, and it was from this sense of tracks as specific places of embodied learning that we identified the distinctive pedagogy at Barambah as the pedagogy of walking. The significance of walking to human cultures is also palpably relevant at Barambah in the program that focuses on an Indigenous culture where walking one's country is regarded as part of custodianship. Again we came to understand the profoundly pedagogical nature of place when we reflected on the history of walking the tracks at Barambah for Indigenous and non-Indigenous people. Barambah has been a place of walking for millennia – it has long been known through walking.

Sacred pedagogy

At Paluma (see chapter 6) we accompanied a group of students one morning as they participated in guided walks through the cloud rainforest and later sampled for aquatic animals in a creek. On this excursion we came to understand that the pedagogy at Paluma cannot but evoke the sacred. A sense of sacredness is part of the material affordances of Paluma. Our entry into the rainforest was accompanied by swirling clouds and shafts of sunlight as we passed through an ancient fig tree whose arches and hollowed towering trunk created a space similar in many respects to a church. This portal into the rainforest was deliberately chosen by Linda Venn and Louka Lazaredes to highlight for students the vast age and spectacular beauty of the rainforest and to create a sense of awe as they compared their own (small) size and (young) age to that of the fig tree. In the place-responsive pedagogy at Paluma, the rainforest becomes a text for inquiring into the beauty of nature and reflecting more deeply on the meaning of life. The scientific exploration of the rainforest remains a central aspect of the pedagogy, but it is accompanied by questions about the purpose and beauty of life. Paluma has an Indigenous and a non-Indigenous history as a place for healing and spiritual renewal. Given these material and cultural features it seems unavoidable that sacredness would be central to any place-responsive pedagogy designed at Paluma. However, the challenge of explicitly addressing sacredness in the multifaith and increasingly secular culture of contemporary Australia means that the exploration of sacredness is contained within personal moments of reflective responding. Some students express feelings related to "God" and others wonder at the beauty of "nature". Linda and Louka validate these responses in a nonjudgemental manner to keep open for students their particular door into world of the sacred, however they might understand this notion.

Shifting sands pedagogy

At Nudgee Beach (see chapter 7) we arrived at the environmental education centre via a major freeway from Brisbane and exited on a small road that eventually meandered along the beach front. Immediately we were aware of the extensive intertidal zone at the beach. Arriving at the centre we noticed the wall-chart detailing the timing of the tides. Mary-Ann Pattison told us that the tides determine her planning of activities and programs at the centre. What can be learned at Nudgee Beach on any particular day depends very much on the changing seasons and the daily variations in the tides. Mary-Ann noted that the road we had just driven along is submerged at various times during the year when there are king tides. Coastal erosion is an emerging problem along the beaches in this region. It was in the context of this conversation that we began to consider the pedagogy at Nudgee Beach as integrally related to shifting sands. The materiality of sand defines the beach. Sand is shifted relentlessly as the beach is made and remade each day by the tides. Animals adapt to the daily churn of the tides and leave traces of their activities in the sand. Learning to read the sand is a core part of one program at Nudgee Beach – students are guided to pay close attention to the markings and patterns that are imprinted by animals on the sand as the tide recedes. Another aspect of the pedagogy is serendipity arising from the unpredictability of events at the beach and the appearance and disappearance of animal species. One year there may be an explosion of crab numbers that disappear suddenly. One day there are sea hawks nearby, but the next they are gone and fail to return. Such serendipity is also a material affordance at Nudgee Beach that requires educators to be flexible and opportunistic in their pedagogical practices. In bringing together these various strands of the pedagogy at Nudgee Beach where planning necessarily shifts opportunistically we also were struck by the contrast with current instrumentalist pedagogies and accountability regimes in schools that privilege effectiveness and efficiency. From these reflections the idea of pedagogy as shifting sands was formulated and used as a framework to explore the practices at Nudgee Beach Environmental Education Centre.

Edge pedagogy

At Moreton Bay (see chapter 8) we embarked on the centre's catamaran, *Inspiration*, with a group of primary school students to explore the Bay and particularly its tidal sandbanks where small hermit crabs and other sea creatures can be observed. From the deck of *Inspiration* you can see that Moreton Bay is geographically the edge of Brisbane, and ecologically it is on the edge in terms of sustainability due to obvious signs of silting and pollution flowing into the Bay from nearby river systems. This habitat too is on the edge of destruction due to intensive commercial and recreational use by local citizens. These material affordances of Moreton Bay provoke a pedagogy of the edge, a pedagogy that has to confront these ecological challenges and necessarily must evoke a response from students about their own behaviour at the edge. But edge pedagogy is not entirely about confronting "inconvenient truths" about the destructive human impact on the Bay. Being on *Inspiration* that day was an enlivening experience of seeing over the horizon and feeling the rhythm of the waves and experiencing the beauty of the hermit crabs with their delicate features and colours. Being on the edge of the Bay heightened our senses and aesthetic sensibility. These contrasting material affordances of the Bay were crucial in producing the edge pedagogy that explores multiple material and semiotic edges to reveal fragility and beauty simultaneously.

Conclusion

"I read the news today, oh boy" the song goes (Beatles, *A Day in the Life*), reminding us about choking coal-induced air pollution affecting over 400 million people in North-East China, the on-going clearing of the Sumatra rainforest for palm oil plantations, the approval of a gigantic new coal mine in Queensland's Galilee Basin, the appointment by President Donald Trump of a climate-change denier to head the Environment Protection Agency in the USA, the accelerating rate of species extinction, and coral death from bleaching affecting hundreds of kilometres of reef in North Queensland. In the face of such devastating news it is tempting to retreat to private spaces and personal pursuits. The sheer scale of the challenges reported daily is daunting and might instil considerable doubt about the efficacy and significance of environmental education in the contemporary world. A powerful source of optimism for us (Peter and Ron) comes from reading the accounts of change and commitment provided in the chapters in this volume. Students provide accounts of emotional and transformative experiences arising from the place-responsive pedagogies designed at each of the centres. You can also read stories of advocacy and commitment by local citizens who worked to preserve crucial remnants of forest or wetlands or tidal ecosystems in their local areas. It is at the local level where the efficacy of our actions and commitments can be felt and appreciated. This is why the place-responsive pedagogies described in this volume are so important. The pedagogies reveal the unique features and the inherent value of local sites and imbue students and teachers with a heightened sense of agency and renewed appreciation of the more-than-human world. This is not the whole answer to the wicked problems (Krasny & Dillon, 2013; Rittel & Webber, 1973) we collectively must solve, but to address global processes we need to start at the local level and learn to value the places where we live our everyday lives. *Diverse Pedagogies of Place* is offered as a contribution to this ongoing challenge of designing powerful place-responsive pedagogies that motivate people to act locally for global sustainability.

References

Abram, D. (1997). The spell of the sensuous: Perception and language in a more-than-human world. New York: Vintage Books.
Ballantyne, R., & Packer, J. (2008). Learning for sustainability: The role and impact of outdoor and environmental education centres. St Lucia: School of Tourism, University of Queensland.
Ballantyne, R., & Packer, J. (2009). Introducing a fifth pedagogy: Experience-based strategies for facilitating learning in natural environments. *Environmental Education Research*, 15(2), 243–262.
Berry, W. (1970). *The hidden wound*. Boston: Houghton Mifflin.
Biesta, G. (2007). Why "what works" won't work: Evidence-based practice and the democratic deficit in educational research. *Educational Theory*, 57(1), 1–22.
Biesta, G. (2015). What is education for? On good education, teacher judgement, and educational professionalism. *European Journal of Education*, 50(1), 75–87.
Carr, W., & Kemmis, S. (1983). *Becoming critical: Knowing through action research*. Deakin, VIC: Deakin University Press.
Carson, R. (1962). *Silent spring*. Boston: Houghton Mifflin.
Cohen, P., & Somerville, M. (1990). *Ingelba and the five black matriarchs*. Sydney: Allen & Unwin.
Cornell, J. B. (1979). Sharing nature with children: The classic parents' & teachers' nature awareness guidebook. Nevada City, CA: Dawn Publications.
Dewey, J. (1938). *Experience and education*. New York: Palgrave Macmillan.
Gough, A. (2001). For the total environment: Bill Stapp's contribution to environmental education. *Australian Journal of Environmental Education*, 17, 19–24.
Gough, A. (2014). Ghosts in Australian environmental education. *Australian Journal of Environmental Education*, 30(1), 1–4.

Greenwood, D. (2014). A critical theory of place-conscious education. In R. Stevenson, M. Brody, J. Dillon & A. Wals (Eds.), *International handbook of research on environmental education* (pp. 93–100). New York: Routledge.

Gruenewald, D. (2003). The best of both worlds: A critical pedagogy of place. *Educational Researcher, 32*(4), 3–12.

Kemmis, S. (1980). *Action research in prospect and retrospect.* Paper presented at the annual meeting of the Australian Association for Research in Education, Melbourne, VIC.

Knapp, C. E. (1972). Attitudes and values in environmental education. *The Journal of Environmental Education, 3*(4), 26–29.

Knapp, C. E. (1992). *Lasting lessons: A teacher's guide to reflecting on experience.* Charleston, WV: Appalachia Educational Laboratory.

Krasny, M., & Dillon, J. (2013). Trading zones in environmental education: Creating transdisciplinary dialogue. New York: Peter Lang.

Lingard, B., Hayes, D., & Mills, M. (2003). Teachers and productive pedagogies: Contextualising conceptualising utilising. *Pedagogy Culture and Society, 11*(3), 399–424.

Mannion, G., Fenwick, A., & Lynch, J. (2013). Place-responsive pedagogy: Learning from teachers' experiences of excursions in nature. *Environmental Education Research, 19*(6), 792–809.

Mannion, G., & Lynch, J. (2016). Primacy of place in education in outdoor settings. In. B. Humberstone, H. Prince & K. Hendersen (Eds.), *Routledge international handbook of outdoor studies* (pp. 85–94). Abingdon: Routledge.

Massey, D. (2005). *For space.* London: Sage.

Moggill Creek Catchment Management Group Inc. (2016). *Smith's scrub.* Retrieved from www.moggillcreek.org/projects/smiths-scrub

Newmann, F. M., Marks, H. M., & Gamoran, A. (1996). Authentic pedagogy and student performance. *American Journal of Education, 104*(4), 280–312.

Rittel, H., & Webber, M. (1973). Dilemmas in a general theory of planning. *Policy Science, 4*, 155–169.

Robottom, I. (1987). Two paradigms of professional development in environmental education. *The Environmentalist, 7*(4), 291–298.

Rose, D.B. (2002). Dialogue with place: Toward an ecological body. *Journal of Narrative Theory, 32*(2), 311–325.

Smith, G., & Sobel, D. (2010). *Place- and community-based education in schools.* New York: Routledge.

Somerville, M. (2010). A place pedagogy for "global contemporaneity". *Educational Philosophy and Theory, 42*(3), 326–344.

Stapp, W. B. (1970). A strategy for curriculum development and implementation in environmental education at the elementary and secondary levels. In J. Evans & S. Boyden (Eds.), *Education and the environmental crisis* (pp. 23–37). Canberra, ACT: Australian Academy of Science.

Stevenson, R. B., Brody, M., Dillon, J., & Wals, A. E. (Eds.) (2014). *International handbook of research on environmental education.* New York: Routledge.

Thomashow, M. (1995). Ecological identity: Becoming a reflective environmentalist. Cambridge, MA: MIT Press.

Thomashow, M. (2002). Bringing the biosphere home: Learning to perceive global environmental change. Cambridge, MA: MIT Press.

Thoreau, H. D. (1906). *Walden, or, Life in the woods.* London: Oxford University Press.

Tuan, Y. (1979). Space and place: Humanistic perspective. In S. Gale & G. Olsson (Eds.), *Philosophy in geography* (pp. 387–427). Dordrecht: Reidel Publishing Company.

Van Matre, S. (1990). *Earth education: A new beginning.* Cedar Grove, Greenville, WV: Institute for Earth Education.

Wattchow, B., & Brown, M. (2011). *A pedagogy of place: Outdoor education for a changing world.* Clayton, VIC: Monash University Publishing.

2 Pedagogy as advocacy in and for place

Ron Tooth and Peter Renshaw

Editors' preface

This Chapter addresses the issue of advocacy pedagogy, that is, pedagogy with a clear normative agenda for the environment where students learn about environmental advocacy and are asked to consider how they might live more sustainably and become advocates in the future. The pedagogy is enacted in Karawatha, a 1000-hectare forest remnant surrounded by suburbs, an ecological hotspot for endangered species and a place that contains multiple stories, particularly the story of Bernice Volz who as a local activist in the 1990s helped preserve Karawatha forest from development as a housing estate. Bernice continues to actively participate in the Karawatha environmental education program. Some educators and researchers at conferences have expressed reservations about the Karawatha program, asking, "Are you teaching students what to think or how to think about environmental issues?" Some express the view that the program should have been designed to expose students to a range of balanced perspectives and arguments about Karawatha (including those of developers, house-buyers, conservationists, recreation enthusiasts). This balanced or neutral approach is in line with much of the research literature on teachers' preference for a "neutral" or "balanced" approach to teaching controversial environmental issues (Cotton, 2006).

The neutral chair approach to teaching values in schools was promulgated in the 1970s by Lawrence Stenhouse (Stenhouse, 1971; Elliot, 1971). The teacher, as a neutral chair, was positioned to impartially manage the discussion of values ensuring that everyone had a chance to express his or her viewpoint and rationally consider alternatives. The teacher, however, did not express a viewpoint or indicate a preference for any of the alternatives. Rather the teacher was expected to explain that his or her deliberately neutral stance would enable students to freely consider the arguments without feeling the weight of the teacher's viewpoint (Elliot, 1971). This pedagogical approach continues to attract considerable support within the environmental education community as explained below by Wals (2010).

> Educators, particularly those with a strong pedagogical background, challenge a focus of EE and ESD on behavioral change as they argue that

education should above all be formative and focus on the kind of capacity building and critical thinking that will allow citizens to understand what is going on in society, to ask critical questions and to determine for themselves what needs to be done (Mayer & Tschapka, 2008; Jickling & Wals, 2008). The idea of influencing people's environmental behavior in a predetermined way, they maintain, contradicts the very foundation of education and borders on indoctrination.

(pp. 17–18)

We acknowledge the pitfalls of treating students as if they are incapable of deciding for themselves, but the advocacy pedagogy at Karawatha is not designed this way. Students' understanding of advocacy is based on their personal knowledge of Karawatha's unique flora and fauna, their firsthand experiences in the forest, and the embodied example of advocacy in the story of the local activist, Bernice Volz. These resources provide students with multiple ways of understanding advocacy and the reasons that concerned citizens would decide to protect a place such as Karawatha. Students might come to hold a different view, but this too would be a more informed choice based on multiple experiences and perspectives.

We also agree with critics of the neutral approach who have highlighted the implications of remaining silent or neutral regarding controversial issues (Carrington & Troyna, 1988). Being neutral can be interpreted as endorsing social complacency and a laissez-faire approach to resolving environmental conflicts. Having the appearance of neutrality also suits those more powerful groups in society who seldom have qualms about pursuing self-interest above that of other citizens or environmental values (Shor, 1992). As Freire (1985) noted, an education that tries to be neutral supports the dominant ideology of the society. We also take the position that educational practice is inherently normative. As Biesta (2007; 2015) has persuasively argued, education is not just about learning per se but about worthwhile learning. It is incumbent on teachers to be explicit about their pedagogical agendas and to explain why they have adopted particular values. But teachers cannot just expect students to accept their normative agenda or explanations. Students have to personally understand and freely commit to normative agendas in ways that are authentic for them.

To theorise this kind of authentic pedagogy for advocacy we draw upon Bakhtin's distinction between authoritative discourse and internally persuasive discourse to specify the kind of advocacy that should be incorporated into place-responsive pedagogies (Bakhtin, 1991). According to Bakhtin, authoritative discourse is heard as the voice that cannot be questioned. Internally persuasive discourse, in contrast, arises when there is an open and rich dialogue between established ways of making sense of the world and new experiences and novel voices (Bakhtin, 1991, p. 346). The place-responsive pedagogy described in this chapter uses story and experiences in place to create the conditions for students to connect their established ways of making sense of the world with the new voices and viewpoints embedded in the Karawatha program.

The pedagogy is designed to move students to become environmental advocates by offering them multiple ways of knowing and appreciating the forest, and the many stories it holds. The pedagogy is grounded in the materiality of Karawatha forest and relies on narratives laid over the landscape, that is, the stories of actors who have made a difference to Karawatha and who have imbued it with specific meanings and visions. Using this narrative pedagogy of place creates a space where students can personally understand advocacy and relate it to their own sense of themselves now and in the future. The actual voices of different protagonists are heard by students in different ways depending on their own histories and interests. Bernice Volz is central. She is the voice of the engaged citizen who advocated with passion and tenacity to save Karawatha. Professor Jean-Marc Hero is the concerned scientist whose voice reveals the uniqueness of the ecology at Karawatha. Ron Tooth and Merryl Simpson from Pullenvale Environmental Education Centre represent the voices of environmental educators who mediate the experiences during the day.

This chapter includes accounts of learning that are emotional and moving. In searching for a way to theorise the kind of emotional and significant transformation that students regularly report after the Karawatha excursion, *Vygotsky's (1934)* notion of *perezhivanie* is deployed. It is translated as emotional, lived experience. *Perezhivanie* is marked by heightened emotions and awareness of significant change happening to oneself. The notion of *perezhivanie* seems particularly relevant to the type of complex learning promoted through the Karawatha experience because it draws attention to moments of significant change in how students see themselves and the places around them. Through the analysis of students' emotional experiences in Karawatha we can appreciate how internally persuasive discourse is generated and leads many students to see themselves as advocates for the environment.

Peter Renshaw and Ron Tooth

Introduction

In this chapter we focus on environmental advocacy and its importance within pedagogies of place. Advocacy for the environment challenges the view of education as a value-neutral endeavour that equips students with skills and knowledge whilst distancing them from the need to make personal choices and commitments to action. Advocacy places the normative dimension of pedagogy in the spotlight – it requires educators to think carefully about why, what and how they are advocating. Many educators are still uneasy with pursuing advocacy for the environment as an educational goal; they regard it as equivalent to telling students what to think and what to value. They would rather operate as a neutral chair, standing back from specific commitments per se to provide students with the tools to inquire and reach their own conclusions. We are keenly aware that the voice of the teacher can dominate dialogues with students and prevent them from making their own considered decisions. However, transmissive teaching that treats students as empty vessels to be filled with knowledge and values by the teacher is not part of our place-responsive pedagogy. Our approach to pedagogy is neither neutral nor transmissive. It is designed to engage students actively in the role of an environmental advocate where they will experience emotionally and bodily why somebody might want to "speak for the trees".

Bakhtin's distinction between authoritative discourse and internally persuasive discourse is helpful in considering how advocacy can be incorporated into place-responsive pedagogies (Morson & Emerson, 1990; Holquist, 1990). According to Bakhtin, authoritative discourse is heard as the voice that cannot be questioned. It needs to be accepted and obeyed but it remains distinct and external rather than interlinked with other voices and experiences through which people make sense of their world (Bakhtin, 1991, p. 346). One's relationship with the authoritative voice is hierarchical requiring acceptance and compliance rather than engagement and questioning. Internally persuasive discourse, in contrast, arises when there is an open and rich dialogue between one's established ways of making sense of the world and new experiences and novel voices. Our place-responsive pedagogy is designed to create the conditions for students to interanimate their established ways of making sense of the world with the new experiences and new viewpoints embedded in the Karawatha program. Interanimation is a dynamic and dialogic process that cannot be determined or directed externally. How students transform and make sense of their experiences during the Karawatha program is variable and unpredictable. The advocacy pedagogy is designed to create a dialogue between the students' pasts, their present experiences, and their imagined futures. The students' learning about advocacy is grounded in the materiality of Karawatha forest and their direct bodily engagement with that materiality. It also relies on narratives laid over the landscape, that is, the stories of actors who have made a difference to Karawatha, actors who have perceived and valued Karawatha in a particular way, actors who have imbued the forest with specific meanings and values. By facilitating students' experience of the materiality of Karawatha, engaging them in authentic stories laid over the landscape, and supporting their imaginative reflections, we hope to create a space where students can personally understand advocacy, relate it to their sense of themselves, and deploy it to imagine new possibilities for their futures.

In this chapter, then, we describe how students developed their dispositions and identities as environmental advocates through an extended story-mediated journey into Karawatha forest. The first words spoken to students as they enter the forest foreground the centrality of advocacy; "I speak for the trees for the trees have no tongues." Students learn about advocacy for the forest, particularly about the local resident and activist, Bernice Volz (Bernice), and they experience firsthand the beauty and materiality of the forest for themselves as they walk through its varied ecological zones and landscapes. Advocacy is situated in the context of Karawatha and in the compelling story of what Bernice achieved as a local advocate in speaking for the forest. As well it is linked globally through the scientific work of Professor Jean-Marc Hero (Marc) a research scientist who continues to research Karawatha as an ecological hotspot that can inform our understanding of global climate change. Through the Karawatha program, therefore, students learn about the global significance of local advocacy, and are provided with the opportunity to reflect on how they might become advocates in their own spaces and in relationships at home and school.

Karawatha is a 1000-hectare forest reserve that includes wetlands, a diversity of forest types and micro-climate zones, as well as threatened frog species and a rich variety of wildlife including the endangered glossy black parrots (Garnett & Franklin, 2014). The story-mediated experience of Karawatha explores the life of Bernice, who led a community campaign in the 1990s to preserve Karawatha from development as a housing estate. Bernice later became a citizen hero in the eyes of many community members, key public servants, politicians and scientists who worked with her in the Karawatha campaign. The materiality of Karawatha is central to the story-mediated pedagogy that is enacted by teachers and students during their journey into the forest. The way rocks, water, frogs and trees combine to heighten sensory awareness is vividly illustrated in the following journal commentary by Ron Tooth as he accompanied a group of students on their excursion:

> We'd been walking though the Melaleuca wetlands at Karawatha, and it had been particularly wet in the weeks before so there was a lot of water. It wasn't raining on that day, but there was a lot of water on the ground and a lot of movement of water. What struck me was how clean the water was in every single puddle that we came to as we walked along this sandy track in amongst the Melaleucas. There were multiple puddles and every one of them was layered with ledges and full of tadpoles that we knew were probably Wallum froglets, which is a rare species, and so there was a great deal of excitement amongst the group that we were seeing frog spawn and tadpoles, and as you looked into any one of these puddles the diversity was astounding. There was a lot of life, a lot of colour, a lot of different textures. I think what got us was that you felt like you were looking through a mirror into the place, and it was so clean and so clear that even the simplest things like a little twig or a tiny leaf looked really interesting. So we became quite caught up with this.
> (Ron Tooth, Personal reflection, 2015)

It is astonishing that these occasional puddles with rare frogs can be experienced at all. Karawatha is situated between two major cities in South-East Queensland. The geological reason for this miracle is the sandstone ridge that curves around much of Karawatha's perimeter to create a natural barrier that has protected its lagoons from pollution and kept human incursions to a minimum. The unique structure of the sandstone ridge has created a natural filtration system that purifies much of the rainwater before it reaches the inland lagoons while any overland runoff is filtered as it moves through three quite distinct forest zones. Karawatha's lagoon system is now the centrepiece of an extensive wetland conservation area that was purchased by the Brisbane City Council and the Queensland Government in order to provide a core catchment area for three major creek systems and preserve the rich variety of plant species and animals. In response to the continued advocacy of Bernice and others, the Brisbane City Council has purchased more land in recent times to create a "green corridor" that connects Karawatha to other important bushland areas to the north and the south west.

The Bernice Volz story

As we noted above Karawatha was preserved in the 1990s through the advocacy of Bernice and the community group she led. From the very beginning Bernice knew that she could not save Karawatha on her own, so she turned to the community and others such as Jean-Marc Hero. She has always insisted that it was a group effort but even a cursory discussion with those involved indicated that she played a pivotal role. Bernice is a self-taught ecologist with no secondary or university education. She would have excelled in such formal studies if given the chance. She became respected throughout local government and across a range of scientific circles for her ecological knowledge and ability to facilitate change. The Karawatha excursion is largely structured on Bernice's story of advocacy, and the influence of her story on students is especially poignant and often elicits the most eloquent and insightful responses, such as the following response from a young girl after she had spent twenty minutes at the end of the day sitting and studying one of the many crystal clear puddles in the melaleuca forest.

> One girl described how she had looked at this floating leaf and . . . pushed it and broke the surface tension. She held it down. It stayed there for a moment and then popped back up again. . . . Later she volunteered to speak to Bernice when we phoned her using the mobile . . . and she told this amazing story of how Bernice was this leaf who'd been pushed down and held down but every time she just popped back up again . . . (girl laughed as she said this), and she'd be held down, and she'd pop up again. Bernice was listening on the phone and she just broke into this most joyful laughter. Bernice and this child had this moment on the phone. We all felt it, and we were moved by the experience and the way she brought the image of the leaf into the conversation and intensified that moment.
>
> (Ron Tooth, personal reflection, 2015)

What aspects of advocacy are conveyed by Bernice's story? Importantly she advocated for Karawatha with grace, diplomacy and a steely determination that seemed irresistible, disarming even the most cynical of opponents. Bernice and her local community members were knowledgeable about their local fauna and flora. They compiled a plant list and an animal list showing the rich diversity of species in Karawatha. This information was then presented to those with decision-making power over the future of the forest. Part of the advocacy story is also about concrete actions to engage decision-makers and tell them about Karawatha and why it was crucial to preserve. As Bernice said in an interview with Ron Tooth,

> We had a meeting in my lounge and we formed a committee and Trish and Cathy and myself we got the plant list and animal list and drew a mud map

and we made an appointment to go and see the Lord Mayor . . . we all sat down in the Lord Mayor's office and we told him about Karawatha and I put my vision to him that this is what needs to be.

(B. Volz, personal communication, 2015)

The story of Bernice is interlinked with the story of Professor Jean-Marc Hero, an international expert in frog research. His support of Bernice in advocating for the preservation of Karawatha gave her voice additional legitimacy in the eyes of many decision-makers. This is crucial in understanding advocacy – while Bernice was in fact knowledgeable, the voice of Jean-Marc Hero was that of an expert scientist so his support for Bernice was central in convincing decision-makers that Karawatha was a special place that deserved protection. As Marc noted in an interview recently,

Karawatha has the highest biodiversity of frogs of anywhere in Australia, in one location, with 24/25 species recorded here. So, naturally, it was a place of interest to me. . . . It's isolated fragments surrounded by highways and houses, people; it's what we call peri-urban, so on the fringe of the urban environment. It's critically important to conserve these areas.

(Hero, 2015)

Advocacy is about building partnerships and coalitions of interests between people in different places. In this case there was a coalition of interests between the local and the global. The dual local/global nature of advocacy is explicitly addressed by Marc in reflecting on his partnership with Bernice. The students who come on excursions to Karawatha learn about the importance of local action within the global effort to preserve ecological hotspots and provide space for endangered species to be sustained into the future. Marc notes Bernice's passion for her own backyard, while linking that to his global perspective on amphibians.

She's a person who is very passionate about her local backyard and I think that is incredible, too. I tend to think of conservation at a global scale. I am working on global amphibian declines. Bernice is dedicated to her backyard, Karawatha forest; and we need both of those perspectives. We need people looking at a global scale and people looking at a national perspective; people looking at a State level, local government level, all the way down to the person protecting the forest in her backyard. She's a legend. I don't know what more I can say.

(Hero, 2015)

Global connections

The global connection of Karawatha to other ecological sites is mediated by the Program for Planned Biodiversity and Ecosystem Research (PPBIO). This research program is a long-term biodiversity study based on a process of scientific democratization that empowers communities to collect systematic data on local flora and fauna as part of an evidence-based process of advocacy and social change. During the Karawatha excursion students learn that they can be part of this scientific engagement and contribute to a global knowledge network of evidence about their local environment. In this way the place-responsive pedagogy enacted at Karawatha links environmental advocacy to personal commitments and civic action (as exemplified in Bernice's story) as well as to the development of scientific understandings and inquiry. Marc highlights the significance of Karawatha in the global context:

> So we know these changes are happening but we cannot understand what's happening to the biodiversity in response to these changes, these anthropogenic changes. My idea, and the idea of all long-term ecological research and monitoring programs, is to actually measure the changes in biodiversity in response to climate, in response to fire, in response to other impacts . . . a system that I am working on, which is called PPBio, the Program For Planned Biodiversity and Eco-system Research. And it's all about establishing permanent plots in an environment like Karawatha, where we can go back to – for centuries. I call this "my 4,000 year project".
>
> (Jean-Marc Hero, personal communication, 2015)

The enormous timespan envisioned for the research project is also instructive for students to contemplate in terms of advocacy for the environment. It's more than caring for this or that frog or glossy parrot here and now. It's about sustaining the landscapes for animals and plants across time – a time well beyond our own lifespans. So Marc's story brings these elements of scientific expertise, research and extended timespans to the inter-related stories embedded in Karawatha. There is one other story to be told here. That is the story of how Ron Tooth, co-author of this chapter, became involved in the Karawatha excursion:

> I became interested in Karawatha in the early 2000s when I was working with teachers in a state school nearby. The Principal and staff were keen to expand their environmental focus and begin learning more about their local neighbourhood. I didn't know much about Karawatha except that it was within easy reach of the school and that it had been identified by the council as a biodiversity hotspot. After some preliminary detective work I realized that Bernice was the person I needed to contact because everyone I met mentioned her name. Our first meeting was in a picnic shelter in one of the parkland areas on the edge of the forest and like most people who met her for the first time I was immediately captivated by her enormous energy and commitment. In that moment I knew that it wasn't just Karawatha that I wanted the students to connect with but also this amazing woman who embodied the kind of active, caring citizenry that the school had been talking about, and that I saw as central to the kind of new programs that we wanted to develop at Pullenvale Environmental Education Centre. There

was an enticing overlap of affordances in the circumstances of my meeting Bernice. During my career as an environmental educator, I have worked with other committed teachers at PEEC to design Storythread as a narrative-based approach to environmental education, and so immediately I knew that Bernice's connection to Karawatha needed to be central to any new program. Equally, the beauty and accessibility of Bernice's backyard, Karawatha forest, provided the materiality for students to experience nature in a heightened and embodied manner. It was a pedagogical jewel waiting to be explored. Finally, the coincidence of connecting to the long-term ecological research of Jean-Marc Hero added a global dimension to the place-responsive pedagogy at Karawatha and enabled me to work with other teachers at PEEC to create the Karawatha experience.

(Ron Tooth, personal reflection, 2015)

The Karawatha experience[1]

Students prepare for their visit to Karawatha by listening to and discussing extracts from interviews with Bernice about her life as an environmental advocate. As they learn about the ecologies and microclimates of Karawatha they practice reflection and attentiveness in observing and listening to the world around them. We have begun to deploy an Australian Indigenous term, *dadirri*, to describe this kind of deep attentiveness to country (see below for a fuller description). Students are also invited to take on the *blanket role* of "environmental advocates" in preparation for the excursion. A *blanket role* is a drama convention where all the participants take the same imaginative role within a whole-group role-play or process drama. The way the blanket role is used as part of the *Storythread* experience at Karawatha is to move students beyond the traditional fictional roles of drama practice into a new space where they are invited to see themselves as a new kind of person who is growing and developing the values and skills of the environmental advocate. Through this real-life blanket role of the environmental advocate students focus on Bernice's local knowledge, values, and community actions and why she so willingly committed herself to save Karawatha. In the process, they discover their own voices and sense of agency.

The day in Karawatha

On the excursion day, students traverse Karawatha from one side to the other with the PEEC teachers and their own teachers, passing through diverse ecological systems, noting the sudden changes in the forest zones, and imagining themselves walking in Bernice's shoes as well as in the footsteps of the Indigenous custodians of the land who have lived and walked in Karawatha for thousands of years. Students are scaffolded at their schools and then at Karawatha to experience and explore the multiple aspects of the blanket role of environmental advocacy. This includes developing scientific understanding and knowledge, aesthetic appreciation of the natural environment and the capacity to communicate to others what they have learned so that they can become agents of change in their school and community. To achieve minimal impact we follow established fire trails for much of the time with only a few small incursions into the heart of the melaleuca wetland in the afternoon. This is when we walk along less-defined bush trails, and while the temptation to leave the tracks and enter into the wildness of the place is strong, the idea that as advocates for the place we need to respect and protect its fragility and complexity is easily accepted by most students. They explore the wetlands area for themselves, observing and recording the life of the forest using cameras and journals, and visiting significant places that were important to Bernice.

The teachers from PEEC shape the unfolding experience of students on the excursion by using a wide range of "micro-mediating tools" that are designed to shift student perception, spark the imagination and create alternative mind, body, and sensory spaces where deep learning can happen. The key pedagogical practice that weaves across the day is based on the idea of *dadirri* which is an Indigenous practice that Miriam-Rose Ungunmerr-Baumann of the Ngangikurungkurr people in the Northern Territory (Ungunmerr-Baumann, 1988; 2002) describes as an inner, deep listening and quiet, still awareness. It is a "tuning in" to others and to nature to create a deeper understanding of life. Miriam-Rose sees this practice as something for everyone and not just for Aboriginal people, and this inspired us to explicitly incorporate the idea of *dadirri* as a key lens into our work at Karawatha. In the following journal entry Ron Tooth describes a moment near the end of a day at Karawatha when students sit silently in a melaleuca wetland forest observing the fine detail and searching for any small movements or signs of life. They have been asked to practice *dadirri* in their own way for approximately twenty minutes, thinking about and showing respect for the Indigenous custodians of the place as they observe, listen to and feel the natural systems around them. The following image captures the moment when students settle into this attentiveness moment at the end of the day.

> I'm sitting in a melaleuca forest experiencing dadirri at the end of the day with a class of 25 year 7 students who are sitting silent and alone amongst hundreds of paperbark trees. Honey-eaters are moving through a low canopy, and leaf shadows are sliding back and forth across the paperbarks. Small pieces lift and turn in soft responses to a light breeze that passes through. Powder rises and floats from the trunks, and branches stretch up and out into interlaced patterns that frame strong snatches of blue sky. Twenty-five ephemeral lagoons loop around us and lie hidden in the reeds. Frogs are calling, and there is life everywhere. I can see glimpses of students sitting silently and alone in this ancient place.
>
> (Ron Tooth, personal reflection, 2015)

Following this extended attentiveness episode students gather together in a circle to share what they have experienced. This is the longest *dadirri* encounter of the day when the students spend nearly twenty minutes sitting alone. The experience is challenging for some and liberating for others but most students come back to the group with something that has caught their attention and that they want to share. It's not often that modern urbanized children have the opportunity to sit silently in a forest like this. Attentiveness moments like this provide the thread that holds the Karawatha day together as part of a flowing journey into place. The work of Miriam-Rose Ungunmerr-Baumann and her writings on *dadirri* inspired us to create a series of very explicit reflective experiences to help children make their own personal learning connection to this place. Each of these moments is different, and they are carefully sequenced and scripted to heighten the sensorial experience for students and provide them with many opportunities to grow their knowledge throughout the day as they follow their own reflective learning pathways into the materiality of the place. A detailed description of some of these carefully crafted pedagogical moments follows.

White crystal dadirri

The journey into Karawatha begins at a high point on its northern edge where the students enter the forest for the first time to follow a narrow winding track that is centimetres deep with ancient quartz crystals. We call this the *white crystal dadirri* walk, and it is designed to elicit a feeling that they have entered into a place of high significance and importance to Aboriginal people and others. It's critical for us in these very first moments to acknowledge that this land is Aboriginal country and that as visitors we are privileged to be walking where Indigenous people have traversed for thousands of years, and where Bernice and Jean-Marc Hero came to make their own connections. The walk begins with a story about the rituals that different Indigenous people use to show respect for places and acknowledge their importance. Our white crystal *dadirri* walk gives students the opportunity to slow down, watch closely and begin to make their own sensorial, auditory and tactile connections to the forest they are walking through. This is about highlighting the protocol of respect that continues throughout the day. Students pass a designated stringy bark tree which signals that their talking needs to disappear. They then walk in a single line listening to the sound of the crystals under their boots as they become more aware of the trees all around them where the sandstone ridge falls away on each side of the track. They are invited to stop at one point to pick up a handful of white crystal and then watch it drift and sift through their fingers back to the track as it shines in the sun. They continue walking until we gather them under the shade of a giant tree; their voices return and we are ready for a new story before we move to animal *dadirri*.

Animal dadirri

As the students continue to follow the track along the sandstone ridge it suddenly opens out into a large expansive area of flat sandstone rock surrounded by giant sandstone boulders of various shapes and sizes. Some are partly buried and others lie on the surface near the top of the ridge or partway down the hill. They lie this way and that, strewn about by the massive forces of nature over eons of time. You can easily walk across the top of these giant boulders and then slip down narrow pathways in between them to explore. There are usually birds watching from trees as we approach with students, and it is common to see lizards and other small creatures scampering across and between the rocks to hide in clumps of grass or in leaf litter. It was as we watched these small creatures in our own moments of attentiveness that we first created the idea of animal *dadirri* which requires children to look at the forest from the vantage point of a wild creature. We had recognised early that when students had access to digital cameras their engagement increased and they began to notice fine details that they might otherwise have missed. We combined the use of cameras with the idea of *observing as if you are an animal* to create novel images. In practice the students imagine that an ant, lizard, snake, beetle, bird, marsupial mouse, frog etc. is holding and using their camera. This requires them to place the cameras in logs, amongst grass, between gaps in leaves, flat against the trunks of a tree or facing up to the sky to simulate what an animal might do and what it might see from a non-human vantage point. When students are given this kind of freedom they seem to find the most unexpected locations for taking photos as they crawl, slither and become part of the place in a very tactile, physical and curious way. Many of the resulting images are stunning.

Rock dadirri

On the edge of this expansive area of sandstone is a single large flat sandstone rock with a vantage point that allows you to look down the hill into the heart of Karawatha's internal catchment where the lagoons are hidden amongst dense bushland. It's an obvious place to sit if you want a good view of the forest below and an ideal gathering space for students with its gentle shaded slope that is flat enough for a whole class of children to sit comfortably. The idea of rock *dadirri* grew from our own experience of sitting on this rock and wondering how many people had done the same thing before us. As we sat feeling the texture of the sandstone under our hands we imagined that we'd become the rock. When we learned that it was also a favourite place for Bernice and her friends to sit we decided to make it a key gathering space for our Karawatha journey. Students are asked to allow their bodies to become totally still as if they've become part of the rock itself. No movements of fingers, hands or any part of their body, just slow breathing. They are invited to hold their bodies motionless as they place their hands beside them on the rock to feel its solidness, texture and coolness. They are reminded that Aboriginal people sat on these same rocks thousands of years before them and that their descendants still visit Karawatha today. They are asked to imagine these people now and in the past and to describe what they see and hear. A short historical account provides them with details to populate their own imagined visual imagery. They are given a moment to become comfortable because they will soon sit totally still for over five minutes. Short stories are shared about how Aboriginal people use the area and how other children have discovered that by sitting as still as a stone, forest creatures and birds became inquisitive and often came quite close. They then listen to sounds and watch for any small movements themselves as they sit still and frozen and soak in the experience. This is always a dramatic moment in the day and students often recall it as memorable and significant. Rock *dadirri* culminates as the students gather in a tight huddle to observe water being poured onto their rock and to see it instantly vanish into the porous sandstone on its long journey to the massive aquifers beneath the ridge that in part feed the wild lagoons far below in the forest.

For the rest of the day we use an array of pedagogical tools that focus students on growing their skill of attentiveness that is linked in some way to the idea of *dadirri*. High definition magnifiers are used to look deep into the structure of leaves, rocks, trees and dirt as they move through different forest zones with their digital cameras taking close-up shots. Doing a *fast 180-degree turn* allows students to notice the dramatic difference between two major forest zones – without this sudden perceptual change the transition between forest zones would go unnoticed by most children. The final activity of the day provides students with the opportunity to speak via mobile phone to Bernice and to share their experience of the excursion with her and what it has meant to them. They ask her questions, listen to her responses and almost always refer to how they have grown in their appreciation for Karawatha and now want to tell others about how important it is and why it must be protected. The emotion, thought and passion expressed during this phone conversation is always strong and often compelling. After the excursion, the students continue to talk about their visit to Karawatha, write personal responses to Bernice and reflect on their learning as they consider what it means for them to live as environmental advocates in their own school and community.

Multiple pathways to advocacy

The Storythread pedagogy at Karawatha is designed to hook students into the experiences of the forest through a variety of stories, tools and modes. We previously wrote about this in general terms as follows:

> These elements work independently and together as "hooks" that capture the attention of students and engage different kinds of learners. It might be one pathway predominantly or a combination that leads to authentic engagement and deep learning in different students. Some are captivated by the sensuality and beauty of the place as it is experienced through deep attentive listening, others by the personal, embodied knowledge and values that they create for themselves and others by the imaginative power of the unfolding narrative in space and time.
>
> (Tooth & Renshaw, 2012, p. 128)

Here we consider in more detail how aspects of the pedagogy differentially hook students into learning during the Karawatha excursion. For this purpose, during 2013 we sampled 108 letters written by Year 6 students to Bernice Volz at the end of the excursion to Karawatha. The letters were sampled from four different state schools to allow a broader picture to be painted of how different groups of students experienced Karawatha. Overall there was a similar pattern of topics and issues covered in the letters from the four schools. In composing their letters to Bernice students were asked three questions to guide their writing: what happened on the day of their visit, what they learned and how they felt about what Bernice did to save Karawatha. We examined the letters to identify those aspects of the pedagogy that were explicitly mentioned by the students. These aspects could include reference to: (a) Bernice's story of advocacy; (b) the practice of *dadirri*; (c) ecological and scientific knowledge about the forest; (d) sensory awareness and aesthetic appreciation of the experiences in the forest; or (e) any other events or aspects of the students' experiences.

On average students mentioned three different aspects of the pedagogy in their letters. Unsurprisingly almost all students (93%) explicitly and positively mentioned Bernice's advocacy in the letter and thanked her for saving Karawatha, and many (about 50%) wrote emotionally about their appreciation of what she achieved, and some explicitly mentioned that they would model themselves on Bernice and intended to become an environmental activist or advocate (26%). This is more than just learning about being an environmental advocate. It's an explicit commitment to becoming an advocate. Below, in the extract of a student's letter (Year 6), the influence of Bernice's story of advocacy can be clearly seen. This student has been inspired by Bernice (*That you could spend so many years working to save a forest is truly inspirational);* and emotionally moved (*I cannot thank you enough for all you've done for the environment and the people who treasure it),* and she has also learned to understand nature in a way that Bernice has modelled (*You have helped me learn that nature is more than a flower attached to a branch or a bird in the sky, it is deep and meaningful. It talks to me and it has so many stories to tell).*

> What you've done to save Karawatha is so inspiring and amazing you have no idea how grateful I am that you've conserved something so beautiful. That you could spend so many years working to save a forest is truly inspirational. All the things I have seen in the short time I visited Karawatha proves you have saved bucket-loads of species. The effort you put in to save this forest is a wonderful thing. I could never imagine someone more inspiring and dedicated. You have helped me learn that nature is more than a flower attached to a branch or a bird in the sky, it is deep and meaningful. It talks to me and it has so many stories to tell. The extent of things you've saved and people you've inspired is colossal and constantly growing.
>
> (Year 6 Student, 2013)

About half the students (41%) were taken by the beauty and sensorial richness of the forest and wrote about how moved they were by the aesthetic appeal of the place. This is illustrated in the extract below from one student who uses just a few lines to vividly convey her sensorial awareness of forest sounds,

> The sound of the wind flowing through the leaves and branches was an amazing thing to hear. One of the best sights was the small magnificent lagoon, all the birds chirping, and walking along the road filled with crystals. . . . Every now and then, the wind would blow really fast and loud like the sound of a waterfall, and it was my favourite part of the entire bush walk.
>
> (Year 6 Student, 2013)

In addition, about one-third of the students (32%) seem to be hooked by the practice of *dadirri*, and they explained in their letters how important it had become to them. Many more students wrote about attentively tuning into the forest, but we classified as *dadirri* only those comments that explicitly used the term. Below one student expresses in a few simple words what *dadirri* meant to him. The exclamation marks suggest he is particularly impressed with the practice of *dadirri*.

> Bernice I've learned so much!!! Dadirri – Senses towards nature. Eyes – sight. Hear – audio. Skin – feel, touch. Heart – care.
>
> (Year 6 Student, 2013)

Another student explicitly mentions *dadirri* as changing her attitude towards nature.

> I have always thought that nature was boring. But when I did dadirri I found out that nature is incredible, there are insects under every rock. There are cicada shells on trees too, it's wonderful.
>
> (Year 6 Student, 2013)

Dadirri was mentioned as raising sensorial awareness by many students, and it clearly was a significant influence on their learning during the excursion.

Regarding scientific knowledge, about one in five students in the sample (21%) explicitly mentioned an aspect of the science of the forest that impressed them. Their comments varied in complexity, starting with simple facts and discrete observations to more integrated understanding of relationships in the forest. Simpler comments focussed on specific interesting bits of information such as the distinctive marks left on the scribbly gum tree trunk by the larvae of local moth species (*I learnt many things, I had never seen a scribbly gum tree and I found it very interesting*). Other students wrote about making observations in the forest and classifying species, suggesting they had learned some general processes of inquiry (*Also making keen observations, and classifying things. I too have developed my nature smartness while being at Karawatha*). There were specific insights about the communicative behaviour of animals such as one student's acute observation that all the frogs but one went silent when the class approached the lagoon –

possibly indicating it was signalling a warning to other frogs (*As we approached the lagoon, I heard all the frogs stop but one, I think it was a warning call or something*). Some students found the survival of rare frogs in the lagoons as particularly memorable (*I never heard of green-thighed frogs before but after visiting the forest, I made a new discovery*) and linked the frogs' survival to the absence of introduced species of predatory fish (*all 25 species of frogs could live there without worrying about the gambusia fish*). A few students also articulated an understanding of the ecosystem itself and the conditions that enabled non-polluted water to filter down into the lagoons. The comment below reveals this understanding of balance and chains of relationships between species:

> The life chain is a very delicate balance, if some species are extinct, it will affect more species, so thank you for saving the environment. . . . I learnt about the frog's sound and how they only live in areas where there is no pollution. The most important discovery I made today is about the bowl structure (of Karawatha) that makes water in the forest between the cities clear and unpolluted.
>
> (Year 6 Student, 2013)

A subtext in all these comments about scientific aspects of the forest is the students' appreciation and valuing of the forest. This is explicitly articulated by one student who hopes people will learn about the unique ecosystem of Karawatha and its endangered frogs so that they too will value it:

> I think it is extremely important that people come visit and learn about Karawatha. I found it hard to believe that people wanted to destroy this unique eco-system, it has one of the most diverse ranges of endangered frogs.
>
> (Year 6 Student, 2013)

Finally, one student wrote a simple sentence that conveys something profound about the relationship of humans to the non-human world. She wrote:

> I think the most important discovery I made today was we're not the only living things that live on the earth.
>
> (Year 6 Student, 2013)

Something important seems to have happened in this student's understanding of humanity in relation to other living things.

In summary, the content of the letters to Bernice included reference to all the central aspects of the Karawatha pedagogy. Notably, Bernice's own story of advocacy for the forest was mentioned by almost all students (93%); followed by sensory awareness and aesthetic appreciation of the forest (41%); followed by *dadirri* and the process of attentiveness (32%); as well as scientific facts and deeper knowledge of the ecological systems of the forest (21%). Students' letters included reference to multiple aspects of the pedagogy (3 on average) so the hooks or pathways into learning need to be described as multifaceted – indeed the design of the pedagogy offers students many different opportunities to understand Karawatha through multiple modes and through different kinds of stories written into the landscape – Bernice's story of advocacy, the ecological story, the story of different species of animals and plants, and the students' own stories of experiences and activities on the day. The design of the pedagogy is built on the assumption that moving students towards becoming environment advocates is best achieved by offering them multiple ways of knowing and appreciating the forest, and the many stories it holds.

In reading the letters that students wrote to Bernice – both those sampled here and those that Ron Tooth can access through regularly teaching the Karawatha program – we've noticed that some students in each class express a sense of being a "new person" or feeling that they are embarking on a "new phase in their lives". A couple of extracts from the letters we sampled are shown here to illustrate this new sense of self:

> Thanks to you (Bernice), I have found my inner self, I have found me.
> It is very hard to describe what I feel. I feel magic. I feel like I am not me. I feel like I am a new girl, a new person.
>
> (Year 6 Student, 2013)

> I loved the place, it was amazing!!! It helps me to open my heart more about my surroundings. This has been the best experience in my life.
>
> (Year 6 Student, 2013)

> I have learnt a lot about myself during my time at Karawatha. I now know that everything I do has an impact on the environment and by doing even just little things, I can help protect it.
>
> (Year 6 Student, 2013)

The sense of a becoming a new person or entering a new phase of life is anchored in place and in story, that is, it is their experiences in Karawatha per se, and the story of Bernice in particular, that instigate the palpable and emotional sense of significant change. It's not that students have a detached or abstracted sense of change in themselves. Their transformations are linked to re-lived moments and experiences in the forest. For instance, the student below provides an account of embarking on a new journey of "fighting for what's right" and not "giving up for anything" but this new self is embedded within Bernice's story of advocacy, as well as embedded in an appreciation of Karawatha with its different species of trees, plants and animals, rock formations and lagoons.

> My environmental advocate journey has just begun and it will lead me to many different and exciting adventures. Karawatha with all its different species of trees, plants and animals, all the rock formations and lagoons make up that beautiful haven in the middle of so much hustle and bustle of civilisation.

Thank you Bernice for deciding to stand up and make a difference, to be the voice of Karawatha Forest. You have inspired me to fight for what's right and don't give up for anything.

(Year 6 Student, 2013)

Other students express this sense of being with and in the forest and becoming a new person more directly and succinctly, as illustrated below.

I feel that Karawatha forest has grown on me and I feel as if I'm a part of the environment. I've become a better environmental advocate.

(Year 6 Student, 2013)

I've learned how to bond into the environment.

(Year 6 Student, 2013)

In just a few hours in the forest I already feel like I have bonded and connected to the beautiful biomes and environments that Karawatha offers.

(Year 6 Student, 2013)

Now I know why I really feel the nature coming into me and trying to show me why you had saved Karawatha.

(Year 6 Student, 2013)

Perezhivanie

In searching for a way to theorise the kind of emotional and significant transformation that students regularly report after the Karawatha excursion, we (Renshaw & Tooth, 2016) have begun to deploy Vygotsky's (1934) notion of *perezhivanie*, which is translated as emotional lived experience. *Perezhivanie* is marked by heightened emotions, a sense of significant change happening to oneself and reflection on the process. *Perezhivanie* has been used recently to investigate early childhood play (Fleer & Hammer, 2013) and *storyworlds* created by children and adults to imaginatively explore important events and emotions in children's lives (Ferholt, 2015). In these studies, *perezhivanie* draws attention to episodes of heightened emotional and cognitive engagement within a role. The episodes of play become topics of conversation and reflection between children and adults as they revisit the stories they have created and enacted. It's "as if" they are floating above the experience and learning from the episode as they recall and evaluate the emotional experiences within and beyond the stories. The child is both acting imaginatively, "as if" somebody else, but also able to shift to consider the "as-if self" from the perspective of their past and present self. In these moments they are able to articulate a sense of self, moving through time.

There are parallels between the Karawatha excursion and the context of Fleer's and Fernholt's research on *perezhivanie*. Each situation involves students actively entering into a story and taking on a role – in Karawatha it is the blanket role of environmental advocate. In the role of advocate and through the story of Bernice students have the opportunity to reflect more deeply on their past and present lives and reconfigure the way they see themselves in the future. We've provided a number of examples and extracts above where students see themselves as "new persons" or embarking on a "new journey", or "bonding with nature" to become a committed advocate who never gives up. Below an extended extract from a letter to Bernice is provided to show how the student shifts temporally and emotionally as she reflects on her experiences in Karawatha, reconsiders her past, and begins to plan her future.

> I now know why you wanted to save this amazing place. . . . I found inside this sacred place that all my worries disappeared with the sights and sounds of the city. When we sat still everything that I saw as ordinary I found something so amazing "the extra-in-the–ordinary." Something inside me made me want to stay there forever. Watching the insects and colourful birds swoop and glide through the clean air. I've had a hard life but not as hard as others so in that moment I was reminded of the beautiful things and people that life has given me. I want to say thank you from the bottom of my newly environmental heart. Thank you for saving this gorgeous place. Thank you for making that moment possible. Thank you for all the hard work and love you put into protecting this forest. Also, I loved talking to you on 6.6.13. You are the most inspirational lady ever. Yours truly,
>
> (Year 6 Student, 2013)

The key moment in this account is the student's reflection on her life (I've had a hard life but not as hard as others so in that moment I was reminded of the beautiful things and people that life has given me). Her self-reflection is comparative (but not as hard as others) and this moves her to remember and be thankful for her good fortune (in that moment I was reminded of the beautiful things and people that life has given me). She moves forward in time to reveal her newly environmental heart and to thank Bernice for making this significant moment in Karawatha a reality for her (Thank you for making that moment possible). The affordances for this significant moment – the student's *perezhivanie*, her emotionally lived experience – have been designed into the pedagogy by overlapping the story of Bernice with the stories inscribed in the place itself and unique moments that each child can experience through *dadirri* practices and heightened sensory awareness as they walk through the forest. Not every student will experience *perezhivanie*, but for some the elements of the experience combine to make Karawatha a significant event in their lives.

We were fortunate to recently capture multiple aspects of a *perezhivanie* event for Liam on his excursion to Karawatha. Liam's relationship with his teacher and peers changed during the excursion to Karawatha, and he anticipates he will create a new view of himself with his parents when he tells them what happened on the excursion. Liam was described by his teacher as capable but disengaged at school. She revealed that she struggled to communicate with him and engage him in learning. But something changed at Karawatha. As the comments by Liam to Merryl (PEEC teacher) show, he was inspired and wants to inspire others and eventually work in a forest.

> Karawatha inspired me . . . like I'm going to try and work in Karawatha Forest to, like, inspire other children or work at a different kind of forest that's like sacred.
>
> (Liam, Year 5 Student, 2013)

The PEEC teachers (Merryl and Karl) asked Liam if he'd speak to Bernice on the mobile phone at the conclusion to the excursion because he had shown such a high level of engagement during the day. It was obvious to them that he wasn't often selected as a spokesperson but his enthusiastic response to the invitation and his willingness to talk with Bernice suggested that this was a good choice. Liam was encouraged to speak from his heart and to say what he felt was true for him. There was silence and anticipation as the phone rang and everyone waited for Bernice to answer. Merryl greeted Bernice warmly and commented on how beautiful the day and weather had been in Karawatha even though it was a little hot. Merryl introduced Liam who revoiced her previous comments about the weather and proceeded to speak in a thoughtful and rather mature way.

> Hi Bernice, it's Liam. Umm. We've had, umm, a very good day. Yes, it was very good weather, and I was just mentioning, umm, to Karl and Meryl, it'd be a tragedy if this forest disappeared and, umm, thank you for saving it for lots of future generations of children and adults to see this lovely place.

His teacher later indicated that she became quite emotional during this phone call and had a "little cry" because she had been unable to "unlock him" and now she was witnessing Liam fully present, emotionally and thoughtfully engaged in a way she'd never seen before. At the beginning of the day she admitted that she had quite low expectations of how Liam would participate, but she was still hoping that he would somehow find a way to connect with the place and the story. This teacher is very skilled and compassionate and always gives a great deal of time to preparing students for their Karawatha excursion, and yet she had not been able to catch the imagination of this boy. At the end of the day she reported her astonishment at how powerful the experience had been for him.

Immediately after the phone call Liam was very excited and came rushing towards the PEEC teachers at the back of the group. He talked passionately about being inspired and hoped Karawatha could inspire other children to realise how sacred places like Karawatha are. He revealed how nervous he was to talk to Bernice because she was "like a celebrity", but he'd recorded the whole phone call to play to his mum and dad that night because "they would never believe I done it".

We'd interpret this as a moment of *perezhivanie* for Liam where his thoughts, feelings and sense of self are in flux. Through the Karawatha excursion Liam has begun to reimagine himself as a leader in his class, as an engaged student for his teacher and as a more capable son at home where he believed his parents would be amazed at what he had achieved. In the moment of talking to Bernice he was both anxious and excited, and yet he had the presence of mind to flick his phone to "record" because he wanted evidence of his achievement to share with his parents. Liam's confidence in speaking for the group seemed to be a surprise to everyone, including Liam himself.

Just after the excursion the classroom teacher arranged for the students to write to Bernice. Liam wrote the following words that suggest the Karawatha experience continued to influence how he imagined himself in the future.

> We are so grateful for what you did because a lot of kids have seen forest. And so will the next generation of people and the next because of you. I also learnt a new word to me called dadirri, thanks to Merryl and Karl. Dadirri means speaking to the trees (deep listening). So now I use dadirri all the time. As an environmental advocate I will teach other people dadirri. And one (idea) is maybe get more schools to adventure (to) Karawatha to witness a beautiful (place).

Liam's *perezhivanie* encompassed a change in emotion, thinking and sense of self, a change noted by the teachers at PEEC as well as his own classroom teacher and commented on by Liam himself as significant to his relationships with his parents and to his sense of a future self. This example is one of many such similar transformations that PEEC teachers have noted over the years. Deploying *perezhivanie* to analyse these episodes suggests that such moments may have longer-term significance in the child's developmental trajectory.

Conclusion

In this chapter we drew on Bakhtin's notion of voice to conceptualise advocacy as internally persuasive dialogue that develops as students appropriate and transform voices beyond themselves – voices that are brought to life in stories and activities during the Karawatha program. Students can interanimate their voices with multiple other voices, namely, the voice of the active citizen, the voice of the concerned scientist and that of environmental educators who create opportunities for students to make sense of advocacy in diverse ways. In addition, through the pedagogy of *dadirri*, students are given imaginative access to the voices of Indigenous custodians of country, and the voices of the materiality of the land itself, as represented in their encounter with the rocks, animals, trees and water of Karawatha. These actual and imaginative voices will be heard by students in different ways depending on their own histories and interests. Bernice Volz is central. She is the voice of the engaged local citizen who advocated with passion, commitment and tenacity to save Karawatha. Jean-Marc Hero is the concerned scientist whose voice reveals the uniqueness of the ecology at Karawatha. With his colleague Merryl Simpson from PEEC Ron Tooth represents the voice of environmental educators who orchestrate the experiences and multiple voices that students hear during the day. They present the Karawatha pedagogy as a series of story moments that connect students to the voices of Bernice and Jean-Marc and to the many *dadirri* moments that have been carefully designed to heighten sensory awareness so students notice the finest details and complexity of Karawatha.

This pedagogy frees students and teachers from the strictures of what Bakhtin calls an authoritative discourse, which cannot be questioned. This kind of authoritative pedagogy creates relationships that are hierarchical, accepting and compliant rather than engaged and questioning, and while this might be excellent for certain kinds of training where methodical compliance is important, it cannot lead to the kind of authentic advocacy that is the goal of the Karawatha pedagogy. When students enter into an open and rich dialogue between established ways of making sense of the world and novel experiences and voices, as they do in Karawatha, they can encounter advocacy in a manner that is highly personal and often very surprising. This is very different from the formulaic, dogmatic and even fundamentalist advocacy that might arise from a more authoritarian approach.

The pedagogy at Karawatha is not neutral or disinterested. Over many years of conducting this program Ron Tooth can attest that it both engages students emotionally and heightens their reflective awareness of the value of Karawatha and the need for environmental advocacy. This type of outcome is difficult to capture if learning is treated as a linear process measurable by tracking increases in knowledge or skills or values. The notion of *perezhivanie* seems particularly relevant to the type of complex learning promoted through the Karawatha program because it draws attention to moments of emotional and transformative learning that change how students see themselves and relate to others and the places around them. The analysis of Liam's experiences in Karawatha shows they resulted in him emerging as a new type of student, a leader amongst his peers and (Liam anticipates) as a more capable son by his parents. His *perezhivanie* – emotionally charged experiences and reflections – seemed to generate an internally persuasive discourse where he rethought his ecological identity, his relationship with the natural world, and his commitment to advocate for places like Karawatha in the future.

Note

1 The Karwatha experience described in this chapter with its focus on advocacy and *dadirri* was designed and led by Ron Tooth and Merryl Simpson over the past six years. Karl Fagermo has most recently offered valuable input into this program and has on occasion led excursion days. Other teachers who were very influential in shaping the earlier iterations of the Karawatha experience were Madelaine Winstanley and Simone Firmin.

References

Bakhtin, M. M. (1991). *Dialogic imagination: Four essays by M. M. Bakhtin* (C. Emerson & M. Holquist, Trans.). Austin, TX: University of Texas Press.

Biesta, G. (2007). Why "what works" won't work: Evidence-based practice and the democratic deficit in educational research. *Educational theory, 57*(1), 1–22.

Biesta, G. (2015). What is education for? On good education, teacher judgement, and educational professionalism. *European Journal of Education, 50*(1), 75–87.

Carrington, B., & Troyna, B. (1988). *Children and controversial issues: Strategies for the early and middle years of schooling.* Hove: Psychology Press.

Cotton, D. (2006). Implementing curriculum guidance on environmental education: The importance of teachers' beliefs. *Journal of Curriculum Studies, 38*(1), 67–83.

Elliot, J. (1971). The concept of the neutral teacher. *Cambridge Journal of Education, 1*(2), 60–67.

Ferholt, B. (2015). *Perezhivanie* in researching playworlds: Applying the concept of *perezhivanie* in the study of play. In S. Davis, B. Ferholt, H. G. Clemson, S-M. Jansson & A. Marjanovic-Shane (Eds.), *Dramatic interactions in education: Vygotskian and sociocultural approaches to drama, education and research* (pp. 57–75). London: Bloomsbury Academic.

Fleer, M., & Hammer, M. (2013). 'Perezhivanie' in group settings: A cultural-historical reading of emotion regulation. *Australasian Journal of Early Childhood, 38*(3), 127–134.

Freire, P. (1985). Reading the world and reading the word: An interview with Paulo Freire. *Language Arts, 62*, 15–21.

Garnett, S., & Franklin, D. (2014). *Climate change adaptation plan for Australian birds.* Collingwood, VIC: CSIRO Publishing.

Holquist, M. (1990). *Dialogism: Bakhtin and his world.* London: Routledge.

Morson, G., & Emerson, C. (1990). *Mikhail Bakhtin: Creation of a prosaics.* Stanford, CA: Stanford University Press.

Renshaw, P., & Tooth, R. (2016). Perezhivanie mediated through narrative place-responsive pedagogy. In A. Surian (Ed.), *Open spaces for interaction and learning diversities* (pp. 13–23). Rotterdam: Sense Publishers.

Stenhouse, L. (1971). The humanities curriculum project: The rationale. *Theory into Practice, 10*(3), 154–162.

Tooth, R., & Renshaw, P. (2012). *Storythread* pedagogy for environmental education. In T. Wrigley, P. Thomson & B. Lingard (Eds.), *Changing schools: Alternative ways to make a world of difference* (pp. 113–127). London: Routledge.

Ungunmerr-Baumann, M. R. (1988). Dadirri. *Compass Theology Review, 22*, 9–11.

Ungunmerr-Baumann, M. R. (2002). *Dadirri: A reflection by Miriam-Rose Ungunmerr Baumann.* Retrieved from http://nextwave.org.au/wp-content/uploads/Dadirri-Inner-Deep-Listening-M-R-Ungunmerr-Bauman-Refl.pdf

Vygotsky, L. S. (1934/1994). The problem of the environment. In R. van der Veer & J. Valsiner (Eds.), *The Vygotsky reader* (pp. 338–354). Oxford: Blackwell.

Wals, A. E. (2010). *Message in a bottle: Learning our way out of unsustainability. Wageningen*: Wageningen University.

3 Pedagogy as story in landscape

Ron Tooth

Editors' preface

This Chapter centres on a narrative-inspired pedagogy called *Hoodwinked* that was designed by Ron Tooth and his colleagues at Pullenvale Environmental Education Centre (PEEC). The narrative is situated locally at Pullen Pullen Creek and involves characters and events based on actual historical records. The protagonists are bush kids who played and explored along Pullen Pullen Creek over a century ago. The bush kids of the 19th century were based on reminisces shared with Ron Tooth by an elderly local resident, John Bird, whose parents had lived in Pullenvale in the late 19th century. In dramatizing and reliving the story based on the actual lives of these children, students become "modern day bush kids" with privileged knowledge that is crucial to the eventual resolution of the tensions and conflicts within the story. The narrative dilemma centres on habitat loss at Pullen Pullen Creek and extinction of bird species as the result of illegal trapping and killing of birds for their feathers, which were exported to Europe in the late 19th century for the fashion industry. Students enter imaginatively into the story through dramatic role-play. Their task within the drama is to travel through time to protect the birds from the smugglers by influencing the thoughts and actions of the teacher who owns the land where the birds are being trapped. The historical authenticity of the story is highly motivating for students. When they know that the original bush kids actually played and explored along Pullen Pullen Creek where they are walking, their interest and engagement intensifies. Authentic artefacts from the 19th century allow students to materially experience the way of life of the original bush kids. A fortuitous donation to Ron Tooth of two boxes of preserved rare rainforest birds (largely extinct in the Pullenvale area now) provides compelling evidence of the destructive effects of trapping and killing local birds. The boxes are exquisite pieces of Victorian decoration, yet in the story they are a powerful visual reminder of species loss and habitat destruction by humans.

While recent theorisations of the interconnections between place and story by Massey (2005) and Somerville (2010) were not deployed in creating this narrative pedagogy, there are significant resonances between these theories and the *Hoodwinked* pedagogy. Massey conceives of place as an active process rather than as a passive backdrop for activity. Place is imbued with agency which Massey connects to story, calling place "a collection of stories" and "a simultaneity of stories-so-far" (Massey, 2005, p. 130). Theorising place as multiple stories resonates with the approach taken in *Hoodwinked*. Written into the landscape at Pullenvale are the stories of the local Indigenous people, the colonial settlers, the trappers and taxidermists, and the local children who played along the creek. In re-creating these characters through drama and story, Ron Tooth and his colleagues make visible to students of today some of the stories inscribed in place, and through careful historical research they also reveal that Pullen Pullen Creek was connected to distant places (London, Paris) in an exploitative manner via the feather trade for hats. This trade had a devastating outcome for the birds of Pullen Pullen Creek. Massey (2005) highlights this relational aspect of place, namely, that places are connected through relationships that create hierarchies of power, exploitation and marginalisation. By entering dramatically and imaginatively into the story of *Hoodwinked*, students can come to a deeper understanding of Pullen Pullen Creek as a set of interconnected stories involving competing human goals, personal agency and ethical responsibility that stretches all the way to Europe. The in-between dramatic role of bush kids – then and now – requires students to improvise courses of action and take principled stands to influence the direction of the story. In this process they live and relive the ethical dilemmas of place – how should they make and remake the stories of Pullen Pullen Creek. This dynamic and interconnected notion of place exemplifies Massey's theorising of place as agentic and relational.

Margaret Somerville's (2010) view that stories bring nature into culture also resonates with the *Hoodwinked* pedagogy. Quoting Sinclair (2001, p. 22), Somerville proposes that 'stories bring nature into culture and ascribe meaning to places, species and processes which would otherwise remain silent to the human ear' (Somerville, 2010, p. 336). In *Hoodwinked*, students experience nature firsthand by exploring along the banks of Pullen Pullen Creek. But this is only one version of the Creek. The students also experience the Creek imaginatively as it was in the 19th century, a habitat for rainforest birds. As well they experience the Creek as a site of contest between trappers involved in the feather trade and locals who regarded the birds and habitat as inherently valuable and important to sustain. So the *Hoodwinked* narrative produces various versions of Pullen Pullen Creek that allow students to understand "nature" as a contested cultural concept, intimately related to human intentions and interests. In working with students in the *Hoodwinked* program over many years, Ron Tooth has documented instances where students seem to be "reworked in some way", something that Karrow and Fazio (2010) describe as the co-emergent relationship that exists between nature and culture when we are responsive to place. One child reported during the *Hoodwinked* program, for example, that being next to the water in the creek made him question what it is to be a person. This is not the kind of pondering that one expects of a ten-year-old but it occurs regularly when students engage deeply with place in narrative-based programs like *Hoodwinked*.

Peter Renshaw & Ron Tooth

Introduction

> You would think that by laying a story over a place or a landscape that you would in some way constrain and narrow the experience for children, but in fact, the very opposite seems to occur. It's as if the place comes alive through the story in a new and deeply personal way that heightens understanding and connection much more than simply walking through the place without the support of narrative. This has often struck me as a strange paradox and also surprises both students and their teachers.
>
> —Ron Tooth, Journal entry, 2015

My recent journal observation about *story* transforming *place* reflects Bruner's (1987) notion that story mediates our thinking, feeling and relationships. Story is fundamental to our memory for events; it provides the means through which we can account for ourselves across time, and through which we represent our place in the world. Stories can engage students in complex thinking about themselves and their relationships with place. This chapter explores the role of story both as a template for designing place-responsive experiences and as a specific pedagogical strategy to engage students with the natural world and with questions of how to live more sustainably (Abram, 1997). The specific example explored in this chapter is a *Storythread* program called *Hoodwinked* that engages students in the story of the bush kids living in the late 19th century who face the dilemma of protecting local bird species from illegal smuggling. *Storythread* is a narrative place-responsive pedagogy of place that has been developed at Pullenvale Environmental Education Centre (PEEC) over the past thirty-four years. To understand how *Hoodwinked* developed over many years and why it profoundly influences students' learning today, it is important to know its origins in the *place* where it was created.

The place

Hoodwinked is a program offered by Pullenvale Environmental Education Centre, which is situated on the western outskirts of Brisbane on the grounds of the original Pullenvale State School. The Centre is set against a backdrop of ancient forests and the mountains of the Diagular Ranges. When I first arrived with my family at Pullenvale in 1982 there were three buildings on the old school site: an empty single teacher schoolroom and its accompanying residence, both built in 1874, and an aging demountable building. The rest of the two-acre block was covered with weeds and a few large pine and eucalyptus trees. Today this story hub consists of ten authentically restored historical buildings set amongst native gardens and surrounded by forest trees that connect to a network of urban forests. When students participate in programs at Pullenvale they catch glimpses of characters from various *Storythread* programs as they walk by, or they might meet them face-to-face in a drama and theatre space or when they step through a time window into a carefully restored historical site. As students enter the grounds to participate in *Hoodwinked* they know they are coming to the place of the bush kids of 1897 because that story is already alive in their imaginations due to our pre-excursion preparation and materials. Our job on the excursion day is to further enhance the imaginative engagement of students with the dilemmas of that story and hopefully transform their relationship with the places they live in.

At PEEC we are acutely aware that we work on the ancestral lands of the Turrbul people who lived, traversed and created culture here for thousands of years and who remain the custodians of this country. One of my first meetings at PEEC in 1982 was with a group of Aboriginal Elders who walked with me, and my two young sons, in the local forest. They laughed and joked as we walked, shared stories about their families and casually talked about their connection to the land as we followed an echidna track along a sandy creek. I have never forgotten the emotion of that day. The meeting had a profound influence on my future interactions with Aboriginal people and was a turning point in my journey into place-responsive teaching and pedagogy. Why didn't I notice the echidna tracks on that day as we walked, yet for the Aboriginal women and men, the tracks were quite obvious? It was only when I knelt on the hard sand and looked intently that I could see the delicate pattern of tracks along the water's edge. Close observation was an embodied way of being in the bush for this group. They often moved slowly, deliberately and in silence, much like some of the ecologists I'd worked with. I now see this experience three decades ago as the beginning of my fascination with *attentiveness in nature*, as yet unnamed or explicitly incorporated in my pedagogy.

At this time I also met a long-term local resident, John Bird, and it was his recounting of childhood stories of living a free life in the bush with his friends that became the inspiration for the *Hoodwinked* program. As I listened to John Bird talk about his childhood adventures at the local creek, and looked at the old photographs of his parents and family that he had stored in a timber box, I was transported to the 1860s when John Bird's parents had just arrived in Pullenvale just after the twenty years of the "Black Wars" (Eckley, 2001; Kilcullen, 2009) when an alliance of Aboriginal groups fiercely resisted the invasion of their country. They fought for their lands across southern Queensland just as Indigenous people did all across Australia (Reynolds, 2006). I read *An Imaginary Life* by novelist and poet David Malouf in that period and scribbled down the following quotation because it captured what I was feeling at the time about *place* and the kind of program I wanted *Hoodwinked* to become.

> The spirits have to be recognised to become real. They are not outside us, nor even entirely within, but flow back and forth between us and the objects we have made, the landscape we have shaped and move in. We have dreamed all these things in our deepest lives and they are ourselves. It is our self we are making out there.
>
> (Malouf, 1999, p. 28)

I carried this quote with me in my backpack for many years and often shared it with visiting teachers when they asked me why I thought children became so engaged with *place* through stories. My answer was always the same: *I think these narratives are allowing children to discover something new about themselves as they connect to particular places and become intrigued by the stories of others who have been here before them.* Many voices arose for me from this place, providing the seeds of what would one day become the *Hoodwinked* program. There were the voices of John Bird and the original bush kids of Pullenvale and the attentiveness to place embodied in the local Aboriginal women and men. Traces of these voices are experienced by students today when they participate in the *Hoodwinked* program.

Understanding the authentic history of *place* is crucial to *Storythread* programs, such as *Hoodwinked*. In researching the history of the area around Pullenvale, I visited the Queensland State archives looking for the original letter written by Adam Walker to the Department of Public Instruction in 1873 asking for the Pullenvale State School to be built. I can still recall the texture of the pale blue paper with the meticulous and beautifully executed copperplate script documenting the hopes of this community for their children. I could sense the person behind the words and how important this school was to Adam Walker and the other families. Finding the original letter gave me a sense of the community that John Bird's family was part of and what the other children and families in the community might have been like.

The *Hoodwinked* program[1]

The centrepiece of the *Hoodwinked* experience is an excursion to PEEC where students step into the lives of John Bird and the original bush kids of the 1890s as they attempt to solve a difficult environmental problem. The excursion is structured as an evolving detective journey across the day. In the morning they visit the bush kids' creek where they spend time practicing attentiveness, imagining the children from the past and writing personal reflections. The middle session is structured around reflective encounters with authentic artefacts used by story characters in the 19th century. The day concludes as the students step into an intense one-hour story drama where they must advocate and fight for the creek in role and as agents of change as they struggle to convince Miss Dove of the danger that she and the birds at the creek are facing. Students prepare for this excursion day by contracting to become modern day bush kids as they consider what this might mean for them in their current lives at school and at home. The excursion day brings all the pre-visit threads together into a rich storytelling, reflective and nature experience at PEEC. The central purpose of the day is for students to connect to the place, especially the local creek, and to use this to enter a story adventure that brings them to a point where they leave PEEC with a strong feeling of their own agency, which is succinctly captured in the following quote.

> The connection to place starts the day because once they have connected to that place they care about what's going to happen, and the story concerns that place. They feel like bush kids, and it takes them deeper into the blanket role (modern day bush kid). So once they step into the story and find out

something is threatening the characters they love, and the place they love, they're "in". They want to help. It's exciting, there's mystery, and they are in a position of power where they are the only people who can help because they are the only people with all the information. They feel empowered, they love the detective skills and it's fun going through the sites and finding the clues and putting them together. . . . So they leave with such an amazing feeling of agency and what they've done together in the group.

(Interview with PEEC Teacher, April, 2015)

The *Hoodwinked* story is one of hope, trickery, danger and betrayal that imaginatively engages modern day bush kids in a journey through time to rescue Miss Dove, the original bush kids, and the rare birds at Pullen Pullen Creek. The story centres on a notorious criminal called Paddy McKinney who has been secretly trapping rare birds on Miss Dove's land near the creek and then selling them in London and Paris as part of the feather trade for women's hats in the high fashion industry. He is the kind of person who lets nothing stand in his way, and he has created what appears to be the perfect plan. Paddy has taken on the false identity of a travelling Reverend who claims to be a committed naturalist. This has guaranteed him access to Miss Dove's land and to her trust, which will allow him to deliver a constant stream of birds to his clients in Europe. As a final safeguard he has created false evidence that points to the bush kids as the environmental vandals killing the birds at Pullen Pullen Creek. Miss Dove believes the Reverend (Paddy in disguise) and the plan seems complete. What Paddy hasn't factored in is that a group of modern day bush kids have just arrived at Pullenvale in the twenty-first century and have discovered clues and then listened and looked through time to see the truth. Paddy is unaware that as he makes his plans these children are also planning to step through time to stop him and save the birds from extinction.

Key pedagogical features of the *Hoodwinked* excursion day

Hoodwinked, as a typical *Storythread* program, combines five key pedagogical elements:

1   the use of historical and environmental stories grounded in the issues of the local area;
2   the use of multiple levels of cultural artefacts and materiality to engage students in inquiry;
3   the use of story and drama to engage students with the significant others who have been there before them and with whom they can interact in the place to become agents of change;
4   the use of "deep attentive and reflective listening" that allows students to be open and receptive to the complexity, beauty, and surprises of the natural world;
5   the use of the "real life blanket role" as a device to enhance personal agency and advocacy in students and to initiate positive change in their school community.

Hoodwinked *is grounded in the authenticity of historical story*

The *Hoodwinked* experience is based on the actual stories of John Bird. His memories of playing with his friends at the creek and of Aboriginal people living nearby and singing in the distance at night as he tried to fall asleep has proven to be compelling for students, which is evident when they hear that the bush kids of Pullenvale actually existed. Once this has been revealed either at school or on their arrival it only requires a PEEC teacher to ask if they'd like to visit the creek for them to be on their feet ready to go. There is a sense of expectancy and excitement that comes from knowing that they are about to visit the place where the original bush kids met and played. The intensity of the response depends to some degree on the amount of preparation at school, but even when this has been minimal the idea is still sufficient to hook students in and bond them emotionally to the bush kids. We have seen this many times and have noted that fiction based on real stories creates a level of authenticity that takes students to new levels of engagement.

When students visit John Bird's creek and spend time soaking up the sounds, textures and colours and then sit in silence watching the birds and listening to the sounds of the forest as the bush kids once did, they experience the creek as transformed by story. It feels right to talk about the bush kids as if they are only a breath away. If we then ask them to peer back through time to imagine they can see the bush kids in this place, they always appear to be able to do this and eagerly describe in detail what they saw. It feels natural to ask why the Aboriginal children have stopped coming to the creek, something the bush kids wondered about as well, and why the adults are silent about this. This dialogue can lead to rich and productive conversations and critiques in the moment and back at school. In these moments the students become co-creators with us as they enter imaginatively and intellectually into the historical world of bush kids to think about various issues and possibilities and to physically scramble up logs, wade across the creek and build cubbies. The pedagogical power of such moments is striking when imagination and history meet the materiality of place.

While *Hoodwinked* is the central narrative, a number of other related stories allow us to develop a broader narrative concerned with the extinction of rainforest birds and the loss of their habitat in the area. One story arose from a donation by a local family of two exquisitely crafted red cedar cases full of rare rainforest birds that are now extinct in the area. These birds had been trapped, killed and preserved by a local taxidermist in the late 19th century. While the boxes are very beautiful as pieces of Victorian decoration they have become a powerful visual metaphor in our pedagogy on habitat loss. These boxes remain at the front of the Old Classroom where they are part of every *Hoodwinked* program. Two other pieces of research fed into and sharpened this focus on birds and habitats. I read a series of articles on the trapping of rare birds in the 1890's to supply feathers to London and Paris for ladies' hats and the resistance to such trade mounted by early naturalists and by nature educators at the time. This detail entered into the *Hoodwinked* program to give the story an authentic point of conflict between people wanting to exploit the creek for profit and people wanting to sustain the creek ecologically.

In addition to these historical narratives there is the story of Pullen Pullen Creek and the fact that it sits at the centre of the "Macleay-McPherson Overlap Zone" which stretches north and south from Brisbane and is significant for its rich biodiversity. The northern Torresian and southern Bassian floras and faunas of Australia meet and overlap at this point which explains the unusually high abundance of bird, bat, amphibian and snake species found in the area although many of these species are now classified locally as "vulnerable" or "endangered". It was this final ecological frame that tied everything together and allowed the story of the bush kids to become a story, not only this place, but of every place where children have met and played in creeks and created their own connections to that place. The themes of bird life and habitat loss have maintained their vitality over thirty years and continue to engage students. This reinforces how important it is to tie stories to the history and materiality of specific site because this is what will provide even richer authentic experiences of place for students.

Hoodwinked *embodies multiple levels of cultural artefact and materiality*

The *Hoodwinked* excursion allows students to touch, handle and use a wide range of material artefacts and objects as part of an extended problem-solving investigation. Over time we have come to appreciate the efficacy of using arte-facts in this way to engage students at all three levels described by Wartofsky (1979). He identifies the first level as consisting of *primary artefacts*, which include those tools used in production, for example, axes, ploughs, industrial machinery, school pens, slates etc. The second level consists of *secondary arte-facts*, which include primary artefacts and the modes of social action associated with the use of primary artefacts. The third level is *tertiary artefacts* or the imagined worlds that constitute an arena of creativity or free play. As part of the *Hoodwinked* excursion day, students engage at all three levels through carefully designed "I Wonder" encounters that reveal the thinking, values and motiva-tions of key story characters. "I Wonder" invites students to handle and analyse artefacts as detectives who decipher clues, make inferences and draw conclusions based on what they discern from handling particular objects. In this way they collectively decide what they think could be happening in the story and make decisions about the next step that they should take. "I Wonder" is a very tactile and participatory experience, scaffolded through questioning by teachers, that allows students to enter into the mind and environmental motivations of charac-ters. By engaging with the materiality of artefacts in this reflective way students can also be given access to the environmental visions that drive characters and how these are shaping their relationship with nature and their choices in the story.

For example, at one point in *Hoodwinked*, the teacher and students enter the bird trapper's camp and see a white canvas tent modelled on a 19th century design with rough bush poles and ropes. The tent is furnished with bush tables, tins, saddles, blankets, harness, a metal trunk, items of clothing and personal trinkets. There are also various letters and notes that reveal key information about their true motives and plans, of which Miss Dove and the original bush kids are unaware. At this moment, there is always a feeling of expectancy because they know that the bird trappers could come back at any moment. Two very important clues are hidden from sight so that the students must search for them. One is a hessian sack containing a preserved azure kingfisher ready for export to England and a poster that reveals that Paddy McKinney is wanted for forgery in England. The poster also lists his many aliases, one of which is the Reverend. The second clue is a wrapped gift. When it is opened, the students find some jewelry and realize that it is intended for Miss Dove. It takes only a moment for them to realize that Paddy is in disguise and that he is deceiving Miss Dove. A third critical clue, Miss Dove's diary, is revealed later when the students search her classroom. This is when they discover how committed she is to protecting the creek and that she has been tricked by the Reverend into thinking that the children in her class are the ones killing the rare birds. The realness of these objects used in *Hoodwinked*, especially those artefacts owned by key characters, engages students and results in curious and authentic learning.

Hoodwinked *uses story and drama to awaken student voice*

A striking feature of *Storythread* pedagogy is the way that it applies elements of story, drama and theatre craft to awaken student voice and sense of agency. In *Hoodwinked* this is most clearly seen in the last hour of the excursion day when the complex story drama comes alive in the classroom re-enactment and students take control as they advocate for the creek and for the rare birds that they know are in critical danger. They improvise costumes and step into their roles as Miss Dove's students in 1897 where they work to resolve the environmental dilemma that she and the bush kids are facing.

> That I can truly let the voice inside me yell out. Even though I was nervous talking to Miss Dove I tried hard to be confident.
>
> (Year 5 Student, 2013)

Everything comes together in these moments when students, like the young girl above, find the courage to speak out to convince Miss Dove not to sign the contract and sell the creek land to Paddy whom she thinks is her friend, the Reverend. I have seen this kind of response many times in *Hoodwinked* and it is always impressive. This young girl has not been asked to stand up and speak. It is her decision, and the passionate words she speaks surprise her as much as those around her. However, this moment of agency is no accident. The PEEC teacher who is playing Miss Dove has created the space and time for students to freely express their views. Two strategies are especially important and an analysis of them is presented here as a way of illuminating the power of the drama process as the means for releasing and focusing student voice and agency.

The first is "Teacher in Role" which in the case of the *Hoodwinked* involves a PEEC teacher taking on the part of Miss Dove. Taking on the role of Miss Dove is very challenging and requires a great deal of skill on the part of the teacher/ actor to know when to push forward and when to hold back so that the students experience their power to intervene and influence key characters. The teacher who is in role as Miss Dove must continually create obstacles that force the students to think on their feet, reflect and improvise as they search for ways to stop Miss Dove selling her land. They have just discovered that Miss Dove thinks that her class are environmental vandals killing birds, and this belief gives the teacher in role a great advantage. It's not as simple as just telling Miss Dove the truth because she will not believe them. This means the children must find creative and clever solutions. Only Miss Dove has the power to decide what happens to her land and only the bush kids from the future know the truth. The young girl who wanted to *let the voice inside me yell out* reveals the urgent embodied sense of agency that students experience as they try to convince Miss Dove. While the technique of "Teacher in Role" provides the opportunity for student voice and agency to emerge it is the technique of "Role within Role" that provides the means.

I discovered "role within role" through a workshop offered by Cecily O'Neill in 1990 when she visited Australia (Ackroyd, 2006). O'Neill, a highly respected drama theorist and educator from England, introduced this technique by reworking "Red Riding Hood" as a process drama. I was part of a small group enrolled as villagers in the fairy story and given secret knowledge and an important task that the others didn't know about. This placed my group in a very powerful position within the drama where we were able to work in two roles simultaneously; the first more mundane and ordinary role (villager) worked to hide and shield the second influential role (villagers with secret knowledge). My group experienced a heightened commitment to the story and a sense of being agents within the drama. Until we introduced "role within role" into the *Hoodwinked* day, the students had a limited part to play in solving problems or shaping the adventure, and while it was certainly fun to be part of the story per se, the students were really only outsiders looking into a clever piece of storytelling. Since the introduction of "role within role", we have seen hundreds of children find their voice, like the young girl described earlier, and make the very personal and quite difficult decision to take action within the drama activity. In some instances children who have been silent all day suddenly speak out and act. On one occasion, another young girl, who we later discovered to have severe learning difficulties, took control of the whole group and began to organize an action plan. This took her teacher totally by surprise because this girl struggled in her classroom and rarely participated – certainly never as a team leader. When students experience "role within role" they often become very passionate and demonstrate a heightened urgency to communicate and act. To someone watching it might look like a simple re-enactment, but when the action begins students respond in quite emotional ways that they and their teachers do not expect.

Hoodwinked uses attentiveness to develop deep nature connections. Dadirri can teach you how to feel nature without touching it. Wherever I go I know that Aboriginal people have been here too.

(Year 5 Students, 2015)

Being attentive to nature requires more than just remembering, recounting or reproducing knowledge and facts *about* nature. It's noticing fine detail, complex patterns, and interconnections between elements and aspects of place. Attentiveness leads to surprising and aesthetic observations that create a desire to share the experience with others. Attentiveness expands our vision of place from something material that exists only "out there" to be watched and touched as opposed to something "in here" that we create through emotional "place attentive" and "place-responsive" encounters with nature. My thinking about attentiveness was informed by the work of the biologist Mary Clark (2004) and her commitment as a scientist to what she calls "profound attentiveness". Clark claims that "profound attentiveness" is at the heart of all great science and art, an experience she equates to falling in love again where our emotions and intellect come together in our experience of the world (Clark, 2004). More recently attentiveness has been given further force within *Hoodwinked* and other programs at PEEC as we have focused on the writings of Miriam-Rose Ungunmerr-Baumann. She is an elder of the Ngangikurungkurr people from Daly River in the Northern Territory, Australia, who speak about the ancient practice of *dadirri*. They describe this as an inner deep listening to country or quiet, still awareness, which Miriam-Rose says is not just an Aboriginal practice but belongs to all people (Ungunmerr-Baumann, 1988; 2002). *Dadirri* is now central to the *Hoodwinked* experience. Hoodwinked creates new identities through the "blanket role".

We all feel like it is what the bush kids did. Yeah, it feels like that we are the bush kids.

(Year 5 Student, 2015)

Blanket role has its roots in educational drama and is sometimes known as the "mantle of the expert" (Heathcote, 1984). Collectively, students assume the imagined role of an expert in a designated field, for example, as a journalist, author, or archaeologist, but always in the knowledge that it's part of an imaginative role-play. At PEEC we use the device to move students from the space of fiction into reality and back again. We ask students to consider how they might move past the imaginative world of story and think about how the role can become a part of their everyday lives. Part of the appeal of blanket role is that it encourages students to first imagine themselves as agents of change within a story before they are asked to consider themselves in real situations at school or home. In this way it works as a transitional device, in a very similar way to what Winnicott

(1971) calls a transitional object. Like a transitional object in Winnicott's terms, the blanket role enables students to play in the space between fiction and reality as they consider what kind of person they might want to become within a story and beyond. In *Hoodwinked* students are invited to see themselves as "modern day bush kids" and to then decide what this might mean for them. They spend a considerable amount of time talking about the qualities of this person and deciding which qualities appeal to them. We no longer view the blanket role simply as a drama strategy but as a transitional device that can empower students to reflect on their relationship to themselves, to others and to nature.

Evidence of change from participating in *Hoodwinked*

In a class reflection during my time at Eco State School I asked the Year 7 students the question: "What was your stand-out moment over your entire school life (1–7)". All the students said that the *Hoodwinked* Excursion at PEEC was the best thing they ever did! This was not one or two students but the entire class that gave this answer! As a visiting pre-service teacher it attested to the power of the *Storythread* approach and experiential learning which in the near-future I was to become a part of (PEEC Contract Teacher, 2015).

For years we have been monitoring the learning arising from *Hoodwinked*. The comments above about students' enthusiasm for *Hoodwinked* (*the best thing they ever did!*) are typical of the reports we regularly hear from teachers. Over the past five years we have collected evidence of change directly from students who have participated in the *Hoodwinked* program using a range of sources such as:

1   "student passports" (each student returns a single A2 sheet to PEEC before the excursion explaining why he or she wants to grow his or her skills as a bush kid);
2   reflections by students as part of sharing circles at the creek on the day of the excursion;
3   on-the-spot statements made by students as the *Hoodwinked* story drama unfolds; and
4   small group interviews with selected students after the excursion.

In our initial examination of the data we were surprised by the heart-felt responses from students. For example, one student expressed herself as follows:

> You need this experience in your life. If you don't have it, you won't be complete.
>
> (Year 5 Student, 2015)

In categorising students' responses to *Hoodwinked* we searched through the data for dominant themes regarding the kinds of change and learning that had occurred. Some students referred to a new understanding of themselves. For others, it was the realization that their thinking had changed through attentiveness. Some students became aware of a growing sense of wellbeing associated with their feelings of oneness with nature, and others were captivated by the aesthetics, beauty and wonder of the experience in place. Finally, there were those who became more aware of their sense of agency and realized that they wanted to advocate and influence others. Below I illustrate and elaborate each of these themes with extracts form the data sources.

Changes in student understandings of themselves

The first area of major change that we identified was in relation to the way students viewed themselves. For example, in the vivid images that follow, a Year 5 student imagines that she has changed from a state of being "normal" on the way to the creek to becoming a new, more invigorated and curious person who feels so alive, with a cleared mind, like a wild animal moving through the forest. This is a remarkable response from a young child, especially her ability to remember with such clarity how her body and senses responded to the experience when she entered the creek for the first time. The interview was three weeks after the excursion, and she is still speaking here with enthusiasm about how her curiosity was awakened.

> So we were walking down normal, but when we went to the creek, the smell just went into my – up my nose, into my brain and my mind and cleared it. And I turned into a different person; like an animal . . . the eye gets bigger, something like that, like a change. And then I was like . . . so that's how my curiosity came.
>
> (Year 5 Student, 2015)

A PEEC teacher shared the following moment – she had asked a departing group of students what had changed for them since they'd arrived in the morning. One girl, who had hardly spoken all day, turned and answered as she stepped onto the bus, "*Today I was the most myself I have ever been*". It is evident that for her the day had been very significant and that she'd moved into a place of deep personal appreciation and insight. This unexpected and eloquent response captivated her teacher and the PEEC staff.

As part of the *Hoodwinked* program, students are asked to sit silently for ten minutes and think about the bush kids being in this place a hundred years earlier. Their reflections are then collected in an unedited form and worked into a single class poem. Below is one example of such a collective poem – it is quite typical of the responses from different groups of students. Students always enjoy the creek experience and their emotions and authentic voice are evident in this group poem where a number of them explore different visions of themselves. What they say could have been said by the original bush kids, and this realization often becomes a point for ongoing reflection that helps to build the bond with the story characters.

> Nature brightens the place up, bird calls, so many animal noises
> Calming the place down, calling to each other.
> Peaceful cool air, trees, wildlife, little insects
> Sun gleaming out of leaves and vines

A cool breeze, feathers and creatures
Full of life I want to see everything.
This place teaches me to deep listen.
Sit in a shady area
Look! Different plants. They have something different about them,
See the ripples, the reflections on the water, appearing on trees
Being next to the water makes me question what makes me a person.
This place makes me feel calm and relaxed.
Solitude, like I'm in a dream. No distractions
I'm not worrying or scared, but safe.
I feel emotional, special, refreshed!
Relieved from stress.
Happy and active, like an adventurist!
This place teaches me how to create different things
Skip rocks, play before school, a meeting spot
Play in the bush with my friends.

(Year 5 Class)

In this poem one student has re-envisaged the group and himself as "adventur-ists" who can skip rocks and play with their friends at the creek, just like the original bush kids did. The poem is infused with a sense that students are being "reworked in some way", at least in that moment, something that Karrow and Fazio (2010) describe as the co-emergent relationship that exists between nature and culture when we are responsive to place. One child recognizes that being next to the water makes him question what it is to be a person. This is not the kind of pondering that one expects of a ten-year-old but it occurs regularly when students engage deeply with place in programs like *Hoodwinked*.

What is particularly striking in the following set of responses is how the imag-ined presence of the bush kids is so significant in helping students to think about themselves differently as a new kind of person within the story. This bonding with the fictional characters is something students often refer to as significant. For example, in the joyful recount that follows, a young boy imagines he is becoming a whole new person as he and the group begins to feel that they are the bush kids.

Karl (PEEC teacher) told us that bush kids were here and it felt so special because we heard what the bush kids did and it just – it felt so, like, real. We felt like we were bush kids. And then everyone – we went back to the classroom and we got dressed and everything. And I was a whole new person when I did that (laughs.) . . . . We all feel like it is what the bush kids did. Yeah, it feels like that we are the bush kids.

(Year 5 Student, 2015)

We have seen the motivational effect of this bond with story characters over many years, and have been struck by how it carries over into how students see themselves as learners at school and at home. For example, in the following writ-ten response a boy links the experience of becoming a bush kid to insights which include recognizing the importance of deep listening, critiquing the use of electronics in modern life, realizing that we all need to spend more time outside and being inspired to reach his personal goals. This is an impressive synthesis of ideas that demonstrates the kind of insight that an experience like *Hoodwinked* can enable for students. The bush kid role has worked so powerfully here that this boy feels compelled to affirm that he doesn't want to leave and will never give up. This is strong language and suggests a desire to change.

> I believe it's very important to be a bush kid no matter where you are or where you come from. Because of the electronics and other distractions kids go outside a lot less. I know now that I'll go outside a lot more. Deep listening, attentiveness, is important. This wasn't just an excursion, it was an experience that I will never ever forget. I wish that I could stay there forever and ever and never leave. . . . I've also learnt to never give up, keep trying, keep approaching your goal. Thanks so much. I will never forget it.
>
> (Year 5 Student, 2010)

Changes in attentiveness

A second category of change was in students' heightened sensory skills, their ability to notice detail and to see and hear in ways that intensified their curiosity and thinking. One student expressed his amazement that attentiveness actually worked, just as the teacher had suggested, and that something as remarkable as birds coming close to you could actually happen. There is an epiphany dimension to his comment as he responds with intense curiosity to being right down close to the ground next to nature and in amongst it. You get the feeling he's seeing the world differently and that this hasn't happened in quite this way before.

> And also, we did attentiveness. We just sat – everybody sat really quiet and we heard all – and we tried to hear all the, uhm, birds. The teacher said, "If you stay still the birds will come closer" . . . And they did. We were right close to the ground. Right next to them, next to nature.
>
> (Year 5 Student, 2015)

Another student was amazed that a bird came so close, swooping past and landing near to him.

> Well, because since there were so many birds – like Karl said, "if we stay still, they will come near us", since one swooped right next to Isabella and one landed next to me, it kind of felt like a really ancient tree, in a way. And it just felt really cool.
>
> (Year 5 Student, 2015)

Teachers often describe a change in students from bored and disengaged learners to enthusiastic participants. Places that students had previously described as boring or ordinary were transformed into extraordinary landscapes full of story and life. The role of *Hoodwinked* in mediating such heightened attentiveness is tenderly captured in the following comment from a Year 5 student. She recognizes that she has gained a whole new perspective by learning to look more closely. What captivates her most is the realization that so much is new to her and that her mind feels refreshed.

> Because when I went down, I felt like walking on grass, going down to a normal creek . . . and then I looked at stuff and I noticed to see more stuff, like a whole new perspective and – yeah. . . . While we were refreshing our mind and everything, we started to see, like, a lot of things that were new to our minds.
>
> (Year 5 Student, 2015)

Other students singled out *Hoodwinked* as the means by which they felt more connected to nature, more than they had ever experienced before. The depth and sincerity of the experience for one boy is reflected in the following comment when he thanks *Hoodwinked* for allowing him to become *more connected to nature* which he elaborates as noticing how the *bark's fallen off* and seeing *the big tree roots* and feeling the leaves *casting over*. He recognizes that something good is happening to him which he describes as connection. It is common amongst children who participate in the *Hoodwinked* program to report that attentiveness makes them feel this way.

> Well, thanks to Hoodwinked, I really got, well, more connected to nature; because, like, it makes me – well, I learnt that I was more connected to nature than I thought, really, because before I just thought, "Oh, that's just a tree. The bark's fallen off. It's going to die soon." And then, now that I have seen a big tree with big roots and, like, its leaves casting over you, kind of, it feels better to go there again. So, like, in a way, I would have my holiday experience at a rainforest because it feels so good.
>
> (Year 5 Student, 2015)

Changes in student's feelings of wellbeing and renewal

A third important category of change was the feeling of wellbeing. The realization that being "in nature" can be a renewing experience was a surprise for many students. This sense that even small remnants of nature like the riparian strip along a creek edge can revitalize and renew oneself is captured in the following account from one young girl as she focuses on the great feeling it gave her and how it made her respect nature more. All this was accompanied by "arm sweeps" around her body and the running of her fingers over her skin and through her hair to communicate how good it felt.

> And nature made me feel alive; like . . . when I went to Hoodwinked, it gave me this great feeling that I was just in a great spot, like, when I went down

to the creek, it is really beautiful. And it was like an experience and it changed how I feel and that I should respect nature more.

(Year 5 Student, 2015)

Not only did it feel good and elicit a feeling of respect but it also gave her a sense of freedom. The liberating current of the place runs through her words below and is present in her conviction that because it's "natural" and "not artificial" she can know and feel the relaxation and the freshness.

Well, the nature is, like – it's very relaxing and we can find a lot of stuff in nature. . . . So then, uhm, in the nature, it is just like – it feels right to do whatever you want to do in nature, because it is just – mmm? . . . . It's just, uhm, relaxing; it's fresh; it's natural. So – it is not artificial, man-made.

(Year 5 Student, 2015)

As she continued to talk about the *Hoodwinked* experience her focus shifted to a deeper realization that it wasn't just the good feelings, relaxation and sense of freedom that she'd enjoyed but also a clearing of her mind. She refers to this on numerous occasions while running her fingers through her hair and touching her head to illustrate what had happened for her. Her thought journey leads her to recognize this change as significant. The importance is captured in the following comment where she reveals how rushed she often feels and how stressed she is by the expectations of others. Now, because of *Hoodwinked*, she has learnt to be less worried. Three weeks after the excursion she is still asserting that this change is real and is continuing, which indicates the depth of the change she believes has occurred.

I used to be so rushed and say, "I need to do instrumental. Oh, no, the test tomorrow." I used to be really, really rushed and a bit worried; I would get worried and sensitive. But I went there; it just cleared my mind and now I'm not worried. I don't go, "Oh, no, what's tomorrow? Or the day after that?" . . . Uhm, yeah, it made me more – less sensitive about days that I am going to be like, "Oh, no. Oh, no." Like, uhm, I kind of a bit worry about, "Oh, no, when is this sheet going to be due? Is it due today? I haven't signed it. Oh, no, I haven't asked mum to sign it, or dad" – yeah.

(Year 5 Student, 2015)

The feeling of relaxation and calm expressed above is quite general (*But I went there; it just cleared my mind and now I'm not worried*). However, below she recalls a moment with Oliver in *Hoodwinked* suggesting that the sense of calmness arises from and remains linked to particular activities and experiences in place.

But it was just relaxing. Like, when we sat down – when Oliver and I dropped a rock in, it sounded so good. It's like – I don't know,,, , (Laughs). It was just so nice. I don't know.

(Year 5 Student, 2015)

Dropping the rock with Oliver is a mundane image, but for her it captures a strong feeling of relaxation, of feeling "good" and "so nice", and some other feelings she can't quite express (*I don't know . . ..(Laughs)*). The general and episodic grounding of her feelings shows that this calming effect of *Hoodwinked* could be evoked regularly over time by recalling different moments or even just by recalling the experience of *Hoodwinked* in general.

> Changes in student's sense of aesthetics, creativity and wonder. The smell. The fresh beautiful smell of flowers and everything, and the bird sound, it was really good.
>
> (Year 5 Student, 2015)

A fourth area of change reported by students was their awareness of the aesthetic beauty associated with being immersed in a natural place (*it was really good*) and recognizing that this unlocked creativity in them and sometimes prompted them to advocate for change. The idea that creativity can be released through engaging with a natural place is captured in the vibrancy of the image below. This young girl visualizes creativity arriving as a sudden explosive force when she enters the *Hoodwinked* creek (*like your creative energy goes "pow" . . . when your creativity, like, exploded*). Her explanation of what happened suggests surprise and the unexpected when her ability to see the rocks, quartz crystals (*gems*) and trees changed and in a completely different way with "*a whole new perspective*". Her elaboration is filled with the joy that the creativity has come so suddenly.

> It was like your creative activity goes "pow". It is like when your – like, when your creativity, like, exploded I saw a whole new perspective; like rocks, gems and trees.
>
> (Year 5 Student, 2015)

A student beside her suggests that it's not really the creativity per se but the place that's most important. What's special for him is how *Hoodwinked* transported him to an earlier time/place of personal significance to him and his whole family. This time/place is re-lived through the *Hoodwinked* creek adventure and very particular experience of hearing a rock hit the water. It is unclear if this simple random event (*you drop a rock in that creek area*) happened then or now but this is part of the intrigue of this image. *Hoodwinked* has created an opportunity for this student to reflect on the sensorial pleasure of being in nature wherever you find it.

> Well, it is not really about creativity but about "place". It is kind of special to me because back when I was in New South Wales, . . . it was – well, I had a creek and I used to go there every day and find little rocks that looked like fossils. And, uhm – well, the canopy stretched over, so that it was dark in a way. That place just reminded me of the place back in New South Wales. And if you drop a rock in that creek area, it will make this awesome sound.
>
> (Year 5 Student, 2015)

There is a long tradition that records how immersion and emotional engagement with the beauty of the natural world can lead to environmental concern and even activism. This can be seen in the lives of individuals like Henry David Thoreau and John Muir in the late 19th century who made key philosophical contributions based on their personal encounters with nature. Influential writers like Rachael Carson in the 1960s drew on their intimate experiences of nature to shape the modern environmental movement and lay the foundation for a generation of environmental reformers. In more recent times in Australia activists like Bob Brown were inspired to fight for the Franklin River because of their feelings of being "in it". This same desire to protect nature because you have experienced the feelings that it can give you is beautifully expressed by this sensitive young girl in the following way.

> It was important because – how would you explain this? Uhm, everything just feels right from then. Like, going into a forest, like, the one – like, going into that creek place, it feels right to go into there. But – well, I think everything that looks really old and ancient, kind of, it should be protected in a way because it just gives you a really nice feeling.
>
> (Year 5 Student, 2015)

She recognizes that when you "feel right" in the place then you want to look after and protect it (*how would you explain this? Like, . . . going into that creek place, it feels right to go into there*). Recognizing when this feeling combines with time that lies beyond her life experience (*ancient*) has impacted deeply on her conviction that something needs to be done and that this place *should be protected*. What is compelling about this response is that the teacher leading the *Hoodwinked* day didn't talk about the need to protect nature. This child sees it as a logical step because she has been captivated by sensing that *everything just feels right*.

Changes in student's ethical sensibility and sense of agency

Finally, we identified change in some students that related to a heightened ethical sensibility that impacted on how they saw themselves living their own lives, and then in some cases how they might influence others and advocate for change. In the following comment a Year 5 student describes how he has changed his mind completely about nature and now cares more. He credits *Hoodwinked* with creating this shift in his thinking which causes him to stop and think more about his actions and to consider if there is a better way to interact with the environment. While this has not moved him entirely into civic action there is a recognition that personal change has happened for him and for others.

> Well yeah it has changed most of us a lot, it's changed me because I care about things more and I like to go out into the garden every now and then and just go water some flowers and stuff like that and like look after my garden. Nope (I wouldn't have done that before.) If I go up to something that's in the way like a branch or something that's in the way like maybe even

a tree that's in the way to get to something at our house well I say "I should ask mum and dad to get that tree to go down because it is in the way", but now I actually stop and think and say "really does this have to go is there something behind the tree that I really need to get to or is it just a little play area or something small". Well it's just like I am thinking I could go around the tree a different way to get to that play area it is just a short cut but that I don't need to be that lazy.

(Year 5 Student, 2010)

In the comment below a student compares how he thought before the *Hoodwinked* experience as an observer (*I used to say wow they are cutting a tree*) to how he thinks now as someone who asks a moral question (*why are they cutting a tree*). He identifies *Hoodwinked* (*Well it's changed me*) as the catalyst, and then credits the experience with creating a shift in his thinking that has now travelled back with him into his own garden where he's daydreaming about how he would respond if a tree he loved was cut down. An observer could hardly guess that these reflective thoughts were turning in his mind as he kicks his soccer ball.

Well it's changed me. When I am in my garden I play soccer and well imagine if that wasn't there like there are these trees in my garden imagine if that wasn't there, imagine if that wasn't there and just like I think it was on Wednesday there was like this huge really, really big tree and it was cut down because people were scared it was going to fall down onto their house and then it was gone it was so different. I am so used to that tree being there and then it's gone and like it was so different the tree is not there. When they are cutting a tree down I used to like say "wow they are cutting a tree down" and now I go like "why are they are cutting a tree down?".

(Year 5 Student, 2010)

Imagination (*imagine if that wasn't there*) creates a sense of loss for this boy and mobilises his awareness that things could be different (*why are they are cutting a tree down'*). His questioning is associated with a revised sense of how he "is" in the world (*well it's changed me*). Similarly the comment below, while recognizing that children have agency (*yeah I thinks kids can make a difference*), recognizes that they require collective action, which is central to the *Hoodwinked* experience when they collectively "become the bush kids" and solve a difficult problem together. You can hear the voice of the political realist here who understands that it *can't just be one kid* because against the whole world they are *nothing* and this in itself indicates insight about how society actually works. It might be argued that this kind of political literacy is one of the most important ideas that a child needs in order to successfully negotiate life.

Yeah I think kids can make a difference but they can't just be one kid because one kid compared to the world is nothing so it would need to be probably like a hundred schools needed to know about the environment and that it's not good to do that stuff to be polluting and stuff like that . . . around the world.

(Year 5 Student, 2010)

Hoodwinked gave these students an opportunity to experience the flow of collective action and to discover something about themselves as agents of change in the process. As this young girl so eloquently explains below, it is when the group suddenly realizes *(Oh my gosh, we need to do this. We need to persuade her)* that agency is released and change happens, although she is not able to fully explain this (*So then all of us thought the same thing, probably.*) There is appreciation that the group was able to "bond" and "work together" easily within the flow of the story with a clear unity of purpose that they had apparently never achieved before. The *Hoodwinked* experience allowed this to happen which is something we have witnessed on many times with a wide range of students.

> So when . . . we stepped into the classroom, we were all like, Oh, my gosh, we need to do this. We need to persuade her. . . . So then all of us thought the same thing, probably, and we just all worked together and bonded. . . . Well, it is just that we were working altogether so well. Normally, we – in our class, we don't have very good group work.

(Year 5 Student, 2015)

The idea of collective agency is taken up in a very specific and concrete way by the following student when he decides to use the *Hoodwinked* experience as a motivation to talk with his family, cousins, friends of the family, and even neighbours. You can sense his satisfaction and hope as he reflects on the purchase of their own "climate safe monitor". There is a feeling that this is an important experience in this boy's life and that he's learnt something important about himself, and his ability to advocate for action and grow his civic responsibility.

> I have told my family and my cousins and lots of other friends not only at school but my next-door neighbours and stuff. I think my family has to and may be a few friends, we got one of those climate smart monitor things and we make sure that all of the lights are all turned off when we are not using them and the TV turned off at the wall when we are not using it.

(Year 5 Student, 2015)

Conclusion

The path that I have travelled with my colleagues at PEEC during the past three decades has been both creative and challenging as we explored how to use narrative pedagogy to support students and teachers in creating their own stories of place. In reflecting on this journey three insights stand out as significant for broader application in other educational settings. The first relates to the power of laying story over landscape to transform students' experiences of place; the second relates to how fiction can intensify student engagement with the materiality of place; and the third relates to how narrative pedagogy enables students to situate themselves as part of a moral world.

We have found that laying narrative over landscape connects students to place in emotional ways. In general, there is a growing realization that many citizens in developed countries across the globe have lost touch with stories of connection to the earth and that these stories must be regained.

> Gone are the rich, metaphor-laden narratives that connected traditional societies to the place/spirit/ecology that provided them with sustenance. Understanding the "real story" of the conditions that sustain life on planet earth is one of the key pedagogical tasks of the environmental educator.
>
> (Sandlos, 1998, p. 5)

Indigenous people all over the world have used story to imbue place with significance. Chatwin (1987) describes how Aboriginal people in Australia used "songlines" for millennia as narratives that carried spiritual and topographical knowledge. Environmental historians like Bolton (1981), Dovers (1994), Greider and Garkovich (1994) and Rolls (1993) have created environmental stories about wild landscapes and the exceptional people who fought to protect them. Sandlos (1998) suggests that it is our lack of engagement with ecologically sensitive stories of place that has created a sense of placelessness and alienation that can result in complacency in the face of the environmentally destructive events of our age. In the *Hoodwinked* program students enter as protagonists into the stories of exploitation and conservation at Pullen Pullen Creek – a degraded and unremarkable part of the landscape to most eyes. Their part in the drama creates an emotionally charged understanding of the creek and helps connect them to place and evoke an ethic of care.

Through designing *Storythread* and deploying *Hoodwinked* as a narrative pedagogy, I realised how fiction can connect students with places in very personal ways. Thomashow (1996) has shown that connecting to place develops an ecological identity in students that impacts profoundly on how they relate to themselves, others and to nature. Responsiveness to place has been explored by Mannion, Fenwick, and Lynch (2013) who followed groups of Scottish students as they participated in the project called *Stories in the Land: In the Tracks of the Highland Drovers*. As students journeyed along ancient pathways and teachers used stories to "teach by means of the environment", Mannion, Fenwick, and Lynch (2013) found that students became collectors, creators and tellers of stories themselves without direction from their teachers. The narrative experience of place resulted in the development of strong place-responsive intergenerational learning that was much more than just history education. Students connected to the places around them in ways that gave them insight into how they might carry a new place-responsive consciousness into their own lives and communities.

I have come to appreciate how narrative pedagogy can intensify students' appreciation of the moral relationship between themselves and place. Attentiveness to/in place is central to such ethical awareness, or what Abram calls a *"renewed attentiveness. . . . A rejuvenation of sensorial empathy with the living systems that sustain us"* (Abram, 1997, p. 69). Abram suggests that attentiveness is what promotes an environmental ethic rather than the logical elucidation of abstract philosophical principles. Payne (2010) also deploys narrative to heighten ethical awareness. He has used story as part of his gnome-tracking adventures where children and teachers join him on narrative journeys that are designed to reconcile the human and the more-than-human world as part of what Payne calls an "eco-pedagogy of the imagination" (Payne, 2010, p. 296). He suggests that by engaging the imagination through narrative, opportunities are forged for connected ethical learning (Payne, 2010). Similarly, our focus at PEEC on environmental stories in place marks *Storythread* as one of the "outdoor" body/mind doing and meaning-making pedagogies (Ballantyne & Packer, 2008; 2009; Tooth & Renshaw, 2009, 2012; Wattchow, Burke, & Cutter-Mackenzie, 2008). *Storythread* is a rich tapestry where narrative and place are folded in upon each other as part of a powerful place-responsive pedagogy. Like all narratives *Storythread* works as a "meta-code" that links us to a "human universal" (White, 1987) and invites us to participate in a moral universe. This is why, now more than ever, we need to appropriate story to address the environmental priorities of today as we search for more authentic and sustainable lifestyles.

Note

1 *Hoodwinked* was originally created by myself (Ron Tooth), and Tonia Pickering, who was the first teacher to be transferred to the Pullenvale Centre in 1984. Over the years other committed and talented teachers have joined the PEEC team and contributed their insights as we have refined this rich and subtly nuanced program. These include Margaret Card, Juliet Cottrell, Suzanne Gulikers, Ellen Appleby, Simone Firmin, Lucinda Shaw, Catarina Hebbard, Madelaine Winstanley, Merryl Simpson, Kate McGoldrick and Karl Fagermo.

References

Abram, D. (1997). The spell of the sensuous: Perception and language in a more-than-human world. New York: Pantheon.

Ackroyd, J. (2006). *Research methodologies for drama education.* Stoke on Trent: Trenthan Books.

Ballantyne, R., & Packer, J. (2008). Learning for sustainability: The role and impact of outdoor and environmental education centres. St Lucia: University of Queensland, School of Tourism.

Ballantyne, R., & Packer, J. (2009). Introducing a fifth pedagogy: Experience-based strategies for facilitating learning in natural environments. *Environmental Education Research, 15*(2), 243–262.

Bolton, G. (1981). Spoils and spoilers: Australians make their environment 1788–1980. Sydney: Allen & Unwin.

Bruner, J. (1987). Life as narrative. *Social Research, 54,* 11–32.

Chatwin, B. (1987). *The songlines.* London: Jonathan Cape.

Clark, M. (2004, May 1). *Falling in love again.* Produced by Jackie May for the Australian Broadcasting Corporation. Interviewed by Alexandra de Blas on Earthbeat.

Dovers, S. (1994). *Australian environmental history.* Oxford: Oxford University Press.

Eckley, W. (2001). Guerrilla warfare. In J. Powell (Ed.), *Magill's guide to military history, Vol. 2* (pp. 636–639). Salem: Corunna-Janissaries Salem.

Greider, T., & Garkovich, L. (1994). Landscapes: The social construction of nature and the environment. *Rural Sociology, 59,* 1–24.

Heathcote, D. (1984). Drama as a process for change. In L. Johnson & C. O'Neill (Eds.), *Dorothy Heathcote collected writings.* London: Hutchinson. Pp 114-125

Karrow, D., & Fazio, X. (2010). Educating-within-place: Care, citizen science, and ecojustice. In D. Tippins, M. Mueller, M. van Eijck & J Adams (Eds.), *Cultural studies and environmentalism: The confluence of ecojustice, place-based (science) education, and Indigenous knowledge systems* (pp. 193–214). Houten: Springer.

Kilcullen, D. (2009). The accidental guerrilla: Fighting small wars in the midst of a big one. Oxford: Oxford University Press.

Malouf, D. (1999). *An imaginary life.* London: Vintage.

Mannion, G., Fenwick, A., & Lynch, J. (2013). Place-responsive pedagogy: Learning from teachers' experiences of excursions in nature. *Environmental Education Research, 19*(6), 792–809.

Massey, D., (2005). *For space.* London: Sage.

Payne, P. G. (2010). Remarkable-tracking, experiential education of the ecological imagination. *Environmental Education Research, 16*(3), 295–310.

Reynolds, H. (2006). The other side of the frontier: Aboriginal resistance to the European invasion of Australia. Sydney: UNSW Press.

Rolls, E. (1993). *From forest to sea: Australia's changing environment.* St Lucia: University of Queensland Press.

Sandlos, J. (1998). The storied curriculum: Oral narrative, ethics, and environmental education. *The Journal of Environmental Education, 30*(1), 5–9.

Sinclair, P. (2001). *The Murray: A river and its people.* Melbourne: Melbourne University Press.

Somerville, M. (2010). A place pedagogy for global contemporaneity. *Educational Philosophy and Theory, 42*(3), 326–344.

Thomashow, M. (1996). *Ecological identity.* Cambridge, MA: MIT Press.

Tooth, R., & Renshaw, P. (2009). Reflections on pedagogy and place: A journey into learning for sustainability through environmental narrative and deep attentive reflection. *Australian Journal of Environmental Education, 25,* 95–104.

Tooth, R., & Renshaw, P. (2012). *Storythread* pedagogy for environmental education. In T. Wrigley, P. Thomson & B. Lingard (Eds.), *Changing schools: Alternative ways to make a world of difference* (pp. 113–127). London: Routledge.

Ungunmerr-Baumann, M. R. (1988). Dadirri. *Compass Theology Review, 22,* 9–11.

Ungunmerr-Baumann, M. R. (2002). *Dadirri: A reflection by Miriam-Rose Ungunmerr Baumann.* Retrieved from http://nextwave.org.au/wp-content/uploads/Dadirri-Inner-Deep-Listening-M-R-Ungunmerr-Bauman-Refl.pdf

Wartofsky, M. (1979). Models: Representation and scientific understanding. Dordrecht: Reidel.

Wattchow, B., Burke, G., & Cutter-Mackenzie, A. N. (2008, November–4 December 30). Environment, place and social ecology in educational practice. In P. Jeffrey (Ed.), *AARE 2008 Proceedings: International education research conference*, Brisbane, QLD: Australian Association for Research in Education.

White, H. (1987). The content of the form: Narrative discourse and historical representation. Baltimore, MA: John Hopkins University Press.

Winnicott, D. W. (1971). *Playing and reality*. London: Tavistock.

4 Pedagogy as slow time in the extra ordinary bush

Noeleen Rowntree[1] and Agatha Gambino

Editors' preface

Chapter Four explores the temporal dimension of place-responsive pedagogy. A compelling image in the chapter is that of the portal between two worlds – the everyday suburban world of fast-paced traffic and noisy activity outside Bunyaville forest compared to the quiet, slow-paced experience inside the forest. It is the forest itself that makes slow pedagogy possible. As they enter, students notice the sudden transition into a different space where time seems to slow. Thomashow (1996) proposed the notion of slowing down and meditating on place. Building on this notion, Payne and Wattchow (2008) wrote about the importance of slow pedagogy in their critique of outdoor education programs. They were critical of programs that treated places merely as a backdrop to the energetic exertions of students on personal quests and group challenges. Such programs centre attention on students per se and their goals rather than on place per se and their relationship with the environment. They are journeying through and passing over the land to fulfil a quest or challenge, and the quicker and more effectively the journey is concluded, the better. Slow pedagogy in contrast is designed to pause and dwell in the environment in order to connect to the history of the place and to sense the layers of meaning that have been inscribed there over time. Slow pedagogy invites students to decentre and be open to experience. Slow pedagogy involves emplacement, that is, being able to place oneself within a system of relationships to other living entities and material things. One becomes a part of the place rather than simply passing through. The sense of emplacement is captured vividly in this chapter in the account provided of one young student who arrived with her Year 1 classmates for an excursion at Bunyaville with images of the forest as frightening and dangerous, yet at the end of the day reluctantly departs wishing she could remain as a part of the forest, that is, "by becoming a plant" to live permanently in the forest. This is a moment of fantasy, but it suggests the power of slow pedagogy to move young children from a fearful and detached understanding of the forest to one where they can imagine themselves being part of it.

Slow pedagogy contrasts with the typical teaching regime experienced by students at school. Many students currently report the pressure of time as they struggle to meet the expectations of a demanding curriculum (Howell, 2016, p. 174). Teachers can feel harried and hurried by the pressures to cover curriculum content and meet accountability requirements (Thompson, 2016). It seems now that more curriculum content needs to be covered in less time. Schools are governed by timetables and the sound of bells that segment learning into specific periods that interrupt the flow of experience. This neo-liberal framing of education in terms of efficiency and effectiveness is challenged by the notion of slow pedagogy. Slowing down could be perceived simply as opting out of the responsibility to ensure that students have learned the required curriculum content. However, slow pedagogy re-orders the way educational goals are ranked, without ignoring the importance of knowledge per se.

The distinction between content knowledge and inquiry process is a long-standing tension in education (Robertson, 2006; Kock et al., 2015). At Bunyaville the tension is managed by privileging inquiry processes so that students are inspired to want to find out more, rather than always seeking to hear the right answer from the expert. "The right answer is not always a noun" the authors concluded when they shifted to slow pedagogy. Their decision to adopt the inductive approach of following-in and supporting students' interests is richly exemplified in the chapter.

The construction of time as kairos is also relevant to understanding the slow pedagogy at Bunyaville (Petruzzi, 2001). Kairos is subjectively experienced time that is relative to the intensity of one's experiences. The intent of the educators at Bunyaville is to create emotional engagement for students expressed as "wow" moments – moments when students are enthralled by an observation, a discovery, or an unexpected encounter in the "ordinary bush" as the authors describe the forest at Bunyaville. These moments can be regarded as kairotic moments where time becomes more intense, more filled with significance, more memorable for the students. Kairos is a personal sense of time that contrasts with chronos, which is the objective notion of time measured by the regular movement of the hands of a clock (Petruzzi, 2001, p. 360). While chronos captures time as it is quantified generally for everyone, kairos captures time qualitatively as it is personally experienced. When the authors chose the notion of "slow" to describe their pedagogy, they began to look for moments where students could be more intensely engaged and emotionally responsive. Kairos is afforded at Bunyaville partly through its location in the heart of suburban Brisbane, making the extra/ordinary bush an easily accessible part of students' lives. The authors recount the story of two youngsters (about five years old) who had come on an excursion to Bunyaville and later turned up on two separate occasions with their parents to show them the places that had become special to them. As another student noted, "maybe all learning can have time. Maybe you just have to think about it and have to relax and stay calm". This is kairotic time – time for students to pause and dwell in place and be open to the experiences they are offered there.

Peter Renshaw & Ron Tooth

Introduction

The forest we know as Bunyaville Conservation Park (BCP) is on a small part of traditional *Turrbal* country, and we acknowledge the *Yagerra/Yuggera* language group. Hidden in the embrace of the forest's dominant tall eucalyptus trees is the Bunyaville Environmental Education Centre (BEEC), surrounded by sculptured gullies, rocky outcrops, seasonally flowing creeks and quiet ponds. We feel extraordinarily fortunate to work in this "ordinary parcel of bush", a place regarded by local Aboriginal people as sacred. Their cultural practices developed in synchrony with the seasonal rhythms of country. Such connection enabled them, prior to the establishment of British colonial rule, to obtain what they needed for everyday life without compromising the land's capacity to sustain them. The forest at Bunyaville would have provided them with wood, bark and resin and was a significant transit corridor as different Aboriginal groups travelled between the D'Aguilar Ranges to the west and the coastal areas to the east to participate in traditional ceremonies and corroborees, particularly the Bunya festival.

During seasonal abundance of particular resources, different language groups were invited onto each other's country to share the resource in feasts. After the feasts, guests would reciprocate invitations to the host so that the consumed resource could replenish (Markwell Consulting, 2010). The main road in front of the BCP was originally a significant walking path forged by Aboriginal people as they travelled between Turrbal country and Jinibara, Gubbi Gubbi and Wakka Wakka countries to the north on their way to festivals such as the Bunya festival. Over time this Aboriginal walking path became incorporated into the transport networks of Brisbane. In the early colonial period of the 19th century when travel was restricted, the pathway was used by horseman. Over time it widened to an unsealed road with added creek crossings for horse-drawn and bullock-drawn wagons and then motor vehicles. Finally from the mid-1990s it morphed into a noisy four-lane sealed highway called Old Northern Road. Knowing the origins of the current highway is a poignant reminder of the multiple histories, cultures and conflicting ways of being that are embedded in the Bunyaville forest and that remain relevant to current and future generations. Along the road's history we see a shifting relationship with this place from one where people were part of and moved through and with country, to one where people are predominantly separate from country and move or manipulate the elements of country for their benefit.

Valuing a forest island: the extra in the ordinary

The hilly 640 hectares of the Bunyaville Conservation Park (BCP) are the headwaters for several creeks, but there is little permanent water, so during British colonisation it escaped intensive agricultural use. The more recent past, however, included extensive logging that was finally stopped only in the mid-1990s with action from the local wildlife group who were concerned about the ecological integrity of the park and increasing urban pressures. A section of the current BCP area was opened as a recreation area in 1972, and it was within this recreation area that the Bunyaville Environmental Education Centre was created mainly through the initiative of local state school principals who recognised BCP as a natural area of significance to the north Brisbane community and as an opportunity for young students to experience a natural setting (see Figure 4.1 below). They advocated for the establishment of education programs focusing on the environment, forest awareness and conservation to address their concern that the rapidly expanding urbanisation of the Brisbane region was reducing children's engagement with the natural environment. Increasing urbanisation and sedentary lifestyles are associated with reduced physical health and wellbeing in children (Louv, 2012); but equally important and critical to our future, urbanisation can create distant and negative attitudes towards nature, particularly a tendency to treat forests as fearful.

It is the vision, advocacy and actions of people, such as the original group of state school principals who established BEEC, which has preserved Bunyaville as a forest island in the midst of suburbia. Wallabies are still glimpsed in the forest as they and other wildlife travel along the *mountains to mangroves* corridor – a corridor created by patches of parkland and forest green connected by creek lines from the D'Aguilar range in the west to the ocean at Moreton Bay. Although the animal and plant life are under pressure from encroaching suburbia and increasing recreational use, dedicated local residents and the students and teachers who visit BEEC value the forest and take action to remove weeds, plant native species and assist the Queensland Parks and Wildlife to manage the BCP. Situated only 15km from the Brisbane CBD, BEEC has become a catalyst for schools in north Brisbane for slow learning in contact with nature. Through its programs, BEEC

Figure 4.1 A richness of sensory experiences is provided by the forest

offers students and teachers a sense of the extended community bridging generations of Indigenous and non-Indigenous people who have and will care for this country.

Personal history – growing up nearby

The bush, trees and the Bunyaville forest have been part of my life since my grandfather carried me into the bush on his back when I was six weeks old. Growing up, the bush was part of my backyard where I'd regularly climb trees to observe what was happening, to find solace and to think. The bush was a place where I felt free and able to be in my own world. It was on the unsealed road at the entrance to BCP that my father (a mechanic) tested bus seals for dust leaks. As a child, Bunyaville forest seemed huge, and it always felt like an adventure coming near the forest driving along bush tracks and dirt roads. As a child I played in nearby patches of bush that were then continuously linked to the larger forest reserve. As an adult I spent more time in Bunyaville Conservation Park walking with my dog, teaching my daughter to drive on the dirt road in the Park, working in the forest for nearly three decades and now living beside the forest. I have always felt connected to the "bush" at Bunyaville and, upon reflection, my appointment to BEEC as a teacher in 1988 felt like destiny.

The Bunyaville experience

Forest magic

The Bunyaville forest remains a magic place with a rhythm of rich sensory experiences that provide the basis of our pedagogy. As winter arrives the angle of the light changes as the sun drops to the north highlighting the golden shimmer of the spider webs crisscrossing through the trees and floating like golden streamers. Migratory forest dwellers such as honeyeaters arrive from lands beyond, adding new melodies to the sounds in the forest. Hoveas and wattles blossom for a fleeting two week show of glorious colour of purple flowers on yellow. Mushrooms, the size of a dinner plate, appear after a fire – the first time in twenty years. With the breaking of the dry season, the first rains change the grey parched bush into an exhilarating array of rivulets with water gushing down tree trunks changing grey bark to green and green to red. As the summer rain continues, water flows along pathways into creeks filling the ponds to the bursting point. Butterflies can be found in the hundreds in one particular gully, appearing across a few months, then not to be seen in those numbers again. Gum leaves of every colour float to the earth below displaying a patchwork of hues. Sugar gliders can sometimes be found dead on walking tracks dropped by owls hunting from the previous night. The rain rushes away rapidly from the headwaters of the creeks, and a drying creek bed appears inviting exploration. Smooth gum trees shed their bark in large chunks displaying bright orange trunks. The roaring crescendo of the cicadas fills the forest for most of the summer. The forest is always changing to create fleeting magic moments. When students are fully present in the place, they experience their own magic moments, their own experience of the *extra in the ordinary*. The art of teaching in the forest is to enable the students to be attentive, to emotionally and cognitively connect to the whole forest and its many parts.

Portal – entering slow time and place

Arriving at BEEC is a sudden transition for students as their school bus turns off the noisy, fast-paced, multi-lane Old Northern Road and drives a short distance into the forest reserve along unpaved roads with increasing density of trees, the enveloping quietness of the forest and the crunch of tyres on gravel and earth rather than the whir of rubber on bitumen and concrete. It takes just a few moments to be transported from the "modern world out there" to the "ancient world of the forest"; from the world of fast-paced time, of time limits and time demands to the world of extended and slow time (Payne & Wattchow, 2008). The contrast is stark and creates a portal experience for students of leaving behind one world and stepping into another. On arrival they immediately sense the difference in place and time and articulate this by contrasting it to the world from which they've come. We recorded the following episode as a group of Year 1 students (aged between five to six years) arrived for a forest excursion.

> Yesterday we had 57 Year 1 students from an inner suburban school visit us for the Possum Bangles program. They were smiling and excited as they got off the bus. One said "I like being here. We don't have to learn anything today. I'm never going back to school".

These youngsters sense that something different is possible here at Bunyaville, and their first response is to contrast it with the routines and expectations of school – "never going back to school", "I like being here", and "don't have to learn anything today".

> Having just declared that they would be doing no learning, the first six or so students who were waiting with me in line as the others disembarked began to exercise their imagination and creativity as they surveyed the nearby pond area. One student announced that he had "seen a swamp monster!" "A swamp monster. What did it look like", I asked. Collectively they wove a description of the swamp monster. "It's got one eye." "And 29 legs." "And three arms." "Three eyes and one mouth." "And it eats school children."

This heightened imaginative responsiveness seemed to arise from the suddenness of the transition. Passing through the portal repositioned the young children initially into a forest of their imaginations where fears about wild and unknown creatures were quite prominent. During the day at Bunyaville they have the opportunity to expand their understanding of the forest through inquiry, observation and shared experiences. On leaving that day, one of this group said she'd like "to be a plant". Again imaginative expression is prominent but initial fear of the forest has been transformed to feelings of being in and with the forest, being part of the forest.

Staff mediating access and learning at Bunyaville

Coming to know the pedagogical affordances of Bunyaville

Initially at BEEC I spent time searching for knowledge and insights from other educators and researchers to develop a pedagogy uniquely relevant to this place. I spoke with many writers and practitioners from across the world. Some approaches such as Earth Education, Gaia theory and Deep Ecology challenged my world views. These approaches made me think more about the earth as a living system and the role of humans within that whole system. I questioned how teaching in a forest that was viewed as "just ordinary bush" could open the eyes and connect the hearts and minds of students, particularly urban dwellers, to the beauty and richness of nature. Today I continue to learn from the local Aboriginal and Torres Strait Islander Elders who have become part of the fabric of BEEC. I try to connect with them, feeling, hearing and seeing the bush as it is for them, tapping into their knowledge and perspectives on the forest. I have come to learn that there are multiple perspectives and ways of knowing the forest.

Continuous trialling enabled us to identify specific places in the forest that matched our goals and elicited more engagement and responsiveness from the learners. It became clearer to me over time that specific sites in the forest had subtle but intense ways of supporting particular kinds of learning and this insight has enabled me to understand the uniqueness of the pedagogy of place at Bunyaville. The pedagogy needs to reveal the *extra in the ordinary*. I came to realise that ordinariness was the unique affordance of Bunyaville. Many visitors perceive the forest from the cultural construct of being "just ordinary bush". There is the assumption that there is "heaps of bush" and that remnant forest is somewhat unimportant. Yet every piece of bush mattered to the Aboriginal people throughout time and the bush mattered to me growing up, and it could also matter to the students and teachers who came to learn here at BEEC. The ordinariness, for example, of watching a single leaf float down to join the other millions on the forest floor could become a moment with aesthetic, emotional and scientific implications. The ordinariness could also consist of imagining the forest as a living room, pretending with the students that we were watching nature TV with the all-round surround sound of birds, insects and the wind moving through the trees. The extra in the ordinariness could be captured, I came to realise, with slow pedagogy where we paused to stay with the experience, then inquired and reflected on nature, at times alone or with others – peacefully, just being in the moment.

My searching is what Peter Senge (Senge et al., 2006) describes as the inner and outer work of sustainability. The outer work is the myriad of things that people believe will "fix" the living systems of the planet. But a sole focus on outer work can restrict a deeper understanding of the interconnectedness of all life, all people and all ecosystems. Instead, Senge suggests that the outer work of sustainability becomes effective "when people start to deliberately slow down their lives to cultivate broader awareness and reflective practice" (Senge et al., 2006, p. 97). For me the Bunyaville pedagogy was about slowing down time so the students could experience the extra in the ordinary, connecting to the forest and themselves, reflecting on their inner and their outer world.

Listening to students and their forest experiences

The pedagogy at BEEC evolved by listening to children intently as they chatted to each other and to the teachers about their experiences in the forest. Listening revealed the distinct affordances of specific locations in the forest. As noted above, it became clear that various places brought about engagement from students and more complex learning. For example, during one part of the excursion called the Earthwalk, students are divided into smaller groups to experience the forest. After a couple of hours the groups come together on a bridge in the forest to reflect on their different experiences. The bridge is deep in the forest in a gully well away from areas frequented by the public. Students can sit as a large group together in a relaxed manner along the bridge, legs dangling down, looking into the forest yet also able to see the BEEC staff and their teachers. Its quietness and seclusion seemed to encourage students to openly share their observations, stories and feelings. The degree of openness to sharing was related to this specific site. Across the years various sites in the forest had been tried to better capture the group's experiences. Eventually the bridge site was found to evoke richer accounts of what students were experiencing and learning. The bridge still affords high quality reflective moments for diverse groups of students to this day.

Key elements of our slow pedagogy

Everything is connected – a systems thinking purpose

Over time we explored and questioned our own world views as we moved to a systems approach to learning that underpins our pedagogy (Sterling, 2004; Gough, 2013). We thought about our role on the planet seeing ourselves as a small, equal part of the earth's community of life and not accepting the dominant paradigm of a hierarchy of life forms that are valued along a graduated scale of worthy and unworthy forms. Systems thinking focusses on patterns, connections and processes and how seemingly separate things form coherent wholes. The challenge for environmental educators is to enable awareness of the whole through engagement with the parts. At BEEC we design our slow learning to consider the parts in order to deepen our understanding of the whole system. For example, after spending time exploring the parts of the whole forest, a group of Year 3 students recalled what they had heard and seen in the forest, such as a wallaby, a golden orb spider weaving a web, birds singing, insects crawling and so on. The conversation moved on to "the forest being amazing", and "nature is really beautiful", to "I need to care for forests as animals live here" and "the forest belongs to everyone" and "it is a habitat for living things". Students' comments articulated the parts as necessary to the functioning of the whole forest.

Like a natural forest system, knowledge is multifaceted and created by a multitude of parts interrelating – child learning from child, teacher from child, child from forest. Teachers at BEEC model being a learner alongside the student instead of taking the role of expert. Students are acknowledged as capable of gathering knowledge from the environment and each other. The process of questioning and inquiring is more important than getting the right answer and this approach underpins all our programs. For example, in a recent excursion, two groups of Year 7 students were investigating their prediction that an undisturbed area would have more invertebrates in the leaf litter than an area frequented by park visitors. They found the opposite result. Adopting an inquiry approach as outlined later in the chapter, we encouraged them to consider other explanations for the unexpected result and consider additional factors such as soil moisture. Such episodes of inquiry can create awareness of complexity and multiple possibilities.

The Centre teachers craft unfolding activities to reflect students' interests and allow them scope to participate in their own ways. One Year 4 student on a recent excursion had been silent all morning. She seemed interested, but she was quiet for the two hours we were together exploring the forest. I had used a range of strategies to include her in the discussion, but she had remained silent. As we gathered on the bridge to reflect on our morning in the forest I asked the whole group, "so what do you think about the forest?" Unexpectedly the silent student responded immediately raising her hand to answer. Wonderful, I wasn't going to miss this opportunity to ask her to speak. She explained that she wondered about the future of the forest and was concerned that her children's children may not see the beauty that she had seen today. This was a real lesson for me, the teacher. So much was going on inside her throughout the experience, and her silence now could be interpreted as deep thinking, the inner work. She had moved beyond the here and now to look forward across generations and the possible threats to the future of the forest. Her temporal reflection reveals her understanding of the longevity of the forest as well as her caring about the forest and its aesthetic richness. This episode highlighted for me that where students are free to participate as they want to, and are accepted as capable contributors, complex thinking and feeling can be evoked.

Immersion – being present in the environment

Children who've previously come to the forest with their families tell us about the party they had with their soccer friends, or of running along the road. Awareness of the forest per se is largely absent from their stories. It is the slow pedagogy that creates immersion. There are many pedagogical tools which take students from the "outside world" through the portal to be present in the forest. Immersion is an experience crafted to provide students with opportunities to learn through whole body-mind engagement. For example, for students to learn about erosion, we take them to the middle of an eroded creek or gully where they physically examine the soil, repair the riparian zone, and closely observe erosion profiles. We encourage questions and inquiries by digging in the earth to sense texture and density. This use of the whole body anchors their understanding of erosion, how it looks and feels and what they personally might do to prevent it. These material experiences make sense of abstract concepts that are otherwise disconnected from one's senses.

We love the unexpected moments of immersion – the spontaneous occurrences in the forest that will remain with students for years. One day a student spotted a tawny frogmouth lying motionless and camouflaged among leaf litter and branches. The teachable moment had appeared. Why is the bird on the ground? Is it dead? What happened to it? The questions came thick and fast with no one really waiting for an answer before asking another question. Each child was emotionally in the moment. After some discussion and hands-on exploration, touching the bird, we noticed a flicker of its eye and found that it was barely alive with a poisonous toad in its throat. We discussed options about what we could do. A collective decision was made by the students to take the bird to the local vet. It was saved and returned to the forest. From being attentive, that is, really seeing and emotionally connecting, students engaged in real life decision-making. This dramatic event also anchored their understanding of the hazards for native animals of introduced species such as the cane-toad that is spreading unabated across Australia.

The "wow" factor: emotional engagement

No matter what the group or their age, until you hear "Wow, look at this" or "Wow this is amazing", we feel we haven't done our job as teachers. The *wow* factor hooks students into being attentive and into a new relationship with the forest. It conveys "this is unbelievable," "can't get my head around it," "what is it?" "ah, it is scary to look at," or "how beautiful". Whatever the emotion, the students are fully present in that moment in the forest. Such emotional engagement is a goal of our slow pedagogy. This might entail modelling a sense of awe and curiosity about the forest microstructure using magnifying annayloupes. This simple magnifying device brings the students into contact with the forest and the earth through emotion and touch as well as sight. For example, walking with students in the forest I periodically look at the ground with my annayloupe, modelling emotional connection through use of imagination, sharing aloud such thoughts as, "If I was an ant, I could fall through that crack and get lost in that *ginormous* cavern down there!" or "I feel as if I am flying over a mountainous region as I look into the bark on this tree". Many "wows" then follow as the students discover for themselves the detail in the microstructure, the parts of the forest they had never noticed before. For example, I recorded the following comments from three Year 6 students during such an activity:

> I could see the texture and patterns of the bark. I saw things in 3D.
> A leaf with three raindrops – so beautiful!
> Not all flies look the same. Some have different colours and shapes; I lifted up a rock and saw worms eating the leaf litter.

The following comments we recorded from Year 3 students while exploring parts of the forest:

> A leaf that had a smiley face on it which made me glad.
> Why haven't I seen this before?
> That's so interesting, I didn't realise that could happen.

These moments of heightened emotional engagement arise from increased sensory acuity that creates a sense of awe, wonder and respect for natural processes and a questioning attitude of wanting to know more. The experience is embodied and students' faces light up and they turn to share experiences with friends. This creates a snowballing of discoveries among other students and maintains high engagement for the duration of the activity. When one student talks about a discovery other nearby students are attracted as illustrated in the short interaction below between two Year 4 students.

Student 1:   "I've found a scorpion in the pond dish."
Student 2:   "Hey, where is it? Wow!"
Student 1:   "Ah, you have one too in your dish."

A child drew my attention excitedly calling me to look at the "*giant ant*" (praying mantis) he found under the leaves. Other children hurried over to see it, but it had quickly disappeared under more leaves. These children began searching under other leaf litter, eager to find another "*giant ant*". Instead they found a bush cockroach and excitedly announced their discovery to others. Getting the group away from the leaf litter and back out of the forest for lunch was difficult. And so it goes – students sharing, helping others to see, learn and know. The forest, *the place*, constantly in flux with a great diversity of structures offered to students along every path, is the foundation for these "wow" moments, but the attitude of the teacher in being receptive to students' experiences is also crucial.

Inquiry approach for learning

After many years of identifying, naming and labelling forest parts for both adults and children, I realised this expert-driven approach to learning was ineffective. I was sometimes repeating the process over and over again with the same question being asked by the same cohort. When I named items for them, the response from students was to soon forget the name and to ask the same question again a moment later. I questioned myself, "Why is a noun the response I give when there is so much more to the item than just its name?" From this simple question a differing pedagogical tool developed that encouraged deep inquiry. Questions about "the what" of the forest were answered with another question or investigation. This required students to look or listen closer. So if the question was, "What is this tree?" the teacher would take a step back to look the tree up and down and pause to touch the "tree", attentive but not responding immediately with an answer. Purposeful pausing and feeling the tree would draw all students to explore further, to look, listen and feel it themselves. A conversation would ensue. This simple strategy has students sharing what they know from observations and communications with each other. The teacher acts as the guide on the side staying quiet while the conversation is progressing well and asking questions to elicit more detailed observations or re-examining misconceptions. The following is a typical inquiry questioning approach that I've conducted over many years:

Student 1:	This is a really tall tree. What is it?
	Teacher touches the tree trunk looks upwards and pauses.
Student 2:	Yeah, it feels so good and I can hardly see the top.
Teacher:	What else can you see?
Student 3:	It's sort of grey and a bit pink.
Student 4:	It has dots here and there.
Teacher:	What type of tree grows in the Australian bush?
All Students:	Gum trees or eucalyptus trees.
Teacher:	Well let's give this tree a name then. Let's see, it is a tall tree.
Student 5:	It probably is a gum tree.
Teacher:	I think it is because, look, there is one over there.
Student 5:	There's one other there too . . . and there . . . there are heaps of them.
Teacher:	OK. Well it may be a gum tree. But what sort?
Student 6:	It has dots on it. Maybe we can call it dot gum tree.
Teacher:	What's another name for a dot?
All Students:	Spots. Ah, we could call it a spotted gum tree.
Teacher:	What a great name for this tree. Let's call it a spotted gum.

By acting naïvely, I allowed the students to create a name based on their own attentiveness. Interestingly when using this strategy I found that they no longer ask the name of that tree or that bird over and over as before. They remember the names they've invented and see more examples as we travel along through the rest of the forest.

As a teacher, I initially worried about this technique of not giving information to the students and allowing them to invent names for animals and trees in the forest, but ultimately I have found the inquiry approach to be far more powerful for learning. This approach assisted the students to think for themselves, be attentive, consider alternatives, and to share their experiences and inquiries with others. Different parts of the forest attract the interest of students. Encouraging students to explore parts of the forest while immersed in the whole forest gradually reveals relationships and interconnections between the parts. One day, for instance, a group of Year 3 students were among a patch of paperbark trees looking for animals or evidence of animals. They found tiny holes bored into the bark and long lines of small chew marks which they attributed to insects. In a nearby paperbark they recognised a honeyeater almost at their eyelevel and hurried over to get closer. "What's it doing?" one child asked as she observed it poking its beak into the bark. "Getting honey," replied another child. "What part of the tree makes honey?" I asked. "Flowers, then what's it looking for in the bark?" replied one. "Insects!" concluded another child. Without the inquiry process the children would not have connected the bird and the insect markings. Inquiry sets students on a path to connect their experiences to a sense of the whole forest.

The experience-reflection-representation cycle

Reflection is one of the most powerful teaching tools at Bunyaville (Ballantyne & Packer, 2008; 2009). Reflection takes many forms and is interspersed throughout the teaching day. Often to start the day, we arrange students in *yarning circles* (a term often used to describe culturally safe forms of conversation in Indigenous communities) (Bessarab & Ng'andu, 2010) to share and compare their experiences in forests. Towards the end of the day, students sit alone in silence in the forest in a "magic spot" (Van Matre, 1990) for personal reflection, drawing together their knowledge, experiences and feelings in the forest. Such reflection slows time and provides a way to experience being present (Wattchow & Brown, 2011, p. 185). Silence as part of the magic spot provides space to daydream and let the mind wander while being present in a natural place. But more importantly, a magic spot provides time to process and connect what student have seen, heard and felt. A quiet spot or magic spot is a powerful pedagogical tool for synthesising learning.

The informal personal reflection of the magic spot is formalised when individuals leave their spot to join the sharing circle. Individual expressions of the experience, which seem ordinary on their own, are woven together to build a collective experience of what is seen, heard and felt. The collective experience creates a systems sense of the forest. Some groups of students articulate their thoughts wondering about the future of the forest, and their own futures, recognising that everything is connected, understanding the relational nature of life on Earth. A Year 3 student highlighted this recently when asked why we should care for Bunyaville Conservation Park. She said, "There is only one Bunyaville".

The collective representation is a tangible product that can prompt students to continue the reflection back in the classroom. Wattchow and Brown (2011, p. 195) highlight the non-linear "relationship between experience, reflection and the representation of experience". Experience, reflection and representation are intertwined and ongoing. Students leave Bunyaville with photos, texts and artworks that provide the stimulus for further conversations at school and home. Reflections in forms other than factual texts are more likely to engage parents and carers and are more likely to evoke emotion and affect (Miles, 2010). Children may know they have had a magical experience, but it is not always easy for them to convey what they have experienced in conventional modes. Wattchow and Brown (2011, p. 47) comment that, "language can never fully encompass the felt or embodied qualities of experience". Alternative forms such as prose poems, or drawings or close-up photos, provide the mediational means for students and teachers to recall and reinterpret their experiences and deepen their understanding back in the classroom.

Slow time

Our pedagogy is designed to slow down time for the learner. Payne and Wattchow (2008) suggest that slow time *dwells* on feeling, seeing and hearing. Slow time creates a space for students to experience the micro in the macro. Though time is actually limited in the forest on the excursion day, students are not pressured by time limits. We encourage students to flow with what interests them rather than fixate on the ticking away of time and what has to be done next. A common response of students is to highlight how calming and relaxing it is being in the forest. Various Year 4 students commented that:

> I felt calm because I didn't have to worry about getting work finished;
> You can always remain calm and there doesn't have to be something on your mind;
> calming as the leaves.

Slow time helps students connect to what they are feeling, bringing an awareness to the inner and outer learning. For example, one Year 4 student surprised us with the following comment in an interview we conducted a week after their forest experience.

> What I learnt is that when you just sit down and take the time to notice that the world you're in, like some people don't have this and how lucky you are to have it and you should appreciate it.

Case study: the Bunyaville Earthwalk

The Earthwalk is part of most BEEC programs. It can be 45 minutes to two hours or a full day (depending on the age of the students) of slow time for attentiveness, inquiry, reflection and sharing. Over the three years of this research project, Centre teachers audio-recorded some of the children's responses during Earthwalks and kept journals of the children's responses as well as their own reflections. Some of the children were also interviewed by research assistants a week after their Earthwalk experience. Here we focus on the transformation that was evident in some of their responses to this experience.

A new ethic of care – my dancing leaf

When leaves fall in front of the children or even on top of them, the place provides an opportunity to make what might seem like an ordinary experience special for every child. As a child picks up a leaf that has just fallen, the teacher will say, "You're the only person in the whole world to have ever touched that leaf! No one has touched that leaf". The child will look up and down and contemplate the truth of this, where the leaf has come from and their special relationship to the leaf. The teacher asks the children, "Have a look at your leaf and tell someone near you one interesting thing about that leaf". Children observe the various colours, holes, rough patches and so on of each leaf. They are told these are not just leaves but forest performers – *Wind Dancers*, especially if the day is windy. As each child in turn drops his or her *Wind Dancer* from a height, all watch its performance intently and, with scaffolding from the teacher, rich language flows to describe the leaves floating, tumbling, twirling or sinking, each dancing differently.

Through this activity, the children have formed an attachment to an element of the forest which they initially neither noticed nor cared for. "Can I take it with me?" is a common response from children. When it comes to leaving the leaf behind, an attachment is being severed, so it is done with an ethic of care. Continuing along the track, the teacher asks the children to find a place that is special to them in which to place the leaf. While they are finding a special place for their leaves, they are again being attentive and noticing the forest. The teacher doesn't talk at this stage so as to create a space where the children's voices can be heard. This is when the quiet children will come to speak to you, giving insight into their learning.

> "I want to put my leaf up there. Am I allowed to go up there?" a girl says pointing into the burnt bush on one side of the track. "Sure if that's the best place for it."
>
> (Year 3 student)

She goes up, places her leaf and returns. "That's an interesting place", the teacher comments.

> "Do you know why I put it there? I put it up there because it's been burnt up there so there's nothing to burn and it'll be safe. If I put it over here (green vegetation on the other side of track) it could get burnt."
>
> (Year 3 student)

She had thought quite carefully about the choice she'd made. If we hadn't allowed the child to speak, we may have assumed a different reason for her leaving it where she did. All the children part with their leaves, putting them down with great care, consideration and almost love. A caring relationship has replaced the initial feelings of disconnection.

Immersion enabling new values

When talking about their classroom activities we have noted students using expressions such as "boring" and "have to". The Earthwalk immersion and slow pedagogy instil different attitudes to learning. The following journal entry was made about the Earthwalk experiences of the same group of young children who declared their aversion to school and learning on arrival:

> As they walked and explored through the forest with the purpose of looking for specific plants (violets), students were attentive to the forest parts and their interconnections – noting features of trees, observing sedge frogs sheltering in the reeds and cicada skeletons clinging to the paperbark, and they spent quite a bit of time looking at holes in tree trunks with magnifying annayloupes, determined to know what might live in there. Equally mesmerising for these youngsters was the glossy deep red substance stuck to the side of a large spotted gum, which they learnt was sap, the tree's blood. When scratches were found on a tree, the immediate response was to infer that the marks were made by a possum, "Possum Bangles". These students wanted to go on discovering, to spend more time in the forest, so we were in fact late getting back from the Earthwalk that day.

The relationships between the tree and the possum are concrete and embodied rather than abstractly conveyed in someone else's words. The sensations of the glass-smooth resin and its intense colour, of reaching up to feel the scratches or bending down and parting reeds to see the frogs provide great stimulus and make the learning process intrinsically rewarding. Learning was no longer something arduous and despised (*"I'm never going back to school"*) but joyful and hungered for.

Connecting inner and outer in reflection

For many students, the Magic Spot is the favourite part of the Earthwalk (see Figure 4.2 below). They often can't wait for the sharing circle to form to share what they've experienced during their silent time of attentiveness and reflection. We were surprised during this study when students articulated an awareness of the difference between the demanding fast-paced world outside and slow-time world of the forest. One Year 6 student expressed this idea as follows:

> I felt like much calmer than at school because it's like never really quiet at playtime. There's always someone talking really loud or [inaudible] so it felt very calm and quiet.

The dramatic and sudden change to place and sense of time is a key affordance of the slow pedagogy of Bunyaville - a portal into a previously unknown,

Figure 4.2 Student in her Magic Spot

inaccessible world. A week after their Bunyaville experience, Year 6 students related an appreciation of the whole mind-body learning allowed by slow pedagogy as they talked about opportunities "to explore", "to move around", "to interact with wildlife", "to be quiet . . . and sit there and enjoy everything that was going on" and to take "time to look" and to "stop and think". A young student (about 5 years old) at the end of her visit had a similar realisation. She was in tears because "I love this place, I don't want to leave". She was reminded that she would be back the next year. "What will we be doing next year?" she asked with a smile.

Bunyaville's location as a forest reserve in the heart of suburban Brisbane enables students to experience slow time in a particularly salient manner. Immersion in nature and the slow way of learning become a palpable, accessible part of their lives. Evidence of this connection was seen when two youngsters (about 5 years old) turned up at our door, on two separate occasions last year, with their parents in tow, about nine months after their participation in a program, to show them the place that had become special to them. A Year 6 child expressed it eloquently saying, "Maybe all learning can have time. Maybe you just have to think about it and have to relax and stay calm".

Taking learning back into the classroom and community

The opportunity to reflect, an important part of an Earthwalk, is extended into the classroom by the representation of the reflection. For example, BEEC staff led a group of Year 9 students in a Magic Spot activity in their school grounds (not the forest). Their teacher integrated this experience with the learning they were doing on reducing the school's own human impacts on the environment. A student initiated the composition of a new poem (Figure 4.3), and her classmates helped her improve it. The poem strongly advocates a joyous, loving relationship with the earth and actions for a sustainable future. It was enlarged, printed, framed and proudly shared with parents, with us and with the school community.

Conclusion

Involvement in this research project has helped us take new perspectives on our pedagogy at Bunyaville. In particular we have gained a new temporal perspective, a realisation that time, slow time, is critical to our pedagogy. We have seen how children sense the difference in time between the forest world and their everyday world. However, mere physical presence in the forest does little to help children understand or value this place. Without slow pedagogy many children would continue to perceive the forest with "outside world eyes" as ordinary, of little value or even as dangerous.

Our slow pedagogy heightens children's attentiveness to the micro as part of the macro, the small parts that make up the whole forest. Children also make connections between their learning in the classroom and their embodied learning beyond the classroom, in the forest. Immersion enables students to emotionally connect with the forest. We have seen children value and care for leaves which they first thought of as ordinary and of little regard. In children's joy in learning through exploration in the forest, we have seen a transformation from their previous aversion to classroom learning.

With slow time, learners can be immersed in inquiry to sense patterns, connections and relationships between the parts of the forest system and in reflection

Make a Change

In my dreams there is a place,
Where pain and death have no trace;
All around me, nature lies
Soaring through the soft, blue skies.

I've seen this future in my daze,
Without the awful, smoky haze;
Everybody needs to know
So that the living Earth can grow.

All the people everywhere,
Need to heal this toxic air;
The Earth is sending us a sign
We need to help, it's now our time.

Self-sufficient, we could be,
By saving all our energy;
The Earth would be a better place
If only we would slow our pace.

This clean and future world I see,
Everything lies untouched and free;
The skies are bright, shining blue
The sea is clean, the sun shines through.
The air is light, clear in the rain
The world is here to sustain.

It doesn't matter who we are,
Or how much we can do;
Smaller steps can take us far
Kids can make a difference too.

As the birds fly by,
I know this place will die;
We need to save it now
And live in peace, somehow.
We are the future, we must see
What out planet needs to be.

It's time to treat with joy and love,
The planet Earth and skies above;
So that we have in future days
Enough for everyone always.

By Sarah Loft and NLSC Year 9 SOSE Honours

Figure 4.3 Poem composed by Sarah Loft and the 2012 North Lakes State College Year 9 Studies of Society & Environment Honours students

to make meaning of their learning. In the response of a child wanting to be a plant, we have seen how an awareness of such connections has transformed her initial view of nature as scary. We have seen students making connections between themselves and the place as well as connections to the slow pedagogy it supports, valuing the opportunities to learn through slow time and using their whole bodies.

In the poetic work of the Year 9 students (see Figure 4.3) advocating for others to change their attitudes and behaviours, we have seen learners placing themselves as part of the whole community, as valuable contributors who can be part of an ecologically sustainable and just future world. In a society that is increasingly urbanised, fast-paced and disconnected from the natural world on which it is inextricably dependent, this is the type of learning that education systems need to cultivate.[2]

Notes

1 This chapter has been co-authored. The "I" in section 1.3 and 3.1 represents Noeleen Rowntree's history and experiences while teaching at Bunyaville Environmental Education Centre. The rest of the chapter has been co-authored and the "I" may refer to either author's experiences.
2 The poem in Figure 4.3 was composed by Sarah Loft from the 2012 North Lakes State College Year 9 Studies of Society & Environment Honours class. Reproduced with Sarah Loft's permission. Photograph courtesy Bunyaville Environmental Education Centre.

References

Ballantyne, R., & Packer, J. (2008). Learning for sustainability: The role and impact of outdoor and environmental education centres. St Lucia: University of Queensland, School of Tourism.

Ballantyne, R., & Packer, J. (2009). Introducing a fifth pedagogy: Experience-based strategies for facilitating learning in natural environments. *Environmental Education Research, 15*(2), 243–262.

Bessarab, D., & Ng'andu, B. (2010). Yarning about yarning as a legitimate method in Indigenous research. *International Journal of Critical Indigenous Studies, 3*(1), 37–50.

Gough, N. (2013). Towards deconstructive nonalignment: A complexivist view of curriculum, teaching and learning. *South African Journal of Higher Education, 27*(5), 1213–1233.

Howell, A. (2016). Exploring children's lived experiences of NAPLAN. In B. Lingard, G. Thompson & S. Sellar (Eds.), *National testing in schools: An Australian assessment* (pp. 164–180). London: Routledge.

Kock, Z. J., Taconis, R., Bolhuis, S., & Gravemeijer, K. (2015). Creating a culture of inquiry in the classroom while fostering an understanding of theoretical concepts in direct current electric circuits: A balanced approach. *International Journal of Science and Mathematics Education, 13*(1), 45–69.

Louv, R. (2012). The nature principle: Human restoration and the end of nature-deficit disorder. New York: Algonquin Books.

Markwell Consulting. (2010). *Bunya mountains Aboriginal aspirations and caring for country plan*. Brisbane, Qld: Bunya Mountains Elders Council & Burnett Mary Regional Group.

Miles, M. (2010). Representing nature: Art and climate change. *Cultural Geographies, 17*(1), 19–35.

Payne, P., & Wattchow, B. (2008). Slow pedagogy and placing education in post-traditional outdoor education. *Australian Journal of Outdoor Education, 12*(1), 25–38.

Petruzzi, A. P. (2001). Kairotic rhetoric in Freire's liberatory pedagogy. *JAC: A Journal of Composition Theory, 21*(2), 349–381.

Robertson, B. (2006). Getting past "inquiry versus content". *Educational Leadership, 64*(4), 67.

Senge, P., Laur, J., Schley, S., & Smith, B. (2006). *Learning for sustainability*. Cambridge: Cambridge University Press.

Sterling, S. (2004). An analysis of the development of sustainability education internationally: evolution, interpretation and transformative potential. In J. Blewitt & C. Cullingford (Eds.), *The sustainability curriculum: The challenge for higher education* (pp. 43–62). London: Earthscan.

Thomashow, M. (1996). Ecological identity: Becoming a reflective environmentalist. Cambridge, MA: MIT Press.

Thompson, G. (2016). Teacher perceptions of national testing. In B. Lingard, G. Thompson & S. Sellar (Eds.), *National testing in schools: An Australian assessment* (pp. 57–71). London: Routledge.

Van Matre, S. (1990). *Earth education: A new beginning*. Greenville W Virginia: Institute for Earth Education.

Wattchow, B., & Brown, M. (2011). *A pedagogy of place – Outdoor education for a changing world*. Clayton, VIC: Monash University Publishing.

5 Pedagogy as walking country at Barambah

Sue Gibson and Mark Cridland

Editors' preface

Chapter Five describes the pedagogy of walking as designed at Barambah Environmental Education Centre. Walking is typically perceived as physical activity with health benefits rather than as pedagogy (Bairner, 2011). However, walking is central to many practices that have a pedagogical intent, such as walking on pilgrimages, or the walking of country by Indigenous Australians to renew the land through songlines – a combination of walking and storytelling about the land (Clarke, 2003). Walking has political significance when people come together to march for a cause and communicate collectively their solidarity (Bairner, 2011). In contrast to these purposeful and pedagogical modes, walking can be merely a stroll together, creating a relaxed sociality that conveys to others that the walkers probably have a close relationship and enjoy each other's company (Vaughan, 2009; Solnit, 2001). Walking has a special place in the history of environmental education. Henry Thoreau (2001) regarded walking as a way of accessing the wildness of nature where walkers could experience the freedom of open-ended adventure beyond the fences and roads that defined the constraints of society. The wild for Thoreau is a metaphysical space where nature is dominant and valued and where walking signifies living in tune with natural processes. In contemporary scholarship, Michel de Certeau (1984) explored walking as an instance of everyday practices that created specific places as full of different possibilities. For de Certeau walking in an urban environment varies subtly in pace, direction and purpose, requiring inventiveness and adaptability by the walker to the ever changing material conditions, as well as the gait and pace of other walkers. This is an embodied way of knowing the urban space. Walkers are themselves part of the evolving constellation of activity that is making the place.

Walking as place-making is relevant to the environmental programs at Barambah – it is impossible to know Barambah except by engaging with its tracks and terrain through one's body. The tracks themselves have been formed over time by others as pathways into knowing. So "making the place" is not a single event but a collective and cumulative event of walking where others have been. In this sense the meanings we can make in place necessarily rely on the history of possibilities established by others (their tracks), but our walking will always be distinct and our experience unique. As Bakhtin noted (Bakhtin, 1986), we necessarily re-voice the words of others in articulating and communicating personal understanding. Similarly we necessarily follow another's footsteps as we walk across the land, yet our experience of it will be unique, our way of walking distinctively personal.

The educators at Barambah, Sue Gibson, Mark Cridland and their colleagues, had not read the theory and research on walking summarised above. Their notion of walking as pedagogy arose from professional practices at Barambah. Sue Gibson told us during one of our discussions in 2014 that she used a "walking-talking" pedagogy. Aristotle had created a peripatetic grove where he could walk and talk with his students on philosophical issues (Shell, 2015), so we were intrigued by these parallels between Sue's practice and the long tradition in Western philosophy of walking, talking and inquiring. We asked her to explain further, and she recalled that on many excursions she started hanging back to walk with those students who seemed more reluctant to take part in the programs. She adopted a follow-in approach to the conversation with these students, encouraging them to set the topic and only adding to things that caught their interest as they passed by. It wasn't a guided walk with the teacher providing an expert commentary for the students to remember. It was similar to a stroll with friends along the tracks where any topic or observation was welcomed in a more relaxed and accepting manner. However Sue did begin to take up opportunities to extend the students' interest in the things they saw, the animals they heard and unusual occurrences along the way. At the conclusion of the walk, one student told Sue that he liked it when they walked together along the track and she talked to them about different things. This episode convinced Sue that this more relaxed conversational walk with (reluctant) students was a powerful way of engaging them in learning. From this insight Sue began to reflect on the many walks that engaged students at Barambah.

The variety of walks at Barambah provided insight into the distinctiveness of the pedagogy in this place. Walking in open forest enabled more distant observation of birds and other animals and an easy upright bodily rhythm. As students encountered vines that crossed their paths, they had to break their rhythm and bend their bodies to pass though. Observations in the denser undergrowth were much more difficult as attention needed to be directed at finding a way through. In the denser spaces, students were necessarily aware of the vegetation in a much more tactile manner as they pushed against vines and branches and experienced resistance and flexibility. As moisture increased under the rainforest canopy mossy logs provided a beautiful but more precarious walking trail. Walking uphill towards the lookout engaged the cardiovascular system and heightened the sense of accomplishment as the distant vista emerged, and one could situate oneself in the broader perspective of the whole landscape. The different patterns and physical requirements of walking give a sense of how knowledge itself is embodied in the act of walking. Solnit (2001) expresses this idea beautifully when she writes, "The rhythm of walking generates a kind of rhythm of thinking, and the passage echoes or stimulates the passage through a series of thoughts. This creates the odd consonance between internal and external passage, one that suggests that the mind is also a landscape of sorts and that walking is one way to traverse it" (Solnit, 2001, pp. 5–6). It is this sense of walking as both place-making and embodied knowledge-making that underlies the intuitive pedagogical practices designed at Barambah. Walking also connects students to the ways of knowing practiced by Indigenous people across time – it provides a cultural bridge or point of contact for students of today to experience the way Indigenous people connected to country and continue to connect to their country through walking.

Peter Renshaw & Ron Tooth

Introduction

> They came from the north, from the south, east and west travelling hundreds of kilometres along traditional pathways, across hot dry land, towards the distant blue tinged Bunya Mountains and the promise of cool forests, cold mountain streams and the nutritious flesh of the bunya nuts.
>
> They gathered to feast and celebrate the bounty of the bunya nut harvest – to tell stories and to duel, to pass on wisdom and for many to trade and dance.
>
> When the feast and celebrations ended, they followed the pathways back to their country, to once again move in tune with the seasons and to wait for the message sticks to arrive and invite them back to Bunya Country.
>
> For thousands of years the tribes have been making this journey and now you are part of this story.[1, 2]

Since 2006, Wakka Wakka Elders have come every second year to the Barambah Environmental Education Centre to present this message stick to students who have been selected to be river ambassadors for the *"Bunya 2 Bay River Journey"*. The Elders entrust the students to:

> Take this message stick on behalf of the Wakka Wakka People. Follow the river to the sea and present it to the Elders of the Quandamooka People and invite them to share the next bunya harvest.

The students as river ambassadors carry the message stick from Barambah to the mouth of the Brisbane River, following the ancient journey of the message and travelling through the country on which Barambah Environmental Education Centre now stands. Barambah is uniquely located on this traditional Aboriginal pathway, a fact confirmed by Gubbi Gubbi and Wakka Wakka Elders from the nearby towns of Cherbourg and Murgon. The Elders told us that Aboriginal groups passed through here on their way to major bunya pine forests to the southwest of the Centre. With Wakka Wakka country to the west and Gubbi Gubbi country to the east, the Centre is surrounded by country that is imbued with Aboriginal knowledge and culture.

At the Centre an extensive system of walking tracks provides opportunities to wind from the open forest into the rainforest and back again, to meander along creek beds, to climb to high vantage points, or to silently sit in contemplation of magnificent forest trees reaching towards the sky. Walking along the tracks through diverse landscapes, it is easy to imagine the Traditional Owners of the land walking through country following pathways, using markers on trees for direction and telling stories on their way to the Bunya forests to share the abundance of seasonal food. The act of walking on these long-established tracks creates material and embodied connection between the students of today and the Aboriginal people of today and yesterday.

Representing contested country

The elements of the Barambah logo (see Figure 5.1) represent the history of the local area during the vast period of Aboriginal ownership and post-European contact. The line represents the roads/pathways that lead to Barambah in the mountains. The twin peaks of Mount Mia represented in the line are believed by some Aboriginal Elders to have been a pathway marker for the groups coming from the north along the Wide Bay Creek to the Bunya country. The tall dome-crowned Bunya tree (*Araucaria bidwillii*) represents the richness of the land and the festivals that brought Aboriginal people together across time. The orb partly hidden behind the tree represents both the full moon and mineral gold that was found nearby, initially at Kilkivan and then at Black Snake and later Minya Creek. A red ring around the orb represents "red gold", the red cedar tree (*Toona ciliata*), a very valuable timber resource from the local forests. The Barambah logo, therefore, captures the contested relationships that Aboriginal people and European settlers have had to the country.

From hoop pine forests to environmental education centre

In the early post-contact years in the 19th century, there was a tremendous drain on the natural forests as land was feverishly cleared by European settlers for the

Figure 5.1 The logo of the Barambah Environmental Education Centre

grazing of livestock, and valuable timber was harvested commercially. As early as 1900 the government was forced to set aside some areas as protected timber reserves, which ultimately became state forests. By 1920, hoop pine plantations were being developed to address the problem of severely depleted natural forests. Plantations were expanded after 1945 with various forestry camps and associated facilities built to accommodate forestry workers.

In 1977, the basic buildings and facilities established for forestry workers were transferred to the Department of Education to become field study centres that provided teachers and students with close proximity to natural learning environments. The old forestry facilities at Barambah at that time were very basic with an office, a corrugated iron walled dining room with an open fire-place for cooking meals and three wooden sleeping quarters. There were no gardens and only a few trees in the Centre grounds. In 1980 the Centre was renamed the Barambah Field Study Centre and in 1988 was again changed to its present name: Barambah Environmental Education Centre. The facilities were improved over time, and today the Centre has a principal, 2 teachers and 4 support staff, a sleeping capacity for 63 students and 12 adults, as well as well-established grounds, tracks and learning sites. In 2010 the surrounding area became Wrattens National Park, and the Centre currently sits within Wrattens Regional Park, an area of the National Park set aside for science and education.

Ongoing connections with Indigenous elders

Throughout the history of the Barambah Environmental Education Centre, strong connections have been maintained with the local Aboriginal community, and many locals still call the Centre "*A Flat*", referring to the name of the forestry camp where Aboriginal people from the nearby reserve at Cherbourg had worked as timber cutters. Elders and their families visit the Centre regularly to observe and participate in Centre programs and events. These ongoing relationships are extremely important to the Centre to ensure that the programs reflect the wisdom and cultural knowledge of the traditional owners.

The biennial *Bunya 2 Bay River Journey* strengthens the relationship between the Centre staff and the Aboriginal community, and the privilege afforded to the students who carry the message stick on behalf of the Wakka Wakka Elders is an amazing gesture of trust and collaboration. Another significant event illustrating ongoing connections occurred in 2011 when Barambah was chosen as the site for the Cherbourg Dormitory Reunion, a time of restoration and healing for members of the stolen generations who were removed from their families and forced to live in the dormitory system operated by the administrators of Cherbourg from the early 1900s to the 1980s. Barambah has been called a place of healing and this is why it was chosen for this important event.

Forests

The local area is covered by a variety of forest types including dry schlerophyll, wet scherophyll and aurucarian vine forests. The surrounding pre-clearing vegetation consists of smooth barked apple and narrow leaved ironbark. Adjacent to the Centre the creek flats support a narrow band of forest red gum and rough barked apple. The understory is generally grassy with occasional scattered shrubs. A narrow band of closed forest along the creek bank, a form of gallery forest, contains rainforest species forming a variable canopy beneath an over-storey of sclerophylls, such as black tea-tree and small-fruited grey gum (Flenady, 2015).

A number of Aboriginal artefacts have been found in the vicinity over the 35 years that the Centre has been established, and there is evidence of past use of the forest by Aboriginal groups, for example, evidence of bark harvesting for shields and stone chips produced by knapping. There is a wide range of traditional food plants in the local forests including a large number of mature Bunya trees. It is the unique location, Aboriginal heritage and natural history of this place that sets it apart from other settings and allows us to offer learning experiences that cannot be replicated in other places. It is this *place* that defines who we are and underpins every aspect of what we do.

The Barambah experience

An oasis: "Not what I expected"

Within the grounds of the Centre, buildings blend into the extensive native gardens that have been cultivated by staff for many years. Students often comment that this place isn't what they were expecting, and adults frequently refer to a feeling of peacefulness. Visitors arriving along dusty roads pull into our driveway and comment on having found an "oasis" as they step out of their vehicle. Overall, there is a sense of having found something unexpected. Barambah is a place where, for a time, people re-connect to the natural environment, and it doesn't seem at all strange to be sharing place and space with wandering goannas, scuttling bandicoots and breathtakingly beautiful birds, for example New Holland honeyeaters and Yellow Eastern robins, that flitter about every nook and cranny of the Centre.

Walking to fig tree

> In a couple of steps students walk from the bright open forest over a creek and into the cool, dark, damp forest. They are assaulted with a sensory smorgasbord – cooler temperatures, filtered light, earthy smell, tinkling bellbirds, close green leaves. The students' eyes light up as they look around and comments like "wow" and "this is so cool" abound. Again students close their eyes and feel, breathe and hear the forest. Up stairs, walking along a large fallen tree covered in moss (see Figure 5.2) as they venture further into the forest.
>
> —Sue Gibson, Journal entry 18/9/2012

The students have just walked down the back of One Tree Hill and are entering into the rainforest of Wrattens Regional Park, having recently arrived at the

Figure 5.2 Mossy log provides a walking path through the understory

Centre. They follow a winding track into the forest, climb over logs, clamber through vine tunnels, cross moist gullies and pass ancient tree trunks. There is movement in the understory as birds flit from branch to twig calling to each other. Students notice the abundance of bandicoot holes and button quail plate-lets littering the edge of the track; they become distracted and stop counting bandicoot holes as a rustling in the undergrowth signals that an invisible local resident is on the move. Suddenly they arrive at the Big Fig tree, a majestic forest ancient, estimated to be 300 years old, rising up from enormous buttress roots and dominating this area of the forest.

Materiality of culture in place

Students sit to contemplate the Big Fig before exploring the area around the base where they discover signs of use by the traditional owners of the area. For many students, it is the first time they have encountered any physical signs of use of the natural environment by the Traditional Owners. There are moments of connection that occur throughout Barambah programs when students realise they are sitting under a tree where a stone axe was once found, or they see the footholds which were cut in a large bunya tree to access the cones from the crown of the tree. This connection is evident when students make comments like:

> The best thing was the One Tree Hill walk, because it was inspiring and significant as many people had walked it before and I felt as if I was part of something bigger.
>
> (Year 10 student)

> I learnt about the amazing history. And how the land and culture is so important to protect.
>
> (Year 10 student)

> Everything feels so much more real. In a classroom you hear things and it goes out the other ear, whereas on country, we can feel and experience (that) which will stay with us forever.
>
> (Year 10 student)

Walking and learning

Observing the Big Fig tree closely, students find the last living remnant of the original host tree and comment on the relationship that has existed between the two trees over hundreds of years. They follow a short track down into the creek bed, taking care not to disturb the tracks left by a wallaby drinking from the water's edge the evening before. As they explore the dry creek bed and banks, they realise the large root running along the top of the bank belongs to the Big Fig they have just seen. After a time, the group diverts from the creek bed to follow the track along the bank past flowering native brambles about to burst into fruit and back out into the open forest. On the way back to the Centre students chatter about the experience they have just had, excitedly wondering about what is to come next. We have come to value such incidental but deep learning through walking, and this walking pedagogy is explored further below.

Staff mediating access and learning at Barambah

Sue Gibson's story

In the beginning of my teaching career there was the walled classroom and then there was this other great big learning space outside the classroom – the outdoors. Right from the start I was drawn to the outdoors. As a science teacher there was never any shortage of reasons to take kids outside: to measure things, to time things, to observe things, even to blow things up in the name of science. The one thing I knew was when kids are outside the four walls of the classroom they relax and engage; when they engage their behaviour changes, and when their behaviour changes a different type of learning happens that kids actually enjoy! It never entered my thinking as a beginning science teacher that non-engagement of students could be an option, though I observed that some teachers tolerated it. Perhaps this intuitive sense that every child can and should be engaged arose from my own childhood largely spent exploring and playing in our home paddock of about 100 acres with a flowing creek and a mountain to climb and the branches of trees to straddle to contemplate life.

Throughout my teaching career, whether inside the four walls of a classroom or embracing the teaching opportunities afforded by an outdoor environment, I have always utilised pedagogy that allows students to "experience" the learning through hands-on, context-based activities. I particularly loved allowing students time to "practically play" with a concept, for example, electrical circuits, and come up with their own ideas before we started formalising what they had learnt. This isn't something I ever thought deeply about; it just made sense to me and seemed to work for both the students and for me as their teacher. As I developed teaching experience, I realised my preferred teaching practices revolved around discovery and experiential learning theories, and it is the success I enjoyed engaging students with these practices that paved the way for my transition into the outdoor and environmental education sector and teaching at Barambah.

Arriving at Barambah for the first time, knowing this was my new place to teach, engendered a variety of emotions and reactions culminating in an overwhelming, wonderful feeling and a sense of privilege that I was going to be a part of this *place*. Thoughts of excitement, adventure and exhilaration intertwined with a sensory overload of colour, sound and smell created a sense of amazement that this place was my new classroom. Once I started to follow this track, the journey of teaching at Barambah, I anticipated twists and turns and forks, yet I knew that whichever way I choose to go, deep learning and fun could co-exist in this place. It is about as far from classroom teaching as you can get, and yet it feels so right to be here. It makes perfect sense to be working in a place that changes with the time of day, with the seasons and with the natural cycles of plant and animal life. Why would you be anywhere else?

Not only does the place make perfect sense, the opportunity to engage students in discovery and experiential learning experiences through immersion in the natural environment provides enormous satisfaction and fulfilment. Our students, who are living and learning in an increasingly virtual world, are losing touch with nature to the point that a significant number of students visiting our Centre have never been on a bushwalk before. The walk up One Tree Hill consistently rates as a favorite experience for students with many explaining they have never climbed a hill before. It is no wonder that experiential learning in the natural environment has a profound effect on many students and elicits deep and lasting changes.

It is not only the *place*, Barambah, which seems right; the staff contributes to the sense of fulfilment working here. Despite physically demanding work and long days, there is a sense of shared purpose, peace and well-being. Staffroom banter is inclusive and cheerful, and genuine concern for each other is evident. Regardless of the role each person plays there is a collective responsibility for the overall management of the Centre and people willingly step forward and step up as need arises. As noted above, Barambah has been called a place of healing; there is no doubt the setting contributes to the supportive working environment.

Mark Cridland's story

I vividly remember the moment over 30 years ago when I decided to pursue my passion as an environmental and outdoor educator. Here is my memory of that moment. There was a sharp crack of the bullocky's whip and a shout of "gee up star" to signal to the bullocks to move forward in unison. The collective raw power of the team was obvious as they effortlessly dragged the large log forward. There were audible gasps from the young students as well as the group of pre-service teachers when the old bullocky led his team around the Pullenvale Environmental Education Centre (PEEC). Stories of times long past were shared as strong hands caressed the beloved bullocks. The threads of the bullocky's stories drew together the past and the present, as well as appealing to students' heads, hands and hearts. Connections were made to low impact living and hopes for a sustainable future. As a pre-service teacher, this way of teaching and learning was a revelation. Having entered teaching training after working for eight years in a number of jobs across Queensland, I found all aspects of tertiary education fascinating, challenging and rewarding. However, the holistic view of students and the authentic real world learning embedded in the environmental education programs at PEEC stirred something deep within me. I was hooked, and so my 30-year journey into the field of environmental and outdoor education began.

My first position as a teacher was unexpectedly as a consultant based at the Cairns Marine Studies Centre (now the Holloways Beach Environmental Education Centre). My role was to travel across Far North Queensland to work with teachers and principals in schools to implement environmental education within the school curriculum. This unlikely role for a novice graduate was fascinating but short-lived, and the following year I became the classroom teacher of a group of 33 energetic Year 7 students with a surprising wealth of world experience but impatience at being confined in the classroom. I struggled to engage the students and conform to the structured requirements of a fragmented curriculum. It was during this first year of classroom teaching that I had the opportunity to take my class on an extended eight-day walk in the wet tropics coordinated by the Tinaroo Environmental Education Centre and Outward Bound Australia. The students who struggled in the classroom came alive during this walk. They demonstrated a range of hitherto hidden skills and took on leadership roles in this outdoor classroom. I was surprised by the keen insights articulated by the students during discussions around the campfire at night or during slow canoe and rafting trips down rivers. I forged a relationship with students based on mutual respect and a genuine sense of shared experiences. For the next three years as a classroom teacher and then as principal of a small rural primary school, I eagerly coordinated a number of these rich learning journeys for my students as well as students from other schools. The journeys blended outdoor experiences and personal development with aspects of the curriculum.

After these five years of teaching, an opportunity arose to lead an environmental education centre. The lure of combining my classroom skills, leadership experience and desire to work in both environmental and outdoor education was compelling, even though as a family we were very settled in the beautiful surrounds of tropical North Queensland. So began our new journey to the Barambah Environmental Education Centre. With a great sense of anticipation after hearing from my colleague about the fantastic location of the Barambah Centre with rainforests, creeks and mountain tracks, we drove along a winding road through increasingly dry forests punctuated by sections of open pastures. Our sense of excitement dwindled with each kilometre and our three sons, aged 4, 2 and six months, were oblivious to the trepidation my wife and I felt. We arrived at Barambah EEC on the 23rd January 1993 and our first impression of the Centre, at the end of our 2000 kilometre journey, was somewhat disappointing after living for four years in the lush green forests of the Daintree in North Queensland.

The following day, with a rough map of the area as guide, we explored our new world. As we followed the paths up the valley towards the tall trees, Barambah slowly revealed its hidden treasures, or as I would say now, its affordances for teaching and learning. A sensory overload was created by the wonderful array of colours, a cacophony of bird calls, evidence of a busy night by nocturnal visitors, mossy logs and dry creek beds full of fascinating geological features. With each turn in the track the environment changed; as we climbed hills the vistas opened up, rock crystals gleamed in the sunlight and evidence of tool-making by the local Indigenous people appeared on the tracks, semi-exposed by recent rain. That night in the enveloping silence we heard the mating calls of koalas and possums, while stars glowed intensely in the darkened night sky free from the light pollution of towns and cities.

Over those first few days our appreciation for Barambah grew and has not abated after 25 years. We experienced what all visitors experience when they walk the tracks at Barambah – a heightened sensorial awareness of our inherent relationship to the natural world. The practice of walking along tracks, having relaxed conversations, the sudden and at times dramatic changes that heighten the senses and attuning to the sounds and sights of the forest drove the design and development of the core programs at Barambah EEC. During the 20 years I was principal at Barambah, the rich Indigenous history, authentic relationships I formed with the local Indigenous community and the insights afforded by walking and talking on country heightened my deep respect for Indigenous people and their spirituality. Over time I became aware of being watched, silently guided and nurtured by the Indigenous people who had walked before me in Barambah. I still regard this awareness as a privilege given to me by the generosity of the Indigenous people who walked on country at Barambah as custodians of the land and who shared with me their stories of this place.

Undertaking journeys and following tracks is a recurring theme in my career as an educator. I resonate with the description provided by Joseph Campbell in his classic book *The Hero with a Thousand Faces.* One listens for the call to adventure, accepts the call and crosses the threshold. Once you cross the threshold there is no coming back and the hero must enter the cave he fears because therein lies the treasure one seeks. The hero must complete the journey and return home a changed person. As in the classic legend described by Campbell, when you visit Barambah and walk the tracks, you are changed forever.

At a celebratory function with friends and colleagues (including Sue Gibson the co-author of our chapter) to mark the end of my time at Barambah, my wife and I reflected upon the 20 years we lived and worked at Barambah, and the theme of our speech was simple. It did not focus on what we had achieved over the 20 years but focussed on the effect Barambah had on us as individuals and as a family. For all who visit the centre, Barambah becomes part of your life's journey or your "songline". On the 23rd January 2013, exactly twenty years after I drove through the gates at the Barambah EEC, I walked along the boardwalk up to the office at the Moreton Bay Environmental Education Centre as the newly appointed principal, full of anticipation and ready to extend my "songline" in this place. I brought to this new role a deep understanding that an environmental educator must take the time to walk and listen as the "place" speaks to you. I have learned to be attentive to the sights, sounds, smells and textures of things as well as the people, past and present, in place. I learned through all my journeys that "place" will guide you, give purpose and nurture you as you change and evolve.

Key elements of the pedagogy

Walking is integral to Barambah programs; walking connects students to the culture of the Traditional Owners, walking allows time to become immersed in the natural environment, walking enhances well-being and walking gets students to where they are going. Regardless of the program that a school might choose to do at Barambah, all students are taken on a guided walk up One Tree Hill as their first activity, and this is a deliberate pedagogical decision. The key pedagogy at Barambah provides experiential learning mediated by the bodily rhythm of walking with others, becoming physically immersed in particular places. It is connection to place that opens the door to conceptual knowledge, deep reflective thinking, an ethic of care for the environment and behaviour change.

Sacred walk to "One Tree Hill"

From the moment students arrive at the Centre, clattering off a dusty bus and chattering to each other, they are expecting something exciting to happen, and that something is found when they leave the confines of the Centre and venture into the forest. It seems that heightened senses are the portal to deep learning; when students are excited about place they are receptive to pedagogy of place, and when they are receptive to pedagogy of place deep learning can occur.

The destination of this guided walk is One Tree Hill (see Figure 5.3), which is named for the starkly magnificent bloodwood tree that dominates the apex of the ridge. We create a sense of the sacred through this walk. This isn't just any forest walk. A magnificent tree defines the destination and its size and age creates a poignant moment where students can easily imagine the distant past and can see themselves in relation to generations of people who have previously visited this site and observed this tree in the sunlight. Once they reach the top and meet the bloodwood tree, they find a space in and around the large roots to nestle in, connecting to place through their bodies. Students are asked to close their eyes and feel, breathe and hear One Tree Hill. When they open their eyes students share what they have felt, heard and smelt. Some things they can identify, some things they can't describe, but the fact that they have connected to a sacred place is obvious from their responses.

> The best part of the trip was the walk to One Tree Hill because we got to witness true aboriginal sites & learn about the history.
>
> (Year 10 student)

Hard walking

Students visiting Barambah are typical of their generation, varying greatly in fitness and readiness for demanding walks through the forest. A number of tracks take students up and over hills where they experience changes in vegetation and panoramic views. Part way up One Tree Hill, the students stop to catch their breath, and their faces light up as they look beyond the track and catch the view from the east through to the west. Comments like "you can see the whole world" and "look how far you can see" abound as students respond to the whole landscape that is "Barambah." Their senses are heightened and they are more acutely aware of their surroundings. Knowing they are only part way through the walk, there is a renewed sense of urgency to get to the top and experience the full panoramic view. Even for those students who are physically struggling with the rigor of the climb, the final part of the walk is always achieved. Walking hard has aesthetic and fitness implications and creates a strong sense of achievement and

Figure 5.3 The bloodwood on One Tree Hill at Barambah near dawn

joy for the students when they crest the final rise. Their teachers often comment that they are really surprised these students could successfully complete such a demanding walk.

Walking differently through forests

Change happens from the moment students enter the rainforest at the foot of One Tree Hill. Walking freely with swinging arms along the tracks in open forest contrasts, in a whole embodied manner, to moving through the close rainforest. The connection to place in this dense vegetation is experienced as bodily confinement and being invited to "wait a while" by the snagging vines. Moving through the rainforest requires students to be in very close contact to the different aspects of the forest, resulting in a whole-body tactile experience (see Figure 5.4). It is this immersion in the learning environment, crouching and bending one's body to the demands of the forest, that underpins the philosophy of pedagogy at Barambah. Physical adaptation to place is the key to student learning outcomes.

Walking-talking pedagogy

Whether walking along the creek bed, winding along a forest track, climbing a hill or following a narrow gully, there is a group of students for whom nothing is more important than being first in line behind the Barambah teacher. This has nothing to do with being nervous about the new surroundings or needing

Figure 5.4 Bending to walk through the forest thickets

reassurance that they are safe and can relax and enjoy the experience. These students have energy, a sense of adventure and a thirst for knowledge about their new environment. They question the teacher continuously as the group meanders along and share stories from their own experiences. They are students who have connected to the environment almost before they leap from the bus on arrival and form a close rapport with their Barambah teacher the moment the walks begin. They are happy to share their lead position with other like-minded students as long as they don't lose their immediate proximity to the teacher, and will strategically work their way up through the group if for any reason they are delegated to a position further back in the line. They are the students who thrive with teachers who practise "walking-talking pedagogy".

The idea of walking-talking pedagogy evolved from a discussion that occurred one day when walking with a group of disengaged Year 9 boys. These boys were participating in a "construction camp" building a replacement footbridge on one of the tracks. Rather than conducting a commentary on the flora and fauna, I (Sue Gibson) chose to simply walk with them, listen to their talk and join in their conversational topics. At times I linked their conversation to observations along our walk, and gradually they began to tune into the walk and the changes in the natural surroundings. After a while one of them said, "*We like it when we walk and you tell us stuff*". This incredibly simple statement triggered an insight for me that the physicality and rhythm of shared walking could be the key that unlocked the learning embedded in this place.

Further discussion with these Year 9 boys about their One Tree Hill walk elicited comments like "hiking, walking through the bush, fun and gets you fit, clears your sinuses, physical activity, talking about stuff on the way – anything that popped into your head" confirmed the thinking that for some students, traditional classrooms are at times too still and non-interactive. The transition from the open forest into the rainforest elicited a different response from the same boys, with comments like "I feel relaxed when I go into the forest", "I do too", "peaceful", "shady", "birdsongs", "makes you feel relaxed just by being there", "space makes me feel like I'm at home", "I need space to be calm and keep my head clear", "I didn't think I would be relaxed but it has relaxed me" suggesting that at other times classrooms are too noisy and busy for these same students. It is an interesting conundrum for classroom teachers striving to meet the varied needs of their individual students for calm and excitement. For students who struggle in indoor learning spaces, Barambah offers multiple times and places for students to be excited and relaxed as they need, as their walk takes them.

Another interesting episode occurred recently with a group of Year 12 boys completing a vegetation study in the rainforest as part of a science based field trip. I had walked to the study site with this group and listened to their chat while they walked, surmising that they probably wouldn't be totally focussed on their data collecting activity when we finally arrived. Part way through the activity the majority of the group were urging one boy to play some music on his mobile phone. His response was "*we don't need music, it's peaceful here*". The rest of the group kept urging until he said "*You can listen to music anytime, here you can hear the birds*". It was obvious that this student had connected to the cool, dark forest, and it was equally obvious this boy had a degree of influence over the other students, as that was the end of the discussion. When I reconnected with this group a short time later they were extremely animated and excited as they had seen a dingo on the track only 10 metres ahead of them. I quietly reflected that this sighting would have been extremely unlikely if they had been playing music on the mobile phone.

Upon reflecting more deeply about walking-talking pedagogy, the idea developed that walking is a rhythmic, soothing activity that moderates the excess energy that some students possess. Unlike the concentration and effort needed to sit still when the natural inclination is to be constantly moving, walking takes little or no concentration and therefore the thought processes needed to take in and process new information become available to these sensory learners.

Case study: when cultures meet

The "When Cultures Meet" program was designed in collaboration with local Aboriginal Elders to utilise the rich Indigenous history and culture of the local area by walking and talking the country. Students learn how Aboriginal people lived sustainably in their own country by using the resources of the natural environment. This is achieved through a *Clan Challenge* in which students experience a simulated day in the life of traditional Aboriginal peoples by building shelters, collecting and tasting bush foods and investigating resources for tools and fire making as well as using traditional weapons that would have been used to hunt. The program elements are carefully sequenced to introduce students to the Aboriginal lifestyle of the local area and to ensure authenticity of delivery. Each activity has a big idea, and collectively these contribute to the overall program big idea. Students begin by walking up One Tree Hill and learning about *Belonging to Country*, which sets the context for the rest of the program.

Belonging to Country utilises storytelling to introduce students to the Indigenous notion of country and living sustainably. One story we use in our program is told by a "Nungar" man from Western Australia. He recounts the journey of an Aboriginal man and his pregnant wife walking through country to attend great gatherings and to celebrate and share food, eventually arriving at a birthing place where their child is born. The story continues as the young female child grows, has children and then eventually dies as an old woman and her body is given back to country completing the cycle. The key idea is that Aboriginal people lived and walked within *their* country, except for special festivals, and could not routinely take resources or consume food from another's country because that country would lose a part of itself and become ill. Indigenous ownership or *Belonging to Country* is seen as a personal responsibility to care for country, in contrast to non-traditional cultures, which view land as a resource, something to own or sell or trade or give away. Belonging to and walking in country is regarded as a relationship to land that cannot be severed – one always has responsibility to care for one's country.

In addition to stories of walking the country, another key pedagogical tool was discovered almost by accident when an Indigenous method of weaving string was introduced into the program. The accidental discovery occurred one day when, due to time constraints, story-telling and weaving string were combined. The outcomes for students were immediately very obvious, epitomized by the student who stated: "*I could sit here all day making string*". The weaving is repetitive and easy to master, requiring the progressive interweaving of two separate threads. Having climbed to the top of One Tree Hill, students sit at the base of the tree and make the string during storytelling about Indigenous people walking through country. There is a very obvious change in body language and movement as students become still and totally engrossed in the story whilst continuing the string-making. Although the students appear to be totally focused on the string, they respond to questions and ask their own questions throughout the story. A student stated: "*I am sitting where an aboriginal person once sat*" again reinforcing the sense of connection to place experienced as part of this activity. The tactile action and rhythm of string-making (like walking) seems to have a soothing effect which allows them to slow their thinking, still their bodies and think deeply. There is a significant moment as they finish their weaving of the string and compare it to the string on a traditional axe found under the big bloodwood. They can see the similarity and know that their fingers have followed a pattern of movement originally choreographed by Aboriginal people over millennia.

A beautiful example of how powerfully these two pedagogies work together occurred recently when a group of Year 5 students were relaxed and engaged in string-making. At this point, the *Belonging to Country* storytelling commenced. As always, the students appeared to be totally engrossed in their string-making, and yet we could see that they were tuned into the story as well. At the conclusion of the storytelling the teacher commented that the concept of belonging to country can be difficult to comprehend, as it is very different to how people view land and ownership today. As if on cue, one student, without looking up or showing the slightest break in the twisting, turning motion of the string-making replied, "*Not if you understand it*"; a statement so simple on the surface, but indicative of deeper understanding. For these students, having walked on ancient pathways through moss-filled forests, having connected to the Big Fig tree and the red bloodwood on One Tree Hill, and now sitting quietly in place with focused minds and still bodies creating string, *Belonging to Country* made perfect sense.

Another example of deep understanding arising from learning in place occurred with a group of Year 10 students. After an evening around the campfire telling stories about belonging to country, the students completed a dot painting activity (see Figure 5.5). When asked about his painting, one student stated, "*It's the story you told us about belonging to country: here's the mountains, the river, the ocean*". At that moment it clicked, and the story in his painting was so obvious, as was the absolute concentration and care he had put into its creation. There was no doubt about his understanding of the story and his connection to it.

As students depart Barambah they leave a leaf on our Reflection Tree, and on that leaf they have written about what they have enjoyed at Barambah and what

Figure 5.5   Dot painting representing a student's understanding of country

they have learnt from their Barambah experience. Students are asked to justify their reflections, and it is these reflections that give us an insight into the depth and richness of learning that has taken place.

> This camp showed me the Indigenous peoples' way of life centuries ago. I now have a GREAT respect for them.
>
> (Year 6/7 student)

> Whilst I have been here I have learnt many new things. The main thing that I have learnt is that it wasn't (isn't) easy for the Indigenous people. They don't simply get something if they want it. They have to go out and make it happen for themselves. They can't go buy a house; they have to make their own shelter. Whilst we were making our own shelters it made me realise the amount of things the Aborigines would have to take into consideration, i.e. waterproof, stability etc. This immersion has honestly been a real eye opener and helped me understand and get an interest in the culture and history. . . . My knowledge has expanded a lot and I think more people should be educated and have the chance to take on an opportunity like this.
>
> (Year 10 student)

Between the excitement of the beginning of a Barambah experience and the reflections at the end, there are many points in time in which deep learning is evident, either in individual students or the whole group.

> I learnt all about the yarning circles and the importance of a circle to include everyone.
>
> (Year 10 student)

> My favourite activity I was involved in was eating bush tucker because I was eager to try & was fascinated by the food that is way different to our own. I learnt how hard it was for the aboriginal people to live especially building shelters & hunting for food.
>
> (Year 10 student)

> The best thing was the dot painting on the CD's because it tells a story in your life. It's calm to do if you are stressed. I enjoyed doing the dot painting because we got to tell a story through the artwork.
>
> (Year 10 student)

> Shelter making because it was a new experience and learning curve for me. Learning that aboriginals travel to different places in different seasons for various reasons.
>
> (Year 10 student)

> What I really enjoyed was the hunting & the bush tucker because I've never thrown a boomerang & the bush tucker was extraordinary. What I learnt here was how to make shelters & how hard it was.
>
> (Year 10 student)

There are the telling moments that accompany the discovery of a whole log covered in orange bracket fungi, a tiny fern nestling in the fork of a tree, or a lazy goanna flattened across the path soaking up the sun.

> I loved the huge! fig tree, it was amazing! I loved it!
>
> (Year 5 student)

These are the times when students' eyes light up and "wow" and "awesome" flicker back and forth around the group as students share their excitement.

> I also loved the fig tree, it was awesome.
>
> (Year 5 student)

> What a magical little ecosystem you provide here. Thanks for the venue to learn, laugh, enjoy the wildlife and refresh my enthusiasm to protect this precious environment.
>
> (Science student from the University of the Sunshine Coast)

There are moments of total engagement when every student is focused on the activity at hand and the level of concentration is obvious. There are times of bodily engagement when students twist and climb over, under and around logs in the forest avoiding the myriad of plants which sting, scratch and prick.

> I liked going on the bushwalk because we went through scratchy trees.
> (Year 7 student)

And there are the delightful moments when students come out with incredibly insightful comments and amaze you with the depth of their thinking and understanding of the big ideas.

> I learnt that strangler figs like to hug other trees until they die.
> (Prep student aged between 4–5 years)

> Knowing that so much history lies between the trees is invaluable. May this place live forever!
> (Year 10 student)

> This camp was amazing, history, culture, knowledge. This place felt like HOME!
> (Students from the Aboriginal Centre for Performing Arts)

There are the times when students ask probing, inquiry type questions which indicate they have a thirst for more knowledge and understanding.

> From when I first arrived here, my knowledge about the culture and history was very little. This immersion has given me the opportunity to learn and allow ourselves to understand the history, culture and feelings (pain) the Indigenous people would've gone through. Now I am more interested about learning more and understanding the culture.
> (Year 10 student)

Finally, there are comments that show the power of pedagogy and place in creating deep and lasting change.

> Change to thinking: Being on country has changed the way I view the Australian landscape and the way I regard the environment. Up until now, I always knew that the land belongs rightfully to Aboriginal Peoples, but I never comprehended that they belong to it. The land is a life source and now I want to do everything I can to protect it for future generations to come – just like the Elders have done for us.
> (Year 10 student)

> Change to feelings: I feel as if I belong to the land now. By this I mean I rely on it so much and now I have learnt to appreciate everything about it. I feel at home.
> (Year 10 student)

Change to behaviour: From being on country I am now going to sit and listen more often, whether it's listening to the birds or the sounds of the ocean especially when I am facing times of stress and need to relax.

(Year 10 student)

Being on country has helped me to show more respect easily, to both people, and the environment. I'll be more careful when working with nature and will always lend a helping hand.

(Year 10 student)

Conclusion

Walking is integral to every Barambah experience and takes varied and diverse forms depending on the purpose of the walk and the terrain being traversed. Strolling along a sunlight-filtered track exploring the sights, sounds and smells of the surroundings results in becoming part of the place. Bending, weaving and connecting with the forest flows seamlessly into walking along a fallen log, balancing as you navigate knots and branch stumps along the way, or climbing over or under moss-covered logs while embracing the adventure and challenge! The extended walk, which can stretch your endurance, stamina and resilience as the uphill sections are conquered, leads down into a meander along the dry creek bed. Marvelling at the glittering biotite mica and white quartz, you find yourself taking time to start and stop at will as nature's treasures catch your eye.

It is the trees, the vines, the logs, the tracks, and a myriad of other affordances of this unique place that create the pedagogical platform for walking and talking with students. When students walk, and particularly when students walk in the close confines of the forest, the physicality and rhythmic motion opens a portal to learning through heightening of the senses which are often dulled in the classroom by the need to concentrate and be still.

When students walk and talk, their senses are sharpened by the constantly changing features of the *place*, and their understanding of *place* is enriched through shared conversation with fellow walkers. Walking-talking pedagogy can wander off and on task according to whatever grabs the students' attention. As topics shift and attention varies, we (as the teachers) take the opportunity to elaborate comments or follow-up queries raised by fellow walkers. There is no need for my companions to "pay attention" if their interest is elsewhere. The casualness and informality of the conversation offers a sense of freedom and openness that contrasts vividly with the normal classroom lesson. At Barambah we have noticed time and time again how the energetic sensory learners, possibly problematic students in the classroom, inevitably weave their way to the front of the group to chat to me and share in an unfolding and opportunistic conversation about place. For students such as these, being able to walk and talk as part of their regular schooling experience could result in greatly enhanced learning outcomes.

At a deeper reflective level, the walk up One Tree Hill and down through the rainforest is integral to students understanding the *Belonging to Country* story as evidenced earlier in the chapter. The walk starts and ends at the Centre with various stops along the way to have a drink, pick raspberries if they are in season, listen to a story, marvel at the forest giants or simply sit to rest. As students hear the story of the Nungar man walking to places of seasonal food abundance, they are able to assimilate the information with their experience of walking earlier that day. They are able to make sense of a culture and concept of ownership that is very different to their own because they have experienced what it is like to walk on country. Similarly the string-making activity mirrors the bodily rhythms of walking country. In both string-making and walking the rhythms of bodily engagement elicit honest and informal conversations among the students that expands their learning.

At the deepest reflective level, the action of walking on country, following pathways which have been traversed for thousands of years by the Traditional Owners of this area and other groups travelling to and from the Bunya Mountains, is a very powerful learning experience for those students who value authenticity above all else. For the students who follow the Brisbane River to its mouth as part of the biennial *Bunya 2 Bay River Journey*, the privilege of carrying the message stick on behalf of the Elders is the ultimate example of authentic experiential learning. These students literally live and breathe the learning, and this is the learning that brings deep understanding and lasting transformative change. In the words generally attributed to Benjamin Franklin: "Tell me and I forget, teach me and I may remember, involve me and I learn". We would add: "Walk with me, and we learn in place together."

Notes

1 Message approved by Wakka Wakka Elder, Aunty Beryl "Tiny" Gambril on 29 August 2010. Permission to use the message in this chapter was given by Wakka Wakka Elder Aunty Vera Sullivan on 24 March 2015.
2 Message stick artwork by Gubbi Gubbi artist Maurice Mickelo.

References

Bairner, A. (2011). Urban walking and the pedagogies of the street. *Sport, Education and Society, 16*(3), 371–384.
Bakhtin, M. (1986). *Speech genres and other late essays* (C. Emerson & M. Holquist (Eds.), V. W. McGee, Trans.). Austin, TX: University of Texas Press.
Clarke, P. A. (2003). Where the ancestors walked: Australia as an Aboriginal landscape. Sydney: Allen & Unwin.
De Certeau, M. (1984). *The practice of everyday life*. Berkeley: University of California Press.
Flenady, B. (2015). *Ecosystem report and rehabilitation plan*.Report Commissioned by Sue Gibson (Principal) Barambah Environmental Education Centre, Wrattens Forest Reserve, Queensland.

Shell, M. (2015). *Talking the walk and walking the talk: A rhetoric of rhythm*. New York: Fordham University Press.

Solnit, R. (2001). *Wanderlust: A history of walking*. New York: Penguin.

Thoreau, H. (2001). *Collected essays and poems*. New York: Penguin Putnam.

Vaughan, L. (2009). Walking the line: Affectively understanding and communicating the complexity of place. *Cartographic Journal, 46*(4), 316–322.

6 Pedagogy in the clouds – between heaven and earth – at Paluma

Linda Venn and Louka Lazaredes

Editors' preface

Chapter 6 explores the pedagogy in the Paluma rainforest, a place between heaven and earth; a place that engages students in experiences of science as well as a sense of the sacredness of the forest. The material affordances of the cloud rainforest at Paluma lead students to consider sacredness and the inherent value of the more-than-human world (Naess, 1995; Abram, 1997). Being high in the mountains, with clouds enveloping ancient trees and shafts of sunlight penetrating through the mist, Paluma is a sensory delight that never fails to transport students from their everyday preoccupations to consider the inherent beauty, timelessness and worth of the natural world – its sacredness. Some are moved to reflect on their religious faith and to thank "God" for creating such a beautiful place. The educators at Paluma accept students' responses without privileging a particular notion of the sacred. The ancient sense of time conveyed by the rainforest is central to the feeling of sacredness that arises for students at Paluma. Rainforests are extremely stable ecosystems that can reproduce themselves across millennia if not disturbed. The students at Paluma learn that some trees are so ancient that their growth rings record the history of Indigenous people in the forest many centuries before colonial explorers entered. They contemplate the immense span of time that the rainforest has been growing at Paluma, and they explore the complexity of the living systems that sustain it. These experiences inevitably draw out words of awe and wonderment from students and enable them to consider more metaphysical questions regarding "reality" and their relationship to "nature".

The Paluma pedagogy opens up consideration of the limits of objective science for appreciating natural systems. Students respond to Paluma in aesthetic and highly subjective ways as they begin to understand the complexity of the forest systems, and they experience moments of transcendent beauty. As noted above, the Paluma pedagogy elicits reflections on "God" and spirituality. But environmental educators have been wary of dealing with religious beliefs or spirituality (Hitzhusen, 2006). The clash between literal creationists and evolutionary scientists shows no signs of diminishing (at least in the USA). In addition, the relation of human kind to nature remains a point of contention, with religious fundamentalists foregrounding the dominion of "man" over nature as recounted in Genesis (1;26–28 King James Version), while religious leaders such as Pope Francis have recently called for a renewed respect for and conservation of the natural world. Pope Francis advocates for the rejection of modern consumerist lifestyles that are pushing species to extinction (Laudato Si, 2015). He encourages a spirituality that finds God "in a leaf, in a mountain trail, in a dewdrop, in a poor person's face" (Francis, 2015, section 233). Pope Francis' encyclical parallels the kind of proposals and values articulated by deep ecologists, such as highlighting our responsibility to live in harmony with natural systems and seeing human kind as part of the more encompassing living systems of the earth (Naess, 1973; Leopold, 1970). For Pope Francis this living system reveals the hand of God, whereas for others it simply reveals the beauty and complexity of living systems per se. This chapter suggests that it may be timely for place-conscious educators to incorporate more discussion of the sacred and the spiritual in their programs. How this is managed in a secular system of education is a challenge that the authors of this chapter have faced.

The authors, Linda Venn and Louka Lazaredes, represent the secular and religious positions regarding nature, but maintain an open and accepting attitude to students' responses to Paluma. They conclude their chapter on Paluma by recounting how they continue to debate their shared experience of awe and wonder in the rainforest – Louka sees the hand of "God" in the beauty of the rainforest while Linda sees the rainforest per se as a beautiful mystery of evolution that can be appreciated for itself. They design the pedagogy at Paluma – between heaven and earth – to inspire a sense of wonderment in students, but they don't enter explicitly into dialoguing with students about their sense of the sacred, whether it is linked to religious observance or whether it is linked to a sense of one's place in an encompassing living system. However, they do foreground for students what might be learned personally and subjectively from contemplating aspects of the rainforest. A salient instance of this type of pedagogy relates to growth and death in the forest. Some trees are caught in a state of suspended growth as they wait for an opportunity to shoot towards the sunlight when a gap opens in the forest canopy. These semi-dormant saplings are called *Oscars* by the authors, referring to the little boy in the novel, *The Tin Drum*, who never grew up. Such saplings may be twenty years old or more, but unfavourable conditions in the understory have halted their growth. The death of an old tree or even the falling of a large branch gives them a gap in the canopy to access the sunlight that they need to prosper. The story of Oscar conveys how trees adapt biologically to niches in the forest, but it also offers students a metaphor they can use to reflect on their personal growth. Like Oscar they will experience growth that happens in spurts, the conditions of their life will change, and they too will have their time in the shade and in the sun.

This example of Oscar is typical of the pedagogy at Paluma. It is designed not only to convey scientific knowledge of processes that sustain the rainforest but also to encourage students to consider metaphysical and axiological questions regarding the purpose of life and transience. It does not seem forced or artificial for such concerns to become the focus of conversation because students are primed by the affordances of the cloud forest to move beyond their habitual ways of thinking and reacting. As with the other pedagogies described in this volume, the place-responsive pedagogy designed at Paluma cannot be explained by focussing only on the materiality of the place per se. The agency and insight of the educators, Linda and Louka, have been crucial. They both have a prolonged history of engagement with Paluma, and it is their sensibilities and specific local knowledge that mediates what students might learn during their excursion. They have designed a hybrid pedagogy that combines an inquiry approach to learning about the biological complexity of the rainforest with a reflective and meditative strategy that invites students to think about their place within the interconnected matrices of life and time.

Peter Renshaw & Ron Tooth

Tasting the clouds

> We are in the dining hall late in the afternoon. The clouds start rolling in over the treetops, slowly filling the oval in cloud. Students ask, "Is it fire?" "Is it mist?" I answer, "No, it's cloud." The kids are captivated and excited by this – they've never been **in** a cloud before. Abandoning our planned learning, we walk outside. Their first response is to stretch out their hands and touch the cloud. I say, "Taste it." Mouths open and they suck it in. "Wow, it tastes like air." "It tastes like water." "It's moist." It doesn't last very long, this initial moment of experiencing. Then we go back inside. However, the next time we see the cloud rolling down, they respond again with the same sense of wonder.
> —Louka Lazaredes, Journal entry, 2012

The striking first impression of Paluma is its stark contrast to the North Queensland city of Townsville, where most of our students come from. "Brownsville" as it is affectionately known, can be hot and dry in the lead up to the wet season, but Paluma is cool, wet and misty all year round (see Figure 6.1). Compared to Townsville and surrounding districts, Paluma is five to ten degrees Celsius cooler – any time of the year. Paluma is alive: filled with lush plants and tall trees, covered in moss and epiphytes, birds calling everywhere. Truly it is a beautiful place to explore.

Visitors to Paluma journey from one season to another: from "the dry" to "the wet". From Townsville, students travel north across the dry coastal plain to the bottom of the Paluma range. Once there, they follow what was possibly an Aboriginal foot track, now a heritage-listed roadway, as it snakes around ridges and gullies, crossing seasonal creeks. From the bus window they may notice that halfway up there is a change in the vegetation; open woodland is interrupted by pockets of rainforest, which soon becomes all that they see. The dry plains are long gone, and they are surrounded by the tall trees of the place that Indigenous Australians called *Munan Gumburu* – "Misty Mountain", or as the area is known today, Paluma. We invite students on a journey of the heart and mind through this timeless place. As clouds roll in over the forest canopy, students are

Figure 6.1 Sunlight between heaven and earth near the Paluma Environmental Education Centre

typically captivated by the experience. We recognise that for some of them this can become a spiritual encounter. After all, the mountains are the place where *earth* touches *heaven*. As the clouds touch the mountains, students and teachers touch the clouds; shafts of light illuminate this in-between place. A Year 6 student wrote the following:

> It's mind blowing. The blanket of moss, the vines reaching from tree to tree. The sudden shower of glimmering drops that, when they reach the ground, [are] so graceful and the light from the tops of the tall never-ending trees reaching in.

Another Year 6 student was moved to reflect on her religious faith in reporting what she liked about this place:

> The animal noises, the clear water streams and peace. Jesus made this place amazing.

As a secular educational institution, spirituality is not our core business. However, we do want our students to gain more than the facts and skills prescribed in the curriculum. We want them to have an *experience*; one that sparks a deeper relationship with the natural world, to develop within them a sense of the sacredness of living systems and their inherent worth. It is our hope that this leads to a change in the way they think, feel and act towards living systems of the Earth.

Paluma's history

Indigenous connection to Paluma

Paluma's almost constant shroud of cloud and filtered sunlight gives the rainforest a mystical, ageless quality (see Figure 6.2). It is not hard to imagine Indigenous people from generations past emerging from the mist as apparitions. Unfortunately, the lives and history of the Indigenous people of this rainforest are largely lost; their artefacts of wood, string and other organic materials have been consumed by the rainforest. There were several Indigenous groups connected with the rainforest (Cairns & Meganck, 1994). The *Guwabara* were based along the mountain range, the *Nywaigi* from around the Herbert River Valley and the *Warungu* and *Gugu Badhun* language group from behind the range. In 1865, the *Nywaigi* population was estimated at about 500; by 1880, that estimate was only 200 (Cassady & Johnstone, 1886). Reports from the late 19th century suggest that the tracks followed by European tin miners were paths used by the *Nywaigi* to access the forest. Indigenous rock art galleries surviving in drier country to the east and west of the rainforest testify to the presence of the *Nywaigi* and *Guwabara* peoples. Ethnographer W.E. Roth studied other groups in similar rainforests north of Paluma around 1900 (Kahn, 2008). It is

Figure 6.2 Clouds drift between the tall trees at Paluma[1]

possible that in their relationship with the forest, the Nywaigi may have practiced something like *dadirri*, "deep listening to country" as practised by Indigenous groups elsewhere (Ungunmerr-Baumann, 1988; 2002). There is evidence that they entered the forest regularly to maintain clearings with fire. These clearings were later appropriated by miners, then timber cutters, resulting in fatal conflicts that are tragically typical of European colonial expansion in North Queensland. Indigenous knowledge of the rainforest was rapidly lost as populations were decimated. What little we do know of Paluma's Indigenous history indicates that this place has been considered sacred for a long time: a place to visit for special events; a place of rejuvenation. Today, the *Nywaigi* still walk the forest, some as national park rangers *caring for country*.

From exploitation to recognition as a special place

The first Europeans into the forests in the late 1800s were nomadic miners, who walked up tributaries of the Burdekin River from the goldfields of Charters Towers. Little gold was found around Paluma, but deposits of tin, first discovered in 1875, kept a small industry going for a hundred years. The forest itself was an economic target for timber cutters from the 1920s onward, so apart from providing opportunities for rest and recreation, early industries in the rainforest were extractive and left their scars on the natural landscape. From the very beginning of European settlement in the Paluma ranges, visitors noted the aesthetic qualities of the forest, the power of crystal clear water rushing down the creeks and the dynamic weather patterns. Tour groups on horseback ventured up the ridges even before the First World War; an account of one expedition mentioned enjoying seventy-five waterfalls during a three-day excursion (Venn, 2002). Anglican Bishop John Oliver Feetham built a house in Paluma in the 1930s and started the tradition of Christian services and retreats in the area (Berryman, 1979). In the Second World War, Paluma's location perched high above the Coral Sea made it a perfect place for radar stations, while its cool climate meant that it was also a perfect location for a medical rehabilitation unit to treat Australian servicemen from the Pacific theatre of conflict. After the war, much of the remaining Paluma rainforest was protected in a national park, recognising its scientific and aesthetic qualities. In 1988, this park was included in the Wet Tropics World Heritage Area. Today, the village of Paluma is a cool mountain retreat for residents of Townsville and surrounding districts. It is a special place that is still experienced by visitors and students as offering physical and spiritual healing (Venn, 2002).

The Paluma experience

Rainforest – more than trees

Many children report that their first impression of Paluma on arrival is "It's all trees". We have not yet unpacked with them the complexity of the ecosystem, or the relationships between trees and cloud and micro- and macro-fauna. Our students have to be *immersed* (Van Matre, 1990) in this place, to see, hear and feel the diversity of living things and their interrelationships. We want them to experience the teeming *life* of the rainforest. This is at the heart of our work as environmental educators. As our students scratch through leaf litter to find macro invertebrates, or as they walk through and taste the clouds of Paluma listening for birds and watching how they interact with the forest, we build on their growing awareness that there is life everywhere up here. Eventually, they come to the realisation that *everything* – all the living things and all the non-living things, including the granite boulders and the clouds that waters the rainforest – *is connected.*

Enabling students to access the sacred

Throughout the world, from Uluru in Australia to the Montmartre in Paris, places at altitude are considered sacred places. Natural places also evoke a spiritual response, maybe due to their flourishing life and beauty, or just the serenity in being disconnected from the busy distractions of towns and cities. Paluma is both a place of natural beauty as well as high altitude and its narrow, winding road isolates it from the noise and traffic of the nearby city. It has provided an ideal place for reflection and attentiveness for Indigenous people practicing *dadirri* and for more recent visitors to the forest who draw upon the Christian tradition to pray and seek renewal of their faith. At the Paluma Environmental Education Centre, we invite young people to this high place and encourage them to learn through experiencing beauty and peacefulness, in the hope they may have a similar experience to those who have walked the forest tracks before them, an experience that is *sacred* to them, however they might understand the notion of *sacred*. The experience starts with attentiveness – a physical sensorial encounter – and continues to a deeper appreciation of beauty that leads to a sense of calm. It goes from recognising the ubiquitous and varied nature of life around them to a sense of amazement that Louv (2005) says is what spirituality is all about. These kinds of experiences go straight to the *heart*. From a curriculum perspective, this emotive response scaffolds deep knowledge and understanding. We also have noted from our experience as environmental educators that it produces change in the way young people think and act towards the natural world.

Staff knowledge mediating access and learning at Paluma

Staff understanding the affordances of place

Teachers and parents who came to Paluma themselves as children remark that their excursion to Paluma was the highlight of their whole schooling. Our personal journeys with Paluma, likewise, are long-lasting and central in our lives. Our deep connections to this place enable us to know Paluma with *heart, head and hand*. Paluma lives in our memories and engages us daily as we guide students and teachers to appreciate and care about this special ecosystem. This intimate knowledge, for example, has enabled us to select specific locations as *learnscapes*² best suited for engaging students in particular learning experiences (Booth, 2001).

Louka's story

I came on excursion to Paluma as a Year 6 student in the late 1980s. Sue Leitch (my class teacher) created an integrated unit of Science and English for the excursion. Much of my fundamental understanding of, and appreciation for, biology came from that year. The rainforest captivated me because of the way the Centre staff presented it to us. The leaders were Allan Carr and Cam Mackenzie. They spoke calmly and quietly and they presented the rainforest to us with a quiet invitation to explore it with them. I remember sitting alone watching the bandicoots come close to nibble. Years later, sitting at a table talking with Cam, I realised how I got rapt in rainforest. We were slowly immersed in the rainforest. I remember it as a sensory journey, not one of facts and figures. I became avidly interested in plants, and although my university studies took me elsewhere, I always loved rainforests and would visit them when I could. Among other things, this appreciation affected the way I voted. I understood what endangered species and habitat were and that they must be protected. When I found out that there was a teaching job available at Paluma, I enthusiastically applied. I regard my appointment to Paluma as a God-given opportunity. It's amazing to be working in a rainforest centre with a fascinating pedagogy that provides students with a significant and meaningful experience. Having read biographies and writings of a few mystics who experienced God through the "glory" of creation and having visited some of their special places - or as we would call them *magic spots* (Van Matre, 1979) – I can appreciate the similarities and differences between our practice and theirs. What is common is that we both appreciate the sacredness of place, and we invite people to have a transformative encounter therein.

Linda's story

My personal relationship with Paluma features in my earliest memories. Like many others brought up in Townsville, Paluma is part of my family history. Photo albums include snaps taken on the iconic stone bridge at Little Crystal Creek, or with the serene waters of Paluma Dam in the background. We went camping, bushwalking, swimming and picnicking at Paluma. Wherever we went, there was always commentary from my parents on this tree, this bird, this frog, "*wow look at that*", and so on. I knew the scientific convention of naming species long before I needed to. One of my earliest memories is of being washed over a waterfall as a four-year-old, into a pool under the iconic stone bridge. I nearly drowned my grandmother, who came in to save me. When I go swimming in the same pool now, the "waterfall" seems so small but the memory is undiminished. I am surrounded by memories wherever I go in Paluma. It was where I first tasted freedom as a teenager with an extended group of friends; it was where I grew to know my future husband and where we had our honeymoon. These deep personal connections give my teaching at Paluma depth and authenticity.

The mountain setting is central to our pedagogy. In Townsville where I grew up, hills and peaks (Mount Stuart, or Castle Hill, or Mount Louisa) defined where one lived – closer to that one or this one, between these two – so my developing "sense of place" evolved in relationship to hills and peaks. Later, when travelling in Europe, I realised how crucial hills and mountains are in the human psyche. It is where we have our churches and cathedrals, temples and castles. It is where people go to seek knowledge and wisdom. This sense of Paluma as a sacred mountain is a crucial aspect of our pedagogy, and it has its roots in my own life as well as being represented in the ways both Indigenous and European peoples have related to the Paluma Range and its forests.

Key elements of the pedagogy

Developing "Paluma Super Powers"

Many students come to us from "screenland", a place of *iClouds* rather than real clouds, where most of their information, recreation and even socialization happens through the medium of a screen. While they may still use some screens with us, we develop their *super powers* as a way of recalibrating their senses to interact with the natural world again. Before their first walk into the forest, we take students through a simple activity where they must consciously use their senses. The intent is that students enter the forest alert and attentive to the textures, sounds, smells and shades of light in the forest.

This focus on the sensorial experience begins when we take students to an open park at the entrance to the rainforest and tell them that we are going to give them *super powers* – well, not really – but we are going to make the powers they have more acute. We ask students what sensory powers they already have, and as they mention them one by one, we use that sense to focus on something nearby. We forecast some of the amazing things students will be able to do with that sensory power by the end of their excursion. Once under the rainforest canopy, only a little dappled sunlight makes its way through to the students. We repeat the activity, inviting students to use their senses to notice the dramatic contrast between the open sky of the park and the closed canopy of the rainforest. At different points along the trail, students are given time to use specific senses – to listen, look, touch or smell something. As the recalibration takes hold, visiting students and adults alike begin exploring for themselves using all their senses. As teachers, we take advantage of this by casually introducing students to desired content knowledge in the trees covered in moss, lichen and bryophytes, or in following lianas with their eyes as they spiral to the canopy where the branches are full of epiphytes. "But wait, there is more to explore." The forest floor is covered in a thick carpet of interesting detritus to turn over carefully and examine. Along the trail, students hear birds calling, see all manner of fungi devouring rotting wood, smell flowering orchids and "stink horn" fungi. The walk ends at a stunning lookout over the ocean, sometimes shrouded in cloud, where students stare into the distance. This focus on sensory awareness leads students to noticing, *really* noticing the natural world. Building curiosity, fascination and amazement culminates in a heart connection. This becomes the basis for the deep learning that happens at Paluma.

"Being" in the forest

An excursion to Paluma has an element of "rehab" for our visiting "digital natives". We are bereft of a Wi-Fi signal and, due to the wet climate, students are encouraged to leave their smart phones at home and deploy their sensory super powers. We do provide small groups of students with a digital camera, a familiar way of engaging with the world around them, and their images offer discussion and reflection opportunities. Having to share the camera scaffolds a "disconnection" from technology so that students are free to connect with the environment and with each other. Early on the first day of their excursion, students are "dropped off" at points along an unmade track to spend twenty minutes alone "*to be*" in the forest, a pedagogical tool that Van Matre (1979) calls *magic spot*. We have found it to be a significant experience, enabling students to connect to "place" emotionally and personally. Some need to overcome their apprehension of being alone, their fear of perceived dangers in the forest, like spiders and snakes, so that they can begin looking with new eyes and listening intently. A student wrote in response to the prompt, "this place makes me feel":

> A bit scared 'cause of the leeches and ticks and poisonous plants, but you get used to it.
>
> (Year 6 student)

Being in the forest requires attentiveness both inwardly and outwardly. Another student wrote in response to same prompt, "this place makes me feel":

> Calm cool and collected. It makes me feel like one with nature and brings out a different side of me; a side that can feel completely calm.
>
> (Year 6 student)

Being engaged

After introducing "Paluma Super Powers" to encourage student engagement, we consciously look for signs of it happening. We've noticed palpable enthusiasm when students are investigating some forest artefact such as a skeletonised leaf, or listening to bird calls, or examining freshwater macro invertebrates. They often exclaim loudly when they discover something novel, and the group quickly moves in to investigate closer. There are "oohs" and "aahs" indicating fascination and amazement. They invite their peers to share their discoveries, often taking photos as a record. This is followed by discussion of what "it" was or how interesting or beautiful it looked, and where it "fitted" in the big picture of the rainforest ecosystem. Throughout this immersion experience, students are asking questions of the nearest adult, soaking up concepts, knowledge and scientific language. Excitement about being in a different place with a different teacher, an openness to learning and the wonder of exploring the place – all are opportunities to develop engagement.

Being "Oscar": *reflecting on time and resilience*

As well as investigations of the ecology of the rainforest, particular features and moments in the rainforest provide opportunities for personal reflection. We use *Oscar* as a metaphor to scaffold students' reflection on time and resilience. An *Oscar* is a semi-dormant sapling, named after the little boy in the novel, *The Tin Drum*, who never grew up. Such saplings may be twenty years old or more, but unfavourable conditions in the understory have halted their growth. The growth rate of an *Oscar* is not constant; they may sit in a state of suspended animation for decades, waiting their chance to flourish. The decline of an old tree or even the falling of a large branch gives them a gap in the canopy to access the sunlight that they need to prosper. We tell the story of *Oscar* for the biological significance of how trees adapt to niches in the forest, but we also offer students this story so they can reflect on their own personal and physical growth. Like *Oscar* they will experience growth and change that happens in spurts, the conditions of their lives will change, and they too will have their time in the shade and in the sun.

   Oscars also let us foreground the timelessness of the rainforest and the passing of time. Looking at a particular *Oscar* sapling with a group of students, we imagine out loud that this tree has been a witness to many groups of school students, tourists and researchers conducting their activities. *Oscar* has heard voices and accents from across the globe as international eco-tourists make their way through the rainforest. The parent trees of an *Oscar* witnessed the airmen and soldiers, American and Australian, who came in the 1940s. Older trees recall earlier European loggers and tin miners. Even older trees recount stories of the *Nywaigi* people walking the forest before the Europeans came. These ancient, weathered trees would recall the name that the *Nywaigi* people gave this place – *Munan Gumburu*. In the earliest rings of their memory, these ancient trees would hold *Nywaigi* language and stories. One of our learning experiences begins with exploration of such an ancient tree, a strangler fig, providing our students not only with detailed scientific information, but a philosophical interpretation of time. We aim for at least mastery of the scientific knowledge and language (Wertsch, 1991), but hopefully achieve a deeper level of understanding of the immense time required for the forest to thrive. We comment to the students as our visit to the strangler fig draws to a close: *We are not here forever, this tree is not here forever, but something will be here forever.*

Ecopedagogy – ecosystem thinking, feeling and doing

Our place-based pedagogy grew both from Paluma itself, and from our personal engagement as professionals in a pedagogical renewal process – thinking, reading, collaborating, debating, experimenting and reviewing. With the natural environment of Paluma as our classroom, we tuned into this rich ecosystem with its dynamic natural cycles and seasonal changes. We chose "ecosystem" as our central conceptual thread, as the "hat rack" on which students could hang all their other ideas and learning. As Louka (co-author) noted in reflecting on our conceptual approach:

> All students seemed to have had an amazing experience. They took away little facts and big ideas. The next step is personal action.
> (Louka Lazaredes, Journal entry, December 2012)

This comment highlights our privileging of holistic thinking and big ideas rather than just interesting facts. Students do remember various facts that they found personally interesting. This is important, but the crucial learning is how these ideas interrelate in a systematic way. To achieve this kind of learning we deploy *ecopedagogy* which entails pausing and dwelling in spaces for more than a fleeting moment in order to attach and receive meaning from that place (Payne, 2005; Payne & Wattchow, 2008). Using *super powers* on the *magic spot* trail lets our students sit quietly and intently to interact with the environment, making connections between the micro and macro processes of the forest. It becomes evident that the tiny invertebrates in the leaf litter make it possible for the giant forest trees to source nutrients and that the summer swarms of termites are actually deconstruction experts taking one tree down so that an *Oscar* can rise up in its place. Such big concepts need time to grow, to make that *head* connection. Although students typically spend only three days with us, this is enough time for the seeds of ecosystem thinking to germinate.

Rapt in Rainforest

Rapt in Rainforest is a biological science program that includes a three-day excursion to Paluma. In documenting the learning during this program we consider students' emotions, knowledge and behaviour by deploying the metaphor of *heart, head* and *hand*. We have collected feedback from students over many years, but the corpus of written responses below was collected in 2012 from 383 students in Year 6. Students were given time to reflect upon their experience of *Rapt in Rainforest* scaffolded by the following prompts:

- This place teaches me . . .
- What I like best about this place is . . .
- This place makes me feel . . .
- This place is special because . . .

Below we present an analysis of these responses in terms of different types of learning associated with the *heart, head and hand*.

Heart

The heart phase of *Rapt in Rainforest* is concerned with engaging students' feelings through immersion in the rainforest, sensory awareness and reflection. This was the focus of our initial phase – to develop a *heart* or personal connection between the learner and the rainforest through developing sensorial awareness, immersing them in the rainforest, and fostering their attentiveness. Before students arrive at Paluma, we visit each class and introduce the central organising idea of the excursion, namely, the rainforest ecosystem as a system of living and non-living things interdependent on each other. This first phase at Paluma itself is a visceral encounter with the cloud forest that is followed by students writing in their journals to reflect on their own experience, note fine details and observations they have made and begin to consider their own actions.

We consistently see the embodiment of heartfelt responses from students as they physically remain still, staring and concentrating on features in the forest. They regularly vocalize their amazement, their voices registering excitement, their faces displaying a sense of wonder and spontaneity. Students begin animated discussions with each other. They physically move in closer to an object or activity. They invite their friends over to look at the object and share their findings. Emotional engagement is written on their bodies and movements. In addition to these observable indicators of heartfelt learning, we found extensive evidence of emotional connection to place in the written data from the 383 students. Twenty-eight percent of responses from students fell into this broad category of *heart* connection. Extracts of the students' written comments are provided below.

- This place teaches me

    That nature isn't just something you get air and other things from. It's a gift, so stop and smell the flowers and it's just not something you find in a forest or bush. It's everywhere.
    Sometimes for the best of things you need to take a break and talk to nature.
    How wonderful our planet is.
    That God still believes in humanity.

- What I like best about this place is

    The mysteries and the serenity.
    Feeling like you're in tune with nature.
    That it's untouched by man.

- This place is special because

    It has a grab on you because it's a fun place. You get to know people better and most of all it's great to get back to nature and smell the fresh air and waking up to trees and more trees and animals.
    Of the different and special kinds of wildlife; but also a special bond with my class that you can't achieve in a confined space like a classroom.

Students wrote from the heart about being alert and responsive to "the art of the rainforest", to the colours which "are really neat . . . green brown and even red . . . when the sun shines down through the canopy . . . like stars, . . . the autumn colour leaves choking the soil like snakes coiling around their prey", where the sounds and movements of the forest are enjoyed in detail as "the birds call to each other and frogs croak in the distance, hearing the birds fluttering their wings. You can also hear the trees blowing with their leaves rustling together and . . . all of those lovely sounds . . . make this place very peaceful and relaxing". Sitting alone in a rainforest elicits a flood of richly descriptive language. Students are there in the midst of it where "it is calm and you can notice every detail . . [like] . . . the amazing spider webs with water on them". Consciously showing students how to recalibrate their senses teaches them "how to really look for things that I wouldn't usually notice; that if I sat down and not said a word, I could hear and see different types of animals and insects; that there's always a time to just use your senses and relax".

For some students, the *Rapt in Rainforest* excursion experience was particularly meaningful. Consider the words of the student below who realised the importance of stopping and appreciating the natural world.

> Nature isn't just something you get air and other things from. It's a gift, so stop and smell the flowers.
>
> (Year 6 student)

Some students' report an epiphany associated with the silence, stillness and serenity of the forest, qualities that are rare in a normal classroom. One student expressed the realisation that, "*sometimes for the best of things you need to take a break and talk to nature*", and the ubiquitousness of nature – "*not something you find (only) in a forest or bush. It's everywhere."* Others enjoyed being part of their group in the forest:

> [This place is special because] Of the different and special kinds of wildlife; but also a special bond with my class that you can't achieve in a confined space like a classroom.
>
> (Year 6 student)

It seems that, for this young person, being totally immersed in a natural setting allowed social relationships to develop in a way that wasn't possible in a "confined space". At the same time as this student is "*forming a special bond with* [the] *class*", she also "*feel*[s] *like you're in tune with nature*". The student is expressing an awareness of the emotional connection among themselves, their group and the natural world.

Head

During the second phase of our program, *head*, we focus on ecological knowledge and procedural inquiry with students and assist them to consider how understanding the rainforest can underpin new attitudes to nature and sustainability. This phase started during the pre-visit when students brainstormed knowledge and concepts regarding the rainforest and ecosystems, recording them in a KWHL chart (*What we Know, What we Want to know, How we can find out, How we will know we've Learnt it*). Learning in this *head* phase is more collaborative, with exploration of how everything is connected within the ecosystem. Such connected understanding is scaffolded through leaf litter investigation and aquatic macro invertebrate sampling. We also develop skills such as the identification and classification of plant and animal species. Towards the end of this *head* phase, students begin to consciously consider human impact on the rainforest and respond through story, drama or other creative-response genres.

We categorised 34% of student responses as relevant to *head* learning such as content knowledge, use of specialised vocabulary and making conceptual connections. Examples of responses from students are provided below.

- This place teaches me

    How trees decompose, about the history of rainforest, about epiphytes and about wildlife.
    How important rainforests are.
    How diverse the rainforest is.
    About the food chain.
    About new dangers, like leeches, the rainforest environment . . . the clouds' true power and inner peace.
    About how the trees, animals and other plants work together in a way and also the fight for survival to get sunlight and the nutrients that the plant or animal may need.

    (Year 6 students)

- What I like best about this place is

    That some wildlife which is commonly found here is usually rare to other parts of Australia.
    All the exotic rare birds and animals that I've never seen before.
    The culture of Aboriginals.
    The beautiful buttress roots and the strangler vine.
    The diverse flora and fauna.

    (Year 6 students)

- This place is special because

    There may be many more rainforests, but none are identical. No other rainforest has the same nature, bugs or animals.
    Of the World Heritage rainforest.
    Of the trees. There are over 300 types of tree in this forest

    (Year 6 students)

Comments from students regarding their *head* learning included facts about tree decomposition, local history and food chains; for example, [this place teaches me] "*how trees decompose, about the history of rainforest, about epiphytes and about wildlife*" and more general statements about ecosystem diversity. Implicit in comments is evidence of embodied understanding of an idea; for example, [this place teaches me] "*how diverse the rainforest is. There may be many more rainforests, but none are identical. No other rainforest has the same nature, bugs or animals. Some wildlife which is commonly found here is usually rare in other parts of Australia*". These students have been able to step back from their experiences and transform specific facts into concepts about the rainforest.

Hand

After students have developed a *heart* connection to the natural world, and spent some time accumulating knowledge and understanding in the *head* phase, we focus on action, the *hand*. In this third phase of the excursion program, students reflect on their own actions and valuing of *place* and its *aesthetics*. We consider with students how personal actions affect local natural systems and global processes, and how their actions could be changed to positively impact the natural world. In the spirit of "giving back" to the environment, students engage in concrete actions such as weed busting, recycling or revegetation. Students are asked to consider what their "job" or "role" is in relation to the natural environment as a way of promoting awareness of their connection to other living systems. Just before leaving Paluma, they are encouraged to commit to one *personal action* towards a sustainable future. The final phase is linked to the maxim of *caring for self, others and place*, in order to develop global awareness and the ethics of valuing place.

Thirty-eight percent of responses were categorised as related to *hand* learning such as developing an ethic of care for the environment. Extracts from students' responses are shown below.

- This place teaches me

    How to treat a rainforest with respect.
    To love nature and nature will love me back.
    That some places are good to keep safe.
    It also teaches me that you have to respect mother nature even if you don't like animals like leeches.
    I love, respect and enjoy God's wonderful and amazing world.
    To respect the rainforest and all bushland.
    To be careful with plants because the animals and plants and stuff are like people, they should be treated just like people.
    It has . . . taught me that lots of people don't take care of the environment and I will try to take better care of it as well.
    I have learnt to also recycle so the environment is in a better condition.
    (Year 6 students)

- This place makes me feel

  So very calm and now I know how beautiful my State is and how precious it really is.

  (Year 6 student)

- This place is special because

  It is secluded and close to nature. You get to experience a rainforest and its values.
  I can be who I am and love the environment.

  (Year 6 students)

Students identified their responsibility to respect and protect the forest, even if some features of the forest still make them apprehensive: "*It also teaches me that you have to respect mother nature even if you don't like animals like leeches*". The statements above were written by students as they sat alone in the forest. In their reflective statements we can see evidence of interrelated learning linking heart, head and hand.

Self-awareness and aesthetic appreciation

An additional insight from the students' comments was their awareness of changes to their sense of self arising from the experience. Sample responses are provided below.

- This place teaches me

  That you don't always have to be stressed and loud.
  That you don't need to be alone to find inner peace in you.

  (Year 6 students)

- What I like best about this place is

  The quietness and serenity; the difference to home. I love the feeling when we're in the forest of being so alone and at peace. I am alone. I have a lot of my own peace and quiet.
  It's nature and it makes me realise how relaxing and calm I can be.

  (Year 6 students)

- This place makes me feel

  Calm cool and collected. It makes me feel like one with nature and brings out a different side of me; a side that can feel completely calm.
  There are no words to describe it. It gives me this feeling in my chest.
  I love the feeling when we're in the forest of being so alone and at peace.

  (Year 6 students)

- This place is special because

> Here nothing cares if you're slow or horrible at maths or any school sub-jects. It just comforts you in your hard times. It has a peaceful relaxing air about it.
>
> It gets your mind to go to a different place.
>
> (Year 6 students)

Almost all students commented on their engagement with the rainforest using words like "calm, peaceful, happy, quiet, silent and serene". This emotional calm prompts heightened self-awareness as expressed by one student as [this place teaches me] "*that you don't always have to be stressed and loud*". Other insights include, "*Here nothing cares if you're slow or horrible at maths or any school subjects. It just comforts you in your hard times. It has a peaceful relaxing air about it. It gets your mind to go to a different place*". Other students were aware of the timeless-ness of the forest, cherishing their experiences: "*There are no words to describe it. It gives me this feeling in my chest. I want to just stand there forever*". [This place makes me feel] "*that I have travelled back in time*". In these responses there is a sense of transcendence both of place (*a different place*) and time (*I want to stand there forever*) that relates to the sense of the sacredness of the forest.

Consistent with our own observations, some responses did reflect students' apprehension at being in unfamiliar territory: [this place makes me feel] "*aban-doned because I'm by myself; alone and peaceful; a little bit scared too, like I'm a small ant and the rainforest is huge; lonely, scared, because, you're all alone sitting in a spot where no one is; this place makes me feel closed in*". (Year 6 students)

Engaging marginal students

We encourage class teachers to bring all of their students, including those exhib-iting challenging behaviours, as we've noticed that our programs engage such students, perhaps more than classroom learning. In our data collection, we acknowledged that requesting written responses disadvantaged students with limited literacy. Students were permitted to respond in other ways. One student's response to the prompt, *this place teaches me* . . . was to draw a detailed diagram of the life cycle of a strangler fig rather than write anything about the life cycle. Another student was y able to write only a few letters that barely suggested what he meant. His written responses have been interpreted as:

> What I like best about this place is . . . "nice and peaceful".
> This place makes me feel . . . "free and alive".

In contrast to these limited written responses, during his interview (see extract below) this student revealed his extensive existing knowledge ("*I noticed some plants that I have seen before in documentaries*"). Recollection of the moment of seeing the white-tailed rat indicates his sensory acuity and his embodiment of attentiveness (*"be quiet, still, listen and watch"*). His responses to two of the interview questions illustrate the effect the excursion program had on him.

Inteviewer: What is the best thing about all the learning that has taken place for you in the last three days?

Student L: All the wildlife, the trees, some stuff in here I have never seen before, so it is good to see it, and while the teachers were talking about . . . [it] . . . I noticed some plants that I have seen before in documentaries. They didn't say much about it, but I noticed something they didn't show. The things I heard were like possums. I could hear something moving in the trees. I thought it was a possum, and I looked up and it was . . . the white-tailed rat. [A] possum-like rat thing came out. Be quiet, still, listen and watch around because sometimes you can see the animals moving. And the bird-watch – that was fun.

Inteviewer: How would say that this experience has changed you?

Student L: Made me smarter. I never knew about all of the plants, trees, everything, even the wildlife, I never knew there was a white-tailed rat.

(Student L, personal communication, 4 May 2012)

Mapping connections

We invite students to take away a personalised record of their experiences that shows the linkages between themselves and the living and non-living features of the forest. To do this we developed a pedagogical tool called the *Connected Map*. This is simply a blank piece of paper in their field workbook, where students make notes or sketch anything personally significant that occurred during the day. In the rainforest, the *Connected Map* builds on student attentiveness and scaffolds reflection on each learning experience. It has proven to be a useful tool in supporting higher-level curriculum-based discussions, for example, on food chains, food webs, trophic levels, natural cycles, ecosystems and our place in the natural world. The loosely structured *Connected Map* frames small group discussions of student observations in the rainforest and individual recordings of these. It prompts consideration of personal values and behaviours as moderating our impact on the environment. Most importantly, our research has given us another tool to use with our students in an exploration of a special place.

Conclusion

All this, and you want heaven too?
—Venn, personal communication, 5 December, 2014

Rapt in Rainforest provided us with an opportunity to document the immersion of students in a sacred, wellbeing experience. An affordance of this place,

Paluma, is that it provides possibilities for exploring really deep ideas and feelings, of becoming "enraptured" with the forest. The teachers involved in this research have differing spiritual views that are not publicly shared with our students. In discussion of the nutrient cycle, however, we can touch on different cultural and religious ideas of death.

> With older students, you can sort of talk about reincarnation or whatever. I just say, "Look, reincarnation is "ashes to ashes, dust to dust". That is reincarnation. Because all these little molecules are going to end up somewhere out there. You know, this could be part of a butterfly. You know, I could be a dog turd. (Laughs).
>
> (Venn, personal communication, 5 December 2014)

We live at a time when our global community is becoming enmeshed with technology. In Western society, 'screenland' has become a permanent facet of education and children's lives; the clouds they normally walk through are the global Internet clouds. These are a necessary part of the modern world in that they make knowledge widely available and foster an awareness of our global community. However, *iClouds* are no substitute for a sacred experience in the life-giving clouds of natural places. Louv (2012) and others have continued to highlight the nature deficit for contemporary generations. For our part, the challenge is to make sure that teachers and students walk through the Paluma clouds, not just to gain facts, knowledge and skills, but to have a transformative experience; one that fundamentally changes their relationship to nature and themselves.

Our students recount feelings and emotions that are typical of sacred encounters – the first of this kind of experience for many of them. As we have noted, participants of several spiritual traditions have visited Paluma where "Heaven touches Earth" to connect with the sacred. Our students recount experiences that are similar to those in these various traditions. Indeed our students join a chorus of artists and poets like Alfred Lord Tennyson and Judith Wright who also encountered feelings of sacredness and renewal in natural places. The common element shared among the experiences of poets, those seeking the divine and our students is the mind and body immersion in the natural world. The experience of one recent student (referred to as M) is typical of many of our students. When we first met M in his class, he was visibly excited, not about the ecosystems of the rainforest, but that he and his friends were off on an adventure together - and rightly so. The class was about to have its biggest slumber party ever!

But something changed for M on the first walk. First the cloud came down, and M's whole class ran outside to touch it. Through our introductory learning experiences, M and his friends became more interested and attentive to the rainforest. The video recorder M was given recounts his amazement at looking at the ancient *grandfather tree*. As M walked down the first hill into the belly of the rainforest, he said, *"Okay, this just became officially awesome."* He spent a lot of time on the walk picking up forest curios like skeletonized leaves, and imbibing the rainforest through his senses. The adventure of the first afternoon's walk gave way to the excitement and wonder of the night walk as M searched for and held a piece of glowing fungi. Another moment of deeper engagement happened at M's *magic spot*. In a reflection time, he shared what he had heard and seen. M had managed to sit still and found his time alone interesting. He talked about feeling calm and peaceful as well as how interesting the things around him looked. M also expressed a desire to protect the rainforest. By the time the bus pulled up to go home on the third day, M decided that he was going to stay in Paluma! He comes from a close family, and he said that they were probably missing him (except maybe his older sister), but it would be okay. Thankfully he was convinced to get on the bus, but other eleven-year-old students have even asked how they can work here in the future.

M's attitudes changed from looking forward to socializing with his friends, to looking back longingly at the rainforest; from a desire to have an adventure, to a fascination with and a concern for protection of natural places. Through the sacred experience of walking through these clouds, something profound happened to M, something good, something that could make a positive change in the future if it happens to more students like M.

In our own personal discussions conducted on long regional road trips, we continue to debate whether the "sacred journey" at Paluma is an example of God's "intelligent design" or from an agnostic view a revelation of the wonders of the web of life. Linda will often say to Louka, "*All this, and you want heaven too?*" As educators we invite students into a sacred experience of their own. We do this so that they develop curiosity for and amazement at the natural world. It is our hope that, at the end of their short time with us, this experience continues to work for them, producing changes in their hearts, heads and hands; that is, in the way they feel, think about and act towards the natural environment.

Notes

1 This photograph was taken by Louka Lazaredes and used with his permission.
2 *Learnscapes* was coined in the 1990s by Malcolm Cox when he was teacher-in-charge at Mount Cootha Botanic Gardens, Brisbane, Australia. See Booth (2001) for a review of literature on *learnscapes*.

References

Abram, D. (1997). The spell of the sensuous: Perception and language in a more-than-human world. New York: Vintage.

Berryman, J. (1979). The educational philosophy of John Oliver Feetham, Bishop of North Queensland. *Melbourne Studies in Education, 21*(1), 155–173.

Booth, P. (2001). Facilitating educators in the design of learnscapes: Research and development of appropriate roles for a learnscaper. Nathan, QLD: Griffith University. Retrieved from http://trove.nla.gov.au/work/153110578

Cairns, M. A., & Meganck, R. A. (1994). Carbon sequestration, biological diversity, and sustainable development: Integrated forest management. *Environmental Management, 18*(1), 13–22.

Cassady, J., & Johnstone, R. (1886). Halifax bay. In E. M. Curr (Ed.), The Australian race: Its origin, languages, customs, place of landing in Australia, and the routes by which it spread itself over that continent, Volume 2 (pp. 424–429). Melbourne: John Ferres.

Francis, Pope. (2015). *Laudatosi': On care for our common home.* Vatican, Rome. Retrieved from http://w2.vatican.va/content/francesco/en/encyclicals/documents/papa-francesco_20150524_enciclica-laudato-si.html

Hitzhusen, G. E. (2006). Religion and environmental education: Building on common ground. *Canadian Journal of Environmental Education, 11*(1), 9–25.

Kahn, K. (2008). The man who collected everything: WE Roth. In N. Peterson, L. Allen, L. Hamby (Eds.), *The makers and making of Indigenous Australian museum collections.* (pp. 163–186). Carlton, VIC: Melbourne University Press.

Leopold, A. (1970). *A sand county almanac.* New York: Ballantine.

Louv, R. (2005). *Last child in the wood.* New York: Algonquin Books.

Louv, R. (2012). The nature principle: Human restoration and the end of nature-deficit disorder. New York: Algonquin Books.

Naess, A. (1973). The shallow and the deep, long-range ecology movement. *Inquiry, 16*, 95–100. [Reprinted in A. Drengson & Y. Inoue (Eds.). *The deep ecology movement: An introductory anthology* (pp. 1–10). Berkeley: North Atlantic Books].

Naess, A. (1995). Self-realization: An ecological approach to being in the world. In A. Drengson & Y. Inoue (Eds.), *The deep ecology movement: An introductory anthology* (pp. 13–30). Berkeley, CA: North Atlantic Books.

Payne, P. (2005). Growing up green. Journal of the Home Economics Institute of Australia, 12(3), 2–12.

Payne, P., & Wattchow, B. (2008). Slow pedagogy and placing education in post-traditional outdoor education. *Australian Journal of Outdoor Education, 12*(1), 25–38.

Ungunmerr-Baumann, M. R. (1988). Dadirri. *Compass Theology Review, 22*, 9–11.

Ungunmerr-Baumann, M. R. (2002). *Dadirri: A reflection by Miriam-Rose Ungunmerr Baumann.* Retrieved from http://nextwave.org.au/wp-content/uploads/Dadirri-Inner-Deep-Listening-M-R-Ungunmerr-Bauman-Refl.pdf

Van Matre, S. (1979). *Sunship earth: An acclimatization program for outdoor learning.* Martinsville, IN: American Camping Association.

Van Matre, S. (1990). *Earth education: A new beginning.* Cedar Cove, Greenville, WV: Institute for Earth Education.

Venn, L. (2002). *Paluma: The first eighty years, 1870s-1950s.* Townsville, QLD: Thuringowa City Council.

Wertsch, J. V. (1991). *Voices of the mind: A sociological approach to mediated action.* Cambridge, MA: Harvard University Press.

7 Pedagogy as shifting sands at Nudgee Beach

Mary-Ann Pattison

Editors' preface

This chapter articulates a vision of place pedagogy as shifting sands that contrasts with the foundational notion of pedagogy as providing the basics and being solid and explicit. Educators often deploy the discourse of "ensuring the basics" or "establishing the foundations" of knowledge. Foundational pedagogies typically consist of step by step, sequentially-designed classroom activities that progressively build knowledge layer by layer. The design of foundational pedagogies is meticulous and reductive so that more complex concepts and skills are broken down into sub-parts and taught piecemeal until the whole structure is completed. Foundational pedagogies establish clear hierarchical relationships between the student and teacher, with the teacher dispensing knowledge block by block and ensuring that students stay on task and on time.

The materiality of the seaside and shifting sands at Nudgee Beach creates a rather different notion of knowledge and pedagogy. The sea is forever changeable, but in its immensity and unfathomability it invites teachers and students to journey forth to investigate. Pedagogy derived from the metaphor of the sea highlights adaptability and serendipity, going with the flow of the tides and currents of students' interests, or adjusting to the unpredictable winds and waves, sometimes running with the spinnaker up when everyone is learning easily and playfully, and at other times zig-zagging into a headwind as learning takes more effort and time than expected. Social relationships "on the sea" are based more on teamwork between teachers and students and mutual assistance to ensure the journey is completed successfully, wherever it might be leading. Certainly any journey on the sea will not be a straight line.

The contrast between foundational and sea-inspired pedagogies provides an insight into the pedagogy of shifting sands at Nudgee Beach. It's a pedagogy that is less concerned with foundations and the basics and more concerned with the flow and movement of experience in a constantly changing context. Teachers at Nudgee Beach Environmental Education Centre are required to opportunistically plan activities for students in relation to the tides, the seasons and the unexpected events on any given day. So the place itself, Nudgee Beach and the surrounding wetlands, calls forth a pedagogy that shifts and changes. In foregrounding the changing nature of place per se, "pedagogy as shifting sands" invokes the spatial theory of Doreen Massey (2005) who contends that places are neither frozen in time nor defined by clear boundaries between the inside and outside. Places are better conceived, she suggests, as processes – sites of interaction that have multiple identities and are unfinished and open. A striking example of this sense of place is Massey's account of Skiddaw, a huge mountain in the Lake District of England that conveys permanence, timelessness and immovability. Yet this mountain is actually a huge rock that has travelled thousands of kilometres from the southern hemisphere over hundreds of millions of years. So our "here and now" experience of the secure foundations of place is an illusion. Nudgee Beach and the pedagogy of shifting sands facilitate this insight. Mary-Ann Pattison, the environmental educator at Nudgee Beach, has elevated this idea of transience (shifting sands) to explicit awareness. Dwelling in place at Nudgee Beach is to experience constant change. Students can see change written into the mud by animals that feed in the shallows of the intertidal zone, or crabs that continually remake their holes after each tide. It is also recorded materially in eroded sandbanks or in the debris stuck in tree-tops from the floods that occurred in the Brisbane River valley in 2011. Change is recorded in longer time-spans for students to appreciate when they walk to the Indigenous bora rings near the wetlands and recall the presence and way of life of the original custodians of the land. Walking further away from the coast they can also see rocky outcrops where the Brisbane River had entered into Moreton Bay thousands of years ago. The contest and negotiation over the identity of this place is also palpable in the noise of aircraft taking off from the nearby Brisbane Airport that is built on landfill over the original expansive wetlands that covered the entire area until recently. Everything about the place at Nudgee Beach highlights change and ongoing contest over what this place means. Looking forward in time, the ocean, rising due to climate change, casts a shadow over the human settlement along the foreshore and heightens awareness of the challenges we collectively must confront in changing lifestyles and patterns of consumption. The motto at Nudgee Beach, "empowering keepers of the wetlands," captures the ultimate pedagogical goal that is built on a heightened sensitivity to the ever-changing nature of the place – fragility and resilience in equal measure.

Peter Renshaw & Ron Tooth

Introduction

> That's what I like about beaches, that you really do see the elements. You get that rawness. Every day is different because the tide comes in and it goes; and every single time that happens, you get a new surprise from the sea. We tell kids about what it was like yesterday and what it might be like from the morning when we are with kids until the afternoon. They can physically see that change in a day because of the change of the tides . . . they get a glimpse into that window of the dynamics of the marine environment.
>
> —M Pattison, personal reflection, 2015

The shifting sands of the beach provide the basis of the pedagogy at Nudgee Beach Environmental Education Centre (NBEEC). Everything is constantly changing, on the move; the tides flow in and out; sandbanks shift and realign from day to day, and migrating birds fly in and out searching for food and nesting spots. One day it's calm, and another is full of fury when the wind roars, and it's raw and wild. To be there in the midst is stimulating, makes you feel alive and in the moment as you connect to what's happening around you here and now. As educators here at NBEEC, we create opportunities for students to engage directly with the beach and the ocean as they experience for themselves the many moods of these dynamic systems and the rawness of the elements.

Most of the visiting students come from Brisbane schools but NBEEC regularly hosts international students from Japan and China and students from far western Queensland who may never have seen a beach or the ocean. We design learning experiences in various places at or near Nudgee Beach including islands, beaches, bushland, mangroves and wetlands where staff and students inter-act first-hand with the biodiversity of the place. This is where students engage with the Indigenous culture and history written into the landscape, while also considering the impact of recent developments such as Brisbane Airport and other nearby industrial complexes. Above all else we want young people to go away with a connection to the place and a sense of joy and wonder about aspects of nature, as well as an understanding of the threat from modern lifestyles based on increasing consumption. To understand the interface between the various visions of this place we consider different relevant stories, in particular the stories of the Indigenous people who are the traditional custodians of this place, the stories of change and development since European occupation and the more recent local stories of environmental protection and activism. Together with their physical experiences on the excursion, we hope these overlapping stories offer students a glimpse into the complexity that is this place, Nudgee Beach.

Indigenous custodianship of Nudgee

Nudgee, which means *place of black duck*, is thought to be a corruption of the Indigenous (Yugarra) name for the area or possibly a dialect of the words *Nar* (black duck) and *dha* (a suffix to indicate location). The first Europeans who entered this place in the 19th century vividly recorded the darkening of the sky as vast flocks of ducks took to the air. As custodians of the country around Nudgee, the Indigenous people were able to feast on plentiful sources of fish, shell-fish, mammals, reptiles and birds. Their cultural practices over thousands of years are etched in the landscape as middens, waterholes and ceremonial sites such as *bora rings* (Strong, 2016). Middens provide evidence today of the artefacts and food consumed in the past by the Indigenous people. Middens appear in the landscape as large mounds of bleached shells with layers of fire charcoal, occasional bones and stone tools. The large *bora rings*, sometimes called *kippa rings*, provided places for people to meet where stories were told, information exchanged, food shared and marriages arranged. Smaller rings were identified by early European explorers near Nudgee Beach, where specific ceremonies such as initiation rites were enacted. Still discernible in the landscape today is circular raised earth and compacted soil from tens of thousands of feet dancing over thousands of years within the boundaries of the main ring. The locations of the smaller rings are not as well-known and increasingly difficult to specify today.

Nudgee Beach sits on an Indigenous system of paths that ran north from the wetlands to other fertile country that is now part of the expanding northern suburbs of Brisbane, including Sandgate, Redcliffe and Bribe Island. These paths allowed the people to travel, to ebb and flow, like the tides, moving back and forth across the country depending on the season and the supply of food. Geological evidence reveals a shifting coastline. The waterholes, bora rings and middens, located some distance inland today, were at one time on the edge of the Bay. The shifting sands of the coastline across thousands of years, as well as the daily tidal shifting of sand are part of the unique affordances that Nudgee Beach offers to students who come to learn about the ecosystem and the relationship of people to this place. Nudgee Beach is a place of abundance and change, abundance in cultural heritage, abundance of life, and constant change across geological time as well as seasonal and daily change based on natural cycles.

Boondall is derived from an Indigenous word meaning crooked creek. The whole landscape now is bisected by the Gateway Motorway and spotted with houses located in the nearby suburb of Banyo, which means *ridge*, which is actually situated along an original headland that at one time marked the mouth of the meandering Brisbane River. Knowing about the changes written into the landscape is important to truly appreciate the affordances of Nudgee Beach for students' learning.

On the margins of developing Brisbane

As the European settlers moved into the area in the 19th century, cutting down trees, fishing in Moreton Bay and ploughing small-plot vegetable farms, this part of outer Brisbane became a sleepy village where the only growth in the area for many decades was the slow incursion of fishing shacks along the shoreline. A few of these earthen floor dwellings still remain. Only the locals were aware of the natural bounty and relative solitude offered by Nudgee Beach. It remained a well-kept secret as Southeast Queensland grew in population, and houses sprawled gradually across the river valley during the 20th century. The winding road into Nudgee Beach was often cut by a higher than normal tide. Being on the margins helped maintain the unique ecological niches of the wetlands, the mangroves and the beach itself. The area was not highly respected by Brisbane residents, however, and was commonly referred to as *swamps* and *mudflats*. The crisis for the future of the wetlands and Nudgee Beach began as Brisbane airport massively expanded across the wetlands from the 1970s. It was at this time that local residents began to advocate for the protection of large parts of the wetlands and the preservation of Nudgee Beach that had been included in plans to expand the airport. The Australian Marine Conservation Society (previously known as the Australian Littoral Society) provided scientific evidence of the complex ecological and productive worth of these areas. In this process advocates explicitly adopted the term *wetlands* and rejected the more common *mudflats* to describe the area. The contest for public and political support crucially involved this linguistic battle to develop an awareness of the place as special and valuable and aesthetically beautiful. Too often swamps and mudflats are devalued and ultimately "filled in" and "reclaimed" by people unable to see beyond the derogatory label to the life-giving abundance where water and land interact. At Nudgee Beach we continue this pedagogical task today by designing experiences for students to see the *mud* as a dynamic life-sustaining mix of water and land.

Local activism for conservation

Local citizens, such as Anne Beasley (1951–2000) a third-generation resident of the area, rallied the community when the expansion of Brisbane airport threatened the area. Anne befriended those who could help her cause and had extensive knowledge of the wetlands and Nudgee Beach to assist in the fight to save the area. Again, when the local state school was closed due to low enrolments, she lobbied the Queensland Education Department to maintain the site as an environmental education centre. She challenged officials in the Department to experience the place as she had as a young child. Anne visited local schools throughout 1988 collecting signatures for her vision of an environmental education centre. The following year the Environmental Education Centre at Nudgee Beach was opened to offer its programs to the children of the greater Brisbane area. Anne was named the most active Brisbane citizen in 1996. Following her sudden passing in 2000 the council named the lookout within the Boondall Wetlands after Anne in recognition of her pivotal role in preserving the wetlands and the beach. Anne's spirit is seen today in the tree planting programs that are organised through the Centre (NBEEC). As children participate in this program they concretely experience the challenges and paradoxes of conservation activism. To make space for the new trees they needed to clear invasive weeds, yet the exposed raw sand can be easily eroded, so it requires preserving some weeds to protect the whole area from erosion. It is in this paradoxical space that NBEEC works with children, balancing the active conservation of native species with maintaining introduced species as required for the whole area to flourish.

The Nudgee Beach experience

Wiping the salt from the leaves of the mangroves, walking on the beach at low and high tide, getting muddy and wet to observe living creatures, catching yabbies and small fish to study and release – these are the experiences that are central to our programs at Nudgee Beach. Students are frequently caught in the moment as they observe a crab scuttling across the mudflats, or wonder at the round sand formations at low tide that were made by the feeding crabs and the stingray holes. Guided walks across the sandflats and along the mangrove boardwalks take different perspectives depending on the age of the students. Early childhood students learn to sit quietly and use their senses – watching and hearing the crabs scuttle about while staff weave stories about plant and animal adaptations to these tidal zones. Students in Year 3 focus on "living", "once living" and "never living" as they walk along the same beach, peek out of the bird hide and observe the variety of birds on the foreshore. The Year 5 program focuses on surviving in the marine environment, exploring adaptations in plants and animals and how their adaptations relate to the dynamic environment. This same topic is then taken deeper in late years. Year 7 students construct complex food web relationships between plants (producers) and animals (consumers) to create a trophic level pyramid on the beach. The guided walks across the sandflats provide a dynamic environment for Year 9 students to understand how to identify and classify organisms using dichotomous keys. For students in Years 11 and 12 the clear patterns of zonation in the mangroves are recorded. It is this unique *place* which engages students of all ages, providing opportunities for students to explore and learn at their own pace in their own way every day.

Apprehension in the tidal zone

Walking in the tidal zone and across mudflats can be fascinating for many students, but for some it evokes apprehension and disequilibrium as they struggle mentally and physically to cope with their fears. We captured this apprehension in a photograph (see Figure 7.1 below) as we observed one student on the mudflats walking in and out, approaching and retreating as a group of her peers investigated the life of the tidal zone. Clearly evident is the student's dilemma of approach and avoidance – *What is it? Oh I can't touch it.* In the photo below you

Figure 7.1 Reluctant student observes group investigation of animals in the intertidal zone

can see the student on the edge of the group. She moved in and out of the circle wanting to participate but not quite being able to overcome her apprehension; her desire to participate was strong but the fear still stronger. Classroom teachers often are surprised by such hesitation particularly from their very able students in the classroom. At Nudgee Beach these students can be ill at ease as they struggle with dirty feet, dark sand between their toes, wet hats on their heads and fear of what lies beneath the mud and sand. Centre staff members are sympathetic to the internal struggles of students as they come to terms with the material realities of studying the environment up close.

Many learning opportunities are offered in the tidal zone. At low tide Nudgee Beach makes up a large four kilometre by four hundred metre sand beach while at high tide only small patches of sand peep between the fringes of mangrove forests. Tidal zones provide rich environments for animals both under the sand waiting to be discovered, on the surface and in the water column. Markings on the beach provide clues to the animals immediately below the surface or to the activity of fish when the tide was in. For example, triangular divots indicate the feeding patterns of schools of *whiting*; two holes with water pushing through indicate yabbies under the sand. The holes left by stingrays like the one below can harbour small translucent splinter-prawn that skip on the sand, as well as the crushed shells and other remnants of their feeding. You learn to read the sand: one notices the image of the flathead fish in the sand behind the stingray hole, knowing that it had taken advantage of the stingray's feeding to provide food (see Figure 7.2 below). Also we see the pattern of the subtle breeze last night, as well as the trail of footprints left by a bird which has flown away.

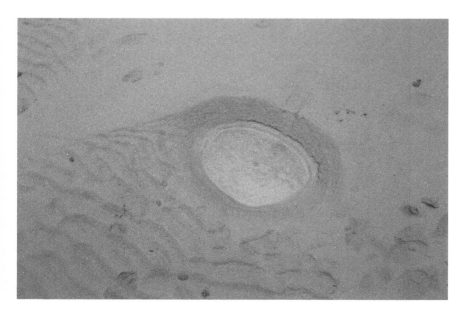

Figure 7.2 Stingray feeding hole with signs nearby of opportunistic fish also feeding

Through a process of exploration and discovery students can find, observe and develop their understanding of food chains and food webs, see adaptation and camouflage of the organisms on the beach and sense the daily rhythms of life on the tidal flats. Just as the sands where we work shift, so too the pedagogy and programs that we offer students shift across the year and even across the day depending on the time of the tides and the changing weather.

Staff affinity with *place* as mediating student learning

I love windy places. Any place that's windy, I will sit on a beach for hours as a storm roars through. I don't care if it is – you know – (wild), I am happy to be in wild and windy places, yeah – always have.
— M Pattison, personal reflection, 2015

Staff at NBEEC have a deep affinity with the place and an understanding of the cultural history of the site, as well as knowledge of the biodiversity of tidal systems, weather cycles, geography and the health and safety regulations related to working in a marine environment. The shifting sands of our programs mean that from day to day we can be working in very different conditions with diverse students from the first year of school through to Year 12, in a variety of curriculum areas, engaging a wide range of pedagogies that bring to life the beach, the mangroves, Indigenous artefacts and stories past and present. One moment it's still and silent, and the next there is strong wind building that then sweeps along the full length of the beach.

The melding of cultural, ecological and historical knowledge of the staff with the ever-changing and shifting nature of the natural systems that make Nudgee Beach a powerful context for learning is not something that has just happened by accident. Rather it is the result of many combined experiences, meetings and influences on key individuals over many years. I have grown and been shaped by this place, and this development has influenced the kinds of programs and experiences that we have created for students and teachers.

Mary-Anne's story

My life has always been associated with wild places, water, beach and sea. My parents were the founding members of the Brisbane Family Bushwalking Society and my childhood was spent travelling to remote parts of Queensland and northern New South Wales for long weekends and school holidays to camp, fish, bushwalk and climb mountains. We revisited beautiful sites year after year where, as children and teenagers, we rambled and explored further and further into the surroundings without a sense of limits to time or where we might go. This connection to specific places remains relevant in my work at Nudgee, as I am able to constantly marvel at the beauty and variability of the tidal environment and pass on that sense of wonder to teachers and students. Sitting and watching the activities of marine animals has been a lifelong interest. I've swum with large schools of fish bumping into me as they head north up the coast, and I've watched such schools of fish cluster together as sharks circled around the outside. In the centre the fish are safe but on the extremities they are vulnerable. These kinds of rich physical experiences are possible only through engagement in natural places. Other staff at Nudgee recount similar stories to mine, of growing up in the outdoors, sailing, fishing, spending time at beaches, engaging actively with place without worrying about time.

Meeting Oodgeroo Noonuccal

As a dedicated sailor across my childhood and teenage years I became immersed in the marine environment, spending whole days sailing on the large lake on the upper Noosa River and many times at dusk waiting hopefully for a lucky breeze to push me back home, or on occasion needing to paddle home. This period cemented my connection to the marine environment, and I began to excel as a sailor in local competitions. I developed a keen awareness of breezes, the tides and the flow of currents in water. With this expertise I was asked to assist the lecturers with the sailing component of the outdoor education course in my teaching qualification in 1979–1981. I came to Nudgee Beach 25 years ago, and sailing was the connection for me. I found that when I was on the water, it was mind-stilling.

It was during this period in the early 1980s that I made field trips with students to Stradbroke Island each semester where I met Oodgeroo Noonuccal (Kath Walker) the Indigenous poet, activist and educator (Noonuccal & Walker, 1992). She talked about Stradbroke Island as *her country*, and she lamented the dramatic changes she had witnessed and what was happening at that time with sand mining on the Island. I think she spent time with me because I was one of the few people who returned each semester for three years with the new students. I remember walking with her around the old missionary site that was near her home on Stradbroke Island. Interestingly, her son lived over the road from my grandmother's house on the mainland in the suburb of Redhill, and I recall seeing her there as well. This serendipitous connection with Oodgeroo gave me a deep respect for Indigenous people and their culture, and this informs our Centre pedagogy today.

Key elements of the pedagogy

Multi-sensory

The experiences we design are multi-sensory. Nobody goes to the beach without engaging their sense of smell, their near and far vision and the feel and texture of sand in shoes and between toes. Visiting teachers work with the Centre staff to help engage their students as they go to the beach and, in the process, find themselves drawn into the whole sensory and changing nature of the experience.

Getting dirty

Mention "beach" to students around Brisbane and typically they imagine a classic white-sanded surfing beach from the Gold or Sunshine Coast. The beach at Nudgee challenges their established image. Students at the beginning of a day typically regard Nudgee Beach with disdain, complaining that "*it's dirty*", or "*why are we here!*", and many walk on tip-toe, trying to jump the muddy puddles or avoiding the water to stay "*clean*". We have students who come back from the beach and say, "*This has been the best day of my life*" because they have been sitting and observing without worrying about time. I am conscious that children today are hurried and are often over-organised by busy parents, so that just to engage with the beach all day is a rare luxury. A lot of what we do here, particularly with our primary school students, is simply going to the beach and having an organic experience – connecting to what's happening there. Our work with international students and newly arrived migrants requires us to work with young people who have had no experience of an Australian beach. They begin a day filled with fear and leave in the afternoon with a feeling of real connection to the place.

> We had (recent migrant) kids who had little or no English. When we had the animals with us (to touch and handle), they had their knees up and they were physically retracting and trying to be out of the group, . . . they couldn't get off their chairs because there was nowhere to go . . . so their solution was to pull their legs up, tuck their chin in, to basically ball up. . . . Then by the end of the day, they are holding a baby crocodile, and that is the transition from this raw fear to engagement.
>
> (M. Pattison, personal reflection, 2015)

Many migrant children who come to the Centre are terrified of water and of getting dirty when they start the day. They certainly can't touch or handle a living creature. By the end of the day they have been captivated by the place. These are the embodied reactions to place that we can record everyday as we see students move from regarding the environment of Nudgee Beach as alien to being at ease and interested in its diverse life.

Long-term engagement

It's difficult at first for many children to notice the subtle changes constantly happening around them or to see the smaller details and intricacies in the most ordinary events. When they are first introduced to an activity on the day of their visit, many want to move on after a few moments and to jump to the next thing. They want to do something different. But at the end of the day they will recognise that by being immersed they have a gained a lot more than by moving from experience to experience every few moments. One group of parents who visited over a number of weeks couldn't see the point at first of allowing students to spend so much time on one activity or in one location. Some of the parents couldn't see that by immersing students deeply over time that they were learning how to connect to place, to take real notice of subtle variations, and observe changes.

Sometimes we ask them to sit totally still and just watch, or stand and be aware of how the elements are interacting with their body, something that many children and adults have never done (see Figure 7.3). We often share our own experiences of being still in nature, watching and noticing, and how this makes us feel. These personal stories seem to resonate with many students. I often share dramatic moments on the water when I've been sailing or when I've been alone just watching. We make a difference for students by focussing on sensory experiences per se and scaffolding moments so they become deeply aware of what's happening to them.

Actively doing

I remember one day when it was rip-roaring windy and the river was wild. There were two young children who joined a river journey excursion for just one day, and they wanted to know if it was going to be all right. "*Are we going to be all right, Mary-Ann?*" "*Yeah, it's going to be great. We are going to have a great time.*" But, the river was wild and at its most challenging. It wasn't dangerous because

Figure 7.3 Quiet observation and writing about the ever-changing sea at Nudgee Beach

the staff and I knew what we were doing. As the group set out into the river they engaged with the elements, and it was exhilarating. The two students knew that they were safe, and they let themselves connect, and they had a wonderful day. We rafted and the wind pushed us here, and the tide dragged us there, and the elements were really "shouting". You could see it in their faces and hear it in their voices that these students were moving beyond what they had imagined they could achieve and they were excited and amazed. The fact that they were surviving and successfully making their way on this great river was for them remarkable.

Care for the place

The shifting sand with every tide challenges us to consider how we can reduce the impact on the beach of student activity. The impact of over five thousand students each year is continually monitored by staff, and we are very conscious of the changes. We continue to monitor our impact through scientific analysis, comparing areas on the beach where we work with those areas in the green zones where people are excluded. This prepares us for the next critical stage of our pedagogy when we consider with students what can be done to protect the place and to foster an ethic of care for the beach and other places. This is where we provide positive messages to student about what they can do. We review the whole experience, encompassing stories and artefacts of the past, their experiences in the present, the reality of the challenges we all face and hope for the future. We talk with students about commitments to concrete actions such as collecting rubbish from beaches, saving water in daily life, planting trees and other actions relevant to their situations.

Case study

In 2012 NBEEC began an extended partnership with *Urban State School*, a primary school located in inner city Brisbane. The principal, with support from the Parents and Citizens Association, decided to send students out of the city into a natural environment over an extended period. The small school has multi-age classes, and this case study documents the work of their senior class (Years 5 to 7) and tracks key learning moments during fortnightly visits to Nudgee Beach over the course of a year. The principal recognised that students' deep understanding developed over time and that this required staying with the journey.

As we worked through the four terms of the year (see below for further description) with the *Urban State School* we spent considerable time reflecting on the lives of the Indigenous owners and custodians, visiting their significant cultural sites nearby, sharing knowledge of their everyday lives such as what they caught to eat, and through quiet attentiveness in place, we tried to connect to their cultural practices. We sat in silence near the bora ring on several different days and then wrote about how we felt. Below is a poem expressing a sense of loss written by one group of students after such an experience:

Silence in the noise
How can we ever understand

What was once here is gone
What we will never understand
I listened for the lost voices
I wanted to understand
So little is known, so much is lost.
   (Years 5–7, Class poem, July 2012)

Students walked the Indigenous tracks through the wetlands, tried to make fire as Indigenous people had, examined the way to collect and treat native foods, and across different times of the year, familiarised themselves with seasonal food sources, thereby gaining a sense of the rhythms of the place as experienced by Indigenous people across time. These were purposefully slow days with plenty of time to think, to connect, to reflect.

Initially we focussed on adaptations of plants and animals in the marine environment. Students used dichotomous keys (yes/no features) to identify mangrove species before making their own keys to identify crabs species found at Nudgee Beach. The idea of using a yes/no dichotomous process to eliminate options and identify characteristics and features of plants and animals is something that students enjoy recreating. It directs their attention to specific features and cumulatively enables them to identity plants and animals for themselves. Initially students commented on the obvious changes they could see such as the tides and changing weather conditions, but by their third visit they were also commenting on the more subtle changes such as patterns in the sand and evidence of the activity of marine animals. We then moved onto sustainable recreational activities that involved canoeing, bike riding, fishing and photography. This highly physical program assisted students to develop their communication, leadership and teamwork skills.

By mid-year the principal of *Urban State School* asked if selected students could be involved in a section of the 340 km biennial expedition *Bunya to the Bay*. These students became "day traveller ambassadors" paddling part of the Brisbane River, meeting older secondary students from other schools who were engaged in the full expedition and documenting various aspects of the journey. The highlight of this experience was to witness the significant effects of the 2011 floods. Students saw timber suspended in treetops just as described in the 19th century by explorer, John Oxley, who made a journey along the same section of the river. The students also saw significant erosion and changes to the flow of the river and damaged public facilities that remained unrepaired some 20 months later. For some students, an echidna sighting in the wild was an unforgettable experience that only a few people are lucky enough to see in their lifetimes. As we travelled down the river there was time to chat and ask deeper questions about what we were doing. The following are quotes from the Year 5–7 students taken as they moved down the river and realised their role in the big picture.

The message is to take care of your environment and don't take it for granted and look after it.

It teaches you that everything in nature is connected and there is nothing that is not connected to another thing.

Almost everything you do every day affects the environment.

When we heard these comments we thought to ourselves, "*These students are starting to get it*". They could see the bigger picture and were connecting the dots about their actions and connections to the environment. One of the teachers reflected on what her class had learnt during their time at NBEEC. She wrote the following,

> The other thing they learnt of course, that they don't know about, is that they have made an emotional connection to this environment and all throughout their lives now, every time there is something about the bay or mangroves, they will have had an experience of that. They will have had an experience that connects, which connects deeply at a human level.

The river trip prepared students for the next phase of their inquiry, namely, to consider the long-term changes to Nudgee Beach. Students visited three sites: the Nudgee waterholes, the boardwalk through the mangroves and the beach itself in early July, August and September. At each site they recorded the temperature, humidity, turbidity of the water, wind speed and direction, as well as taking a basic water sample to look for micro-organisms. Story was used to look at the issues associated with the area over longer periods of time such as the human impacts of road construction on the waterholes and the reduced impact created by the boardwalk on the mangrove area. They also calculated how many feet had walked on the beach during the excursion to estimate our impact on the foreshore sand and its animals.

Students participated in a community of inquiry process (Cam & Rinkel, 1994) to reflect on how they understood the complex environmental issues encountered during the year. Listening to the audio-tape from this process revealed that the majority of the students were far more comfortable talking about rather than writing about their experiences. Extracts from the audio reveal students' sense of change in themselves as a result of the program:

> It makes me feel that I can do better and not do that and do things differently than I usually would, and do stuff that wouldn't hurt the environment instead of hurting the environment in everyday life.
>
> (Student from *Urban State School*, 2012)

> The learning at Nudgee Beach has improved how we answer at school and more questions at Nudgee Beach, it has improved how we learn and how we show what we have learnt.
>
> (Student from *Urban State School*, 2012)

The NBEEC Arts teacher scaffolded students in different drama strategies such as rolling back in time to explore the past and taking on specific roles and perspectives in the present. The different perspectives were explored in role-play with students expressing conflicting ideas for the future of the place. Memorable comments included the girl, in role as a professional worm catcher, who passionately pleaded for the "*saving of the mud.*" Another student demanded that the person in charge "*take some time and just see what is here, and what will be lost before you even knew that you had it!*" These comments were expressed spontaneously in role by students. The thoughts and what they were articulating showed a deep connection and understanding of the importance of the wetlands; they were empowered as keepers of the wetlands.

The students developed an enriched view of this aquatic environment by the end of the school year. The connections being articulated were complex and the language was rich as shown in these comments from Year 5–7 students.

> I think more deeply into the question and answer it more deeply and I give a longer answer and a more developed answer than if I just hadn't gone there.
>
> You can learn more and take in more information out in the open by experiencing.
>
> To learn about nature and how things live in nature and animals. You have more experience and you can see what is happening instead of imagining it in your head.

The program culminated with Nudgee Beach Centre staff working in the school to consolidate the students' learning and to design innovative ways to present their insights to the whole-school community. We dealt with environmental activism, developing writing, media and drama skills. A DVD with images of students at the Centre, their thoughts and written work was created and presented to parents as part of the end-of-year program for the school. In contrast to the beginning of the year when students struggled to write more than a few words on the knowledge of marine life, when presented to parents and the school community they had to condense their extensive knowledge to fit onto the presentation slides. For the graduation ceremony of the students from *Urban State School* I wrote the following comments:

> It's making them think and critically analyse because of the way we are teaching. It's not about the content, it's not about who delivered it, it's not even about the national curriculum. It's about what is going on in their heads. It's making them think even in the classroom and that to them has been a great revelation – that what they learn here at NBEEC is transferred back to their classroom as a method of working.
>
> (*Urban State School* graduation, 2012)

Conclusion

The tides and the ever-changing intertidal zone create the learning affordances at Nudgee Beach. As teachers we have to plan around the tides. Students experience a different Nudgee Beach depending on the day, the season and the weather. So this dynamic aspect of "nature" is a key affordance for what students can learn here – nothing remains the same but life has learned to adapt and thrive. Learning at Nudgee Beach requires attentiveness to the traces and signs of living things. Animals leave traces of their activity. People leave material traces and cultural artefacts that give insight into the past. Students can imagine the scuttling crabs from the sand patterns they see; they can imagine the stingrays from the hollows in the sand. The Indigenous children and past generations of settlers' children also saw these same patterns and hollows and they too learnt to understand the connections, the way the tide and sands shift and replace the image. The sand and mud record these moments only to see the traces washed away at the next tide. What might be learned is that there is serendipity – will a bird of prey swoop down? Will the tide reveal a stranded fish or marine mammal?

In the process of writing this chapter as I reflected on dynamic changes and serendipity, I developed a clearer vision of the Nudgee Beach pedagogy refracted through the metaphor of "shifting sands." *Pedagogy as shifting sands* is a more open and unpredictable journey into learning, like a grain of sand tossed by the sea, drifting with the pull of the tides, being washed ashore and settling for a while, being picked up and swept away again, changing direction as a current of experience sweeps in, sometimes a little uncertain of the outcome, uncomfortable but enjoying the adventure of the ride. *Pedagogy as shifting sands* is less concerned with learning objectives, less concerned with reaching predetermined goals and more concerned with the flow and movement of experience in the present. Of course, this sense of pedagogy as shifting sands is located in *place* at Nudgee Beach and the adjacent wetlands, and the affordances of this *place* have provided me with the courage to go with the flow, to allow students the freedom to explore for hours and be guided by what takes their interest. *Pedagogy as shifting sands* requires time in place to experience change and transitions, to see the beach before, during and after the tides have come and gone, and to be sensitive to the changes that have occurred. As I noted earlier in the chapter, with regard to the reservations expressed by some of the parents (accompanying their children to NBEEC), adults can be uneasy with such pedagogy because it seems too slow, too open and too trusting that students can learn through their own observations and experiences. It pushes against the grain of current educational policy that requires efficiency and effectiveness from teachers in an accountability framework. We know that this can have negative consequences for students and teachers in terms of stress and anxiety. *Pedagogy as shifting sands* is a less stressful way of teaching, one that can look like play and relaxation from a distance. But it is playful teaching and learning with a serious intent, namely to connect students to *place* and to engender in them an appreciation of place that motivates them to care and consider how their own actions might have positive and negative impacts. Our motto, "empowering keepers of the wetlands," captures our ultimate goal but our approach is built around the primacy of experience and a heightened sensitivity to the ever-changing nature of the environment.

My experience as a child and young adult prepared me uniquely for my professional career in environmental education; it prepared me to develop *pedagogy as shifting sands*. I teach the way I learned. This phrase is often meant as a negative comment about teachers simply reproducing transmission pedagogy and treating students as empty vessels to be filled with the required curriculum content. In my case, the phrase captures a rich childhood spent in natural settings learning through open-ended engagement in exploring the world around me. Later when I learnt to sail I had the opportunity to be constantly in touch with the changing winds and currents of the marine environment, and I developed an acute sensitivity to these dynamic natural systems. So when I teach students at Nudgee Beach I don't need to follow a script. What I know now is that I need to trust experiences in place, openness, serendipity and students themselves to be the basis of my pedagogy – the *pedagogy of shifting sands*.

References

Cam, P., & Rinkel, K. (1994). *Thinking stories: Teacher resource/activity book*. Sydney: Hale & Iremonger.

Massey, D. (2005). *For space*. London: Sage.

Noonuccal, O., & Walker, K. (1992). *The dawn is at hand: Selected poems*. London: Marion Boyars Publishers.

Strong, M. (2016). "One ring to rule them all?" Towards understanding the plethora of bora grounds in southeastern Queensland. *Queensland History Journal, 22*(12), 859–877.

8 Pedagogy of the edge at Moreton Bay

Belinda Daly

Editors' preface

The pedagogy of place designed at Moreton Bay uses the edge as a metaphor to integrate different aspects of the Centre's educational programs that focus on history, ecology and marine science. Moreton Bay offers a distinctive affordance for edge pedagogy because it is the site of myriad intersecting edges between sea and land, earth and sky, human design and the more-than-human world. Edge pedagogy foregrounds both the incredible beauty and diversity of life that occurs along boundaries, as well as the conflicts and tensions that occur when different spaces and interests intersect. As briefly summarised below, the edge is a concept that resonates with scientists, activists, artists and educators.

Ecologists are particularly concerned with edge effects where two distinctive ecosystems intersect and interact (Neate-Clegg, Morshuis, & Banks-Leite, 2016; Barnes & Hamylton, 2016; Murcia, 1995). Ecosystem edges are sites for the movement of materials, nutrients and energy across their boundaries, and this is particularly relevant to the current chapter which takes as a specific case study a program that engages very young children with the diversity of shells and crabs of the intertidal zones in Moreton Bay. Shells are washed ashore on sandbanks where they provide shelter for hermit crabs whose life cycle is contained between water and land scavenging for food at the edge.

Moreton Bay is the eastern edge of the city of Brisbane, and like many marginal spaces, it is a place where pollution and urban rubbish accumulates. After the flood in January 2011 vast quantities of silt were washed down the Brisbane River into Moreton Bay threatening the seagrass meadows of the Bay that support turtles and endangered Dugong herds. The Dugong is an amazing species that has more in common with elephants than other marine mammals. It is on the edge in a number of ways: its habitat is on the edge of the Bay, and as a species it is increasingly vulnerable. The EDGE (2016)) is an organisation dedicated to preserving species that appear to be tipping over the edge, and recent reports from scientists studying the seagrass in Moreton Bay suggest runoff from river systems damaged significant feeding grounds for Dugong that further threatens their survival (Connolly, 2009; SEQ Catchments Ltd., 2013). So, the pedagogy of the edge foregrounds these vital issues of species preservation and rehabilitation.

Artists are keenly aware that being on the edge can be aesthetically moving and rewarding. People are typically captivated at the edges and boundaries of spaces, and local artists in South-East Queensland such as Nicola Moss (2016) are drawing inspiration from Moreton Bay in terms of the edge. Moss recently presented an exhibition of hand-cut paper works and drawings, Life on the Edge, that celebrate the biodiversity of Moreton Bay. Her works depict the beauty and fragility of the flora and fauna in Moreton Bay, which depend for their survival on what the waters carry and disperse. Pedagogy of the edge has this aesthetic dimension as well, seeking to arouse students' aesthetic sensibilities regarding the interconnectedness of the myriad edges in Morton Bay.

Being on the edge can be exhilarating but also frightening and challenging. As recounted by the author, Belinda Daly, many students arrive at Moreton Bay with pre-conceived negative ideas about hidden creatures at the edge and need to be coaxed to overcome their feelings that the Bay is a foreign and scary place. Many have never seen hermit crabs or marine creatures up close, let alone been asked to handle one, despite living in the local area. The pedagogy of the edge encompasses this notion of challenging students beyond their comfort zones so that they step beyond the edge of their competence into new experiences and possibilities for the future.

Being on the edge captures the notion of being ready for change. The pedagogy at Moreton Bay is designed to prepare students for change in their behaviour. Through practical activities students are shown how harm to the environment might be minimised even though the Bay is heavily used by the general public. For example, as a part of understanding that "every footstep counts", students engage in the "snake walk" as they cross the edge of the intertidal zone. Students form a line behind the teacher and begin walking, stepping in the footprints of the person in front of them with exaggerated slowness and carefulness in each step. This allows students to embody the need to be attentive to the environment and minimise their impact. Through this collective act of care, students are introduced to the concept that every step we take has a lasting impact on natural places. So the final and perhaps more important implication of pedagogy of the edge is to avoid pushing species over the edge through careless and indifferent behaviour.

The notion of edge pedagogy was named explicitly only recently by the educators at Moreton Environmental Educational Centre, but it has a deep resonance with the material affordances of Moreton Bay, a place that has been continuously formed and reformed over millennia, a place of boundaries and intersections. It resonates too with the aesthetic sensibilities of artists who find complexity and beauty in the rich biodiversity of the Bay. The edge resonates with the anxieties of concerned scientists and citizens who wonder if human activity and negligence might push Dugong and other species over the edge. In the pedagogy of the edge these overlapping stories of biodiversity, beauty and anxiety are told in different ways by the educators to reach students of all ages.

Peter Renshaw & Ron Tooth

Introduction

Stretching 125 kilometres from Caloundra in the north to the Gold Coast Seaway in the south, Moreton Bay is a place of edges continuously remade across eons of time. Volcanos erupted and eroded over millions of years to create the red soiled Brisbane plain. Annual floods have distributed silt across the plain, and the fluctuating sea levels associated with ice ages over the past 200,000 years have dramatically changed the shape of the shoreline of the Bay. Rocky outcrops offshore trapped sand from coastal ocean currents to form large beautiful sand islands, such as Moreton Island and Stradbroke Island, and these in turn have created the contours of the Bay. The pedagogy of the edge is designed to connect students to this place of contours and boundary conditions. To appreciate Moreton Bay students are invited to the edge where land meets sea; they are asked to step over the edge and immerse themselves in exploring the varied environmental niches of the Bay; and they are challenged to move beyond the edge of their comfort zones to become "Champions of the Bay" for themselves and future generations.

Complex ecosystems

This fertile and dynamic marine environment supports complex ecosystems that thrive in and around the Bay. Interrelated habitats include coral reefs, mangrove forests, intertidal zones and extensive seagrass beds that provide ecological niches for 750 species of fish, 6 species of turtles, small herds of endangered dugongs, 120 species of coral, 8 species of mangroves and 45,000 migratory shorebirds each year. Mangroves provide a sheltered nursery for juvenile fish, prawns and crabs that will eventually migrate to the deep ocean. This nursery provides 75% of the seafood enjoyed by the people of Brisbane. Both tropical and temperate plants, animals and corals are able to thrive here, thanks to the unique intersection of climate zones at Moreton Bay.

Indigenous country

Quandamooka, the Indigenous name for Moreton Bay, has been home to many different Indigenous groups speaking the Jandai language. At the time of British colonisation in the late 18th and early 19th centuries Ngugi people lived on Moorgumpin (Moreton Island), the Noonucul and Goenpul people on Minjerribah (Stradbroke Island) and numerous other groups lived along the shoreline of the mainland south of Mairwar (Brisbane River).

Indigenous clans provided access rights to other groups for hunting and fishing. Food supplies were plentiful with seasonal hunting and gathering of plants and animals, including dugong, mullet and tailor caught in fishing nets called towrow nets, sometimes aided by dolphins (Steele, 2015). Turtle, crustaceans and gastropods such as oysters, eugaries, pipis and mussels were also collected from the sea, while on land, kangaroo, lizards, flying foxes, birds, berries and bungwal fern root were collected. Archaeological testing of midden sites on Minjerribah dates occupation to at least 21,000 years before present (BP).

The Quandamooka peoples have a rich and complex spiritual, social and cultural life. Spiritually important places have been found throughout Moreton Bay, and many tracks and travel routes or *songlines* have been discovered on the islands. Corroborees and other ceremonies were an integral part of family and community life, including huge regional celebrations attracting clans from hundreds of kilometres away. Quandamooka people continue to live in Moreton Bay today, despite displacement by colonisation. In 2011, they gained native title over the land, waters and islands surrounding Minjerribah (Nth Stradbroke Island), which recognises the continuous and ongoing traditional laws and customs of the Quandamooka people living on the Island.

A growing community

Moreton Bay was colonised by British convicts, soldiers and later by settlers who pioneered isolated outposts from 1824. Initially the Bay's islands were used as places of banishment where outcasts, prisoners and people of ill-health were isolated in institutions on the islands. A rich fishing industry developed based on fish, prawns and crabs, and this sustained small communities around the Bay, now only evidenced by abandoned docks and partly submerged boats. Dredging of coral reefs for shipping access and minerals did not cease until1998 when the first laws were enacted to provide protection to the various resources of the Bay by the creation of Moreton Bay Marine Park.

Situated on the edge of the expanding city of Brisbane, Moreton Bay has been changed by rapid urbanisation. Rock walls have replaced the natural shoreline, recreational vessels nestle in extensive marinas, houses crowd up to the shore and pollution accumulates in the waterways flowing into the Bay. Boats of every description cruise constantly across the waters. A community of people play, talk, walk and run along the esplanade paralleling the shore. Some residents, like the author, reflect somewhat anxiously on the fragile beauty of the place and search for ways to maintain the Bay. Everyone acknowledges that the Bay is under unrelenting pressure from urbanisation and overuse.

A day at Moreton Bay

Inspiring "Champions for the Bay"

Moreton Bay Environmental Education Centre's (MBEEC's) vision for visiting students is "Inspiring Champions for the Bay". "Inspiration" lies at the heart of our pedagogy so much that we have named our excursion vessel *Inspiration*! It is a 12-metre aluminium catamaran that can transport up to 60 passengers, or have 40 students actively using microscopes, plankton trawls, sediment grabs and underwater video. Working together with schools and classroom teachers, we engage students in firsthand learning experiences that inspire them to want to take action for Moreton Bay. The goal of "Inspiring Champions for the Bay" informs all our programs from Preparatory Year (aged about five years) to Year 12 (aged about 17 years). Our programs reflect the "more-than-human" aspects of Moreton Bay that we as teachers most value. We also necessarily acknowledge that human activity has had a profound effect on the ecological systems of the Bay. There are three types of programs:

- "Champions of the Past" – History programs looking back to past events and perspectives that have shaped the Bay and the relevance today of these events.
- "Champions for the Present" – Science programs researching the integrity and sustainability of the natural and cultural environment of the Bay today.
- "Champions for the Future" – Inspiring students to take action for Moreton Bay today so that it can be sustained for future generations.

All Moreton Bay EEC programs include a specific role for students to ensure that they are active participants during and after the excursion. Roles may be as varied as "junior archaeologist", "marine scientist", "history detective" or "ornithologist". Since its adoption, the implementation of the "student role" has become a powerful tool that gives students a greater sense of ownership of the program and a clear purpose for their excursion. It enables them to feel as though they are an important part of something authentic and that they can make decisions about the progress and outcome of their excursion as well as the future as a "Champion for the Bay".

History in the Bay

History comes alive through our programs at various authentic sites in the Bay. Year 5 students arriving on their excursion to St. Helena Island walk in the footsteps of 19th century convict prisoners, following their personal stories to the places within the crumbling ruins of the penal settlement where convicts worked, slept and died. Students' empathy is aroused as they realise that these convicts were people with thoughts and feelings, struggling with the difficult situations of their time and dreaming of a better life. As one student, William, commented after the excursion,

> There are stories concealed inside everything!

Many of our historical programs also use a dilemma to create the motivation for the unfolding events of the day – "*the fort is closing down!*" or "*St. Helena National Park is to be rezoned and leased for tourism development!*" This evokes consideration by students of the value of historical sites. The following comments are indicative of the commitment many students develop during the excursion.

> We shouldn't close down Fort Lytton because kids love this place and history can inspire people.
>
> (Year 4 student)

> If it got closed down there would be no history memories.
>
> (Year 4 student)

First contact with Indigenous people

Indigenous knowledge and traditional land management strategies are an integral part of our Centre programs. In the "First Contact" program, Year 4 students are placed in the role of three shipwrecked convicts, a true story of the first white men to spend time interacting with the Indigenous people of Moreton Bay in 1823. This story is established in stages, with an initial visit by Centre staff to the school to set the scene and provide historical resources for students to explore. Then on the excursion day they meet a number of Indigenous Noonucul men from Minjerribah (Stradbroke Island). The program follows the historical story of how the escaped convicts were given access to Indigenous knowledge of the land and shown how to survive by using the resources available around them. Students appreciate these insights as noted by two students below:

> I have changed by learning all of the new knowledge and skills of the Aboriginal culture.
>
> (Year 4 student)

> I've got more respect for the Aboriginal people now because of their knowledge of the land.
>
> (Year 4 student)

During one activity on this excursion students are challenged to survive alone by using the knowledge and skills shared with them by the Indigenous teachers. They realise how invaluable the Indigenous knowledge is for planning their survival. Importantly they also get opportunities to reflect on the first contact between white and Indigenous people in Moreton Bay and the decades after, and how important the Indigenous culture is to our local area, to our society and our contemporary culture in Australia. The following student's guarded comment (*I trust them a little more than I did*), reveals the lack of contact many students have with Aboriginal Australians and the negative view of these presented in the mainstream media. It is not surprising in this context that she expresses a somewhat guarded response.

> I now respect the Aboriginal people a lot more than I used to. I trust them a little more than I did.
>
> (Year 4 student)

On the other hand the student quoted below sees that there is a different way of knowing and being in the world represented by Aboriginal culture (*now I look at two ways in culture*), and she sees possibilities for a different future (*It will help me a lot*).

> Well, I have changed because now I look at 2 ways in life, the Aboriginal way and my way. It will help me a lot.
>
> (Year 4 student)

These changes were made possible, according to the visiting classroom teacher, by the knowledge and experiences shared by the Aboriginal men and Moreton Bay EEC teachers during the excursion.

> The wealth of knowledge shared by Mark, Matt and Tim is a valuable resource. They made learning relevant, challenging and fun. These are the types of learning experiences which will continue to resonate with the children long after they leave a classroom.
>
> (Classroom teacher)

The long-term significance of such experiences is expressed in the teacher's notion of resonance into the children's future.

Science in the bay

Our science programs engage students in hands-on learning experiences that focus on real issues facing Moreton Bay today. On board the catamaran "*Inspiration*", students participate in Citizen Science projects, where they conduct fieldwork partnered with real "champions of today" – marine scientists, mangrove specialists, water quality scientists and others whose work contributes to the monitoring and maintenance of the Bay's ecology.

The scientific work on board involves conducting research on the water quality, the abundance and health of animals, plants and coral, and evidence of human effects on ecosystem health. Students conduct research at selected locations, using the underwater video glider to ascertain the structure of the coral and plant life of the ocean floor; they use baited nets to identify (and release) animal species, and they use a remote arm to conduct sediment grabs of the ocean floor. Students' research data is logged and compared to the longer-term trends accumulated over time by other groups. Their data contributes to a larger body of evidence being collated by the local community of citizen scientists. Students can see that there is purpose to their work and therefore that the accuracy of their data and their analysis of trends and patterns can form a part of wider efforts to make a difference for the Bay. This connection between science per se and a sense of obligation to the environment is expressed well by the student below:

> Science is about finding out about places so you can care for them.
>
> (Year 9 student)

Staff mediating access and learning at Moreton Bay

Childhood connection to natural places

I am not a local, but I've lived and worked here for 19 years. When I first arrived in Queensland from Victoria, I headed straight to Moreton Bay despite knowing nothing about it or having any previous connection. Quite simply I was drawn to its vast, open watery spaces where I could lose myself in silence, a pale blue horizon and an isolated shore. My migrant parents journeyed across the world from wet and cool Europe to a hot, dry foreign land that they were determined to make their home. Coming from a line of farmers, their connection to land was ingrained. For me, growing up with a very large extended family with a fascination for natural places meant spending every holiday period exploring new places, walking through eucalyptus forests, building secret cubbies in the rainforest and spending dawn to dusk playing on the banks of rivers. My parents were creating a connection to Australia in the best way they knew how – being in the environment, revisiting special places to make this foreign land a place that was familiar and beautiful to us. I made sense of the unfamiliar world around me by having fun with my cousins, feeding off each other's new discoveries about the intricate and surprising world of nature. What developed alongside this was a sense of collective stewardship over the areas we held dear. We noticed when things died, when the river-bank changed its course and when someone had wreaked havoc on one of our special spots. We were always trying to find ways of being gentle to the environment, and if we saw that there was something wrong, we would be compelled to fix it. These early experiences cemented my relationship to the world of nature around me.

Emotional and intellectual connections

Moving to Brisbane and residing in an urban setting adjacent to Moreton Bay, I realised that I could easily step into a natural place and feel far away from all that was crowding in. For me this was physiological, a place to relax, de-stress and to heal body, mind and spirit. I was also building a keen appreciation of the ecological complexity of the Bay and the richness of the mangrove forests and foreshores that I wandered along. I became preoccupied with learning about the Bay in order to connect intellectually as well as emotionally from just being there. The ecological complexities of Moreton Bay continue to astound me.

Professional insights about place

Professionally too, I was redefining what teaching meant to me and what my life's work would be. I became a national park ranger who specialised in environmental and heritage interpretation, where the focus was on communicating ideas and feelings that would allow people to make meaningful connections to place. It was here that I realised the power of place, the way that it can create new challenges for people, the way it can reveal its hidden stories and open up new concepts, and the way that it inspires people to contemplate and reflect. As a ranger on an island park in Moreton Bay, I also accepted the role of protector and the chance to make a difference. Later, I began working at Moreton Bay Environmental Education Centre; knowing what it was to be a newcomer to the Bay, I sought ways to help students see beyond the surface of the blue ocean vista and open up the fascinating, hidden, and complex worlds that had been opened up to me.

Initially, my pedagogy was inspired by the people around me, other experienced staff who worked in mindful ways in place by asking students to observe closely and carefully, to slow down and to notice the minutiae. I am a loud, busy person, so this was a new way of working for me. I now recall my own challenge to slow down when I ask busy students to step out of their habit of rushing quickly to the next thing and instead to stop, crouch quietly, look and wait. Being enmeshed in the place is the most powerful tool I have in terms of transforming the way students experience Moreton Bay. I regularly see students who treat foreshores, mangroves and creek beds as foreign, alien places. When we walk into these places, squelching through water and mud and being surrounded by a twisted forest, there is an initial revulsion and disbelief that we need to be *in* it. I ask students to see with different eyes, to absorb what this place is offering on a sensory level, and to track the feelings this place engenders within them. I see them light up with interest when we reveal aspects of nature that were previously unseen or unknown. For me, reversing the disconnect between people and places by making a meaningful and emotional connection in the hearts and minds of students has become the core of why I do what I do.

Key elements of the pedagogy

Our discovery of "The Edge"[1]

What makes Moreton Bay EEC unique? This key question was the cornerstone of our pedagogical research journey that began in 2010. Over the years of research and reflection, we discovered that while we could teach great programs, we could not explicitly *express* "how" we did what we did. We collected data to find out what students preferred and we interviewed teachers who brought their classes on excursions. We talked – extensively. Finally, one discussion threw in a new concept: that of "the edge." The "edge" describes the boundaries between air and water, water and land, the borders between habitats, and the zones of comfort and challenge that students face during their excursion to the Bay. We realised we were asking students to step into a vast and unfamiliar place with no concept of what was there or how to connect with it, or that this was daunting. Our programs involved students undertaking a journey, and our task as MBEEC staff was to support them at each step as they crossed over unfamiliar edges and into an exciting new world. The effect of this metaphor in our Centre was immediate as the "edge" concept transformed our pedagogical approach, shaping our pedagogical framework, the structure of our programs and our teaching.

Our journeys across the edge – a pedagogical framework

The Bay is a place with multiple physical and metaphorical boundaries where many different human interests, histories and environments collide. As short-term visitors to the Bay, our students must cross over many edges and boundaries, some of which may not have been crossed before. This "crossing over" can be a physical sensation of stepping off the shoreline and into the water as well as a metaphorical crossing of personal edges through challenge. These edges might be boundaries within natural places, cultural sites or temporal edges that require moving across different time zones of the past, present and future.

Our curriculum encapsulated as *Learning on the edge*, involves learning in authentic places through the lens of history, science, geography, drama, and civics. The *edge* can be applied to multiple aspects of our programs as illustrated below:

- Natural edges – mangroves and foreshore
- Cultural edges – Indigenous and non-Indigenous
- Historical edges – past and present
- Intellectual edges – deep learning and reflection
- Emotional edges – fear and challenge
- Social edges – collaboratively and independently

We recognise that the journey towards becoming a "Champion for the Bay" requires students to develop a connection to this place and that, for this to happen, students will need to immerse themselves in many ways. The edges can be experienced through physical touch and the senses, intellectually and emotionally, alone or in the company of others. This immersion involves undertaking "edgy" experiences that create a dynamic atmosphere for learning where intellectual and emotional shifts can occur. This framework acknowledges that students' personal, social and cognitive growth comes from the affordances of edges and the active process of crossing and reflecting on experiences at the edges in order to become a "Champion for the Bay."

Case study: "Habitat Heroes"[2]

Our Year 1 "Habitat Heroes" program invites the young students to become "junior marine scientists" who need to explore and understand the various habitats in the Bay and what lives there. On board *Inspiration*, students explore what lies above and below the surface of the water through the use of binoculars, a sediment sample, microscopes and an underwater camera. Throughout, students build an awareness of the structure and composition of the ocean floor and the shells and animals found there.

On arrival at the shore of a sandy spit in the Bay, students squelch through the muddy intertidal zone discovering tiny, mysterious creatures scuttling into holes, poking antennae out of their shells or oozing ink within the seagrass beds and sandy habitats. With the support of teachers and accompanying parents, students wade through the wet sand and hold wriggling creatures in their hands, often for the first time, taking the greatest care not to injure the animals whilst overcoming their fear. These hermit crabs are the focus of the children's attention as they learn how to be habitat heroes for this animal. Their knowledge begins to emerge as seen in this brief comment from a year 1 student.

> Crabs have to live in wet places because that's where they get water and food.
> (Year 1 student)

Learning at the edge

"Crossing over the edge" on the excursion day, students become immersed in hands-on, multi-sensory experiences. Novelty heightens students' attentiveness to their environment. The special experience for one child was:

> Finding the little pools – I had never seen one.
>
> (Year 1 student)

Attentiveness to place can also provide new opportunities to see the world aesthetically and appreciate nature on a large and small scale. This may be as simple as a new way of "seeing" a shell or the sand:

> I like it (the shell) because it has a nice pattern of white and black, and it has a nice spiral.
>
> (Year 1 student)

> I like this shell because it looks like a brain.
>
> (Year 2 student)

Apprehension and emotion

At times this new learning is confronting and challenging. Through the feelings of apprehension or fear experienced in a new situation, students have a heightened awareness of their surroundings and are physiologically alert. This creates a learning environment of full attentiveness and deep emotion in which students confront personal edges. Many students arrive with pre-conceived ideas, often received from significant others:

> I'm actually really scared. It scares me a lot. My mum and dad told me yesterday that other crabs are really dangerous and they nip your hand off.
>
> (Year 2 student)

Others need to overcome the feeling that the Bay is a foreign and scary place. Many have never seen the hermit crabs or marine creatures, let alone been asked to hold one, despite living in the local area. Physically connecting to an alien place is an enormous personal challenge that takes great courage:

> Eeeewww, it's alive, it wriggled out! Help me, it's coming out, it's coming out!
>
> (Year 1 student)

> Something's in it! It scared me!
>
> (Year 1 student)

> It's on my hand. I can't get it off, I can't get it off! (shaking hand violently).
>
> (Year 1 student)

Their bodies indicate the fear and distaste as they hold the shell by the tip at arm's length poking out their tongues and screwing up their noses.

Yet connecting to place through emotion is an important part of "crossing over the edge". While a few children are scared, the experience is predominantly one of fun and laughter. The hermit crab tickle touches students in a very meaningful and joyful way:

> I think he's coming out. He is . . . (laughs) See? (laughs) It tickles (laughs). It's come out (laughs).
>
> (Year 1 student)

Her friend responds with equal joy:

> Is this a worm? It's ticklish too! (laughing) It's coming out! (laughs).
>
> (Year 1 student)

The emotions elicited from these new learning experiences can also provide a long-lasting connection to place once students realise that they have made a significant and positive achievement that day. In evaluating the day, one child said she felt,

> Excited because I have never picked up a hermit crab and felt it tickle me.
>
> (Year 1 student)

Full sensory engagement with and physical immersion in the surrounding environment gives students the opportunity to "be" in the environment and this external experience quickly becomes a time for high internal emotions. Walking through the mudflats elicits verbal protests:

> Oh my God! Going in deeper. Nearly pulled me over!
>
> (Year 2 student)

> Aaaagh! Eeeeeewww! How much are we going in?
>
> (Year 2 student)

> I've got water in my shoes!
>
> (Year 2 student)

But these verbal protests are few compared to the smiles, shining eyes, conversations and excited squeals that show how special this is. For the majority:

> This is awesome because we get to go through the mud with our shoes on!
>
> (Year 2 student)

This awesome experience could be simply represented as a naughty transgression of school rules, but for many students it connects them ethically to this place:

> Like, so you can feel what it feels like, and you know how to take care of animals and nature.
>
> (Year 2 student)

Understanding habitats

Whilst they investigate individual animals and cross over natural edges from deep water to beach to intertidal zone, students are gradually being introduced to the understanding of the Bay as "big space", but one in which the elements are connected. New understandings develop about the relationships between animals and their environment:

> If hermit crabs don't have water they will die.
>
> (Year 2 student)

Throughout the exploration, students, as scientists, begin to consider complex ideas such as the connectedness of nature and ecosystems:

> Because animals might not be living in the shells now but they might live in (there) later.
>
> (Year 2 student)

> I learned shells have creatures.
>
> (Year 2 student)

But when we take a handful of sand and magnify it, students suddenly discover a new, minute world:

> It's crushed up shells!
>
> (Year 2 student)

These shells, they realise, form the whole beach, which gives them a sense of the vast scale of time and natural material that is necessary to form a beach.

Decision time

Invariably, students begin to create a collection of the amazing shells and animals they have discovered and begin to question if they can keep them. For some, it is an incredibly difficult decision when it is time to move on. Through discussion with each other, students usually understand that each creature needs to go back to its habitat, where it has all the elements needed for survival. In the case of empty shells, students easily see the need for these to be left behind as homes or shelter for animals in the future. Collecting shells from the shoreline by parents and children is a common, a taken-for-granted activity at the seaside, so deciding to return that shell is a marker of new understanding and, hopefully, a new ethic of care. For most children the experience of caring is one of happiness:

Happy, so then the crabs don't die.
Really happy, I helped the crab and put it back.

Teacher:	Best thing about today?
Child:	Um, holding a hermit crab . . .'cause it was my first time.
Teacher:	How did you feel returning the shells?
Child:	Happy, so then the crabs don't die and that they just tickle a little bit, and I was really scared because I thought they were going to pinch me.

(Year 2 student)

Students reflect on the interconnections between the elements within a habitat – shells for homes, plants for food, a variety of animals and clean sea water. This cements the concept that damaging or removing any element has great effects on the whole habitat and everything within it and that we can all play a part in protecting and caring for this place.

> Well we used to collect them, but now that I know that we are not allowed to because I know they might be homes for other animals that live on the beach, so now we don't collect them anymore.

(Year 2 student)

For many, there is immense pride and a feeling of empowerment in taking action and completing the last, important act of returning the shell. These "Champions for the Bay" realise that they have the ability to be stewards for the marine environment by their own personal actions and by treating other animals and places with care and respect.

> Putting the shell back so other animals can live in it, so that's why we had to put it back.

(Year 2 student)

At this stage of the learning, the students begin to voice their concerns about the fragility and beauty of this place, and they can see the potential for humans to influence the wellbeing of this place.

> Because if the ones that have the babies get destroyed, the young ones will not be able to grow up, and there would be just no more.

(Year 2 student)

> It might be a very beautiful creature, and if there are no more of them we will be very sad.

(Year 2 student)

The snake-line – minimal impact

The concept of minimal impact is addressed at various times throughout the program, but especially and concretely when we cross over into the habitat of the hermit crabs. As a part of understanding that "every footstep counts," students engage in the "Snake Walk" as we begin to cross the edge of the intertidal zone. Students form a line behind the MBEEC teacher and begin walking, stepping in the footprints of the person in front of them with exaggerated slowness and carefulness in each step. Each person watches the ground closely as he or she walks, placing his or her feet very precisely, being careful to avoid the shelled creatures at his or her feet. Repeatedly, the snake line forms a circle to study closely items of interest and breaks back into a long, single line when we move to another site. The formation of the line and careful stepping allows students to embody carefulness, a physical response to the need to be attentive to the environment and minimise their impact.

Through this collective act of care, students are introduced to the concept that every step we take has a lasting impact on natural places. They also comprehend that they have already exhibited behaviours that embody this new understanding and connection to place:

> You have to be careful so you don't tread on animals or shells because they can be trying to live in the homes, or they could be home for other animals.
>
> (Year 2 student)

> Because if you were a hermit crab and someone stepped on your shell it would not be very nice.
>
> (Year 2 student)

By utilising place, giving time and opportunity for students to be attentive to their environment and modelling respect and care, students can synthesise their knowledge, emotions and values making it possible for them to exhibit empathy with something outside of themselves.

> We need to look after crabs because we have homes, and we can't let them not have homes because they are living creatures like us.
>
> (Year 2 student)

> Please don't not care for them. You have to care for them because they are so little and other animals might try and eat them.
>
> (Year 2 student)

Personal and community agency for the Bay

At the end of the day the students are beginning to understand that each of us can act responsibly for the wellbeing of this place, as an individual or collectively. In the student responses, we see concern and an ethic of care emerging as the students widen their intellectual understanding of the fragility of the Bay environment and the survival needs of the animals within it. The development of values around the need for the conservation of species both now and into the future begins, as does the idea of personal and community agency.

Within their reflections, students also acknowledged that while there are many ways of learning, firsthand experience in natural settings has a particular salience:

> because it might be a new experience, we didn't really know that much about the sea and it couldn't have been a better experience for what we hadn't done before.
> I Google stuff a lot and now I am going to see stuff a lot.
>
> (Year 2 student)

The final phase of the "Learning across the Edge" framework is becoming an active citizen. In the "Habitat Heroes" program, the final phase of the learning is where students are inspired to become "Champions for the Bay" by making a pledge to demonstrate future behaviours that will benefit Moreton Bay. This extends the pedagogy of place beyond simply developing abstract knowledge to a sense of personal responsibility for life in the Bay. These students recognise that they have the ability to make personal choices about their behaviour and that these could also extend to influencing others. They recognise that any action (no matter how small) helps maintain and improve the health and vitality of Moreton Bay and will have a direct impact on them and the marine life that lives along and beyond its many edges.

Most students are excited to take the pledge, feeling that this fits with the knowledge and values they have developed. They also feel that they have already taken their first steps towards this goal on the excursion day.

> Some people cannot be Hermit Crab Heroes because they leave rubbish on the beach!
>
> (Year 2 student)

> Take shells back! Put shells back on the beach!
>
> (Year 2 student)

> I have changed because now I'm feeling happy because it was fun being nice to the environment and not taking the shells.
>
> (Year 2 student)

Some will not make the pledge, but this shows that they are deeply considering the implications of taking the pledge and reviewing this against their own personal values. Choosing not to do something also shows deep, thoughtful responses.

One boy's growing awareness of his personal journey from the past and into a future "Champion for the Bay" was clear:

> Because I wasn't that intelligent when I was little but now I am getting more and I have decided to be a scientist. Like doing some research may be. Start doing research and more in my lab.
>
> (Year 2 student)

Conclusion

On the edge of a major capital city, the Moreton Bay of today is globally unique in maintaining healthy populations of dugong and turtles despite widespread urban development. Threatened by the huge floodwaters in 2011, Moreton Bay received the full force of thousands of tonnes of silt laced with pollutants cascading down the Brisbane River and into the Bay. Researchers and scientists are watching closely to see the long-term effects of the flood and continued high silt loads in the Brisbane River on Moreton Bay's complex ecosystems and the myriad forms of life they contain. A loss of seagrass due to lack of light did not result in the rapid decline of dugong populations that was expected, and the Bay's wildlife remains viable.

Of all things, Moreton Bay is adaptable and resilient; coping with the natural changes and fluctuations of its land forms, climate and catchment. But these changes are not all natural, as people have been inexorably entwined with the Bay and form an integral part of its past, present and future. People have made this place richer, with a cultural heritage stretching back over 21,000 years from the Quandamooka people to the soldiers, prisoners and residents of recent times. But the actions of people have also threatened the Bay and we continue to live with the legacy of the past as well as our present actions – pollution, erosion, over fishing, habitat destruction, lack of advocacy for cultural heritage sites and urban development.

Moreton Bay EEC and our students are closely connected with this Bay, and one of the affordances of our Centre is that students are able to experience firsthand the natural beauty of the ocean, coastline and wildlife as they physically immerse themselves within it. Spotting a dugong or turtle is a powerful and memorable moment, witnessed when students catch their breath and stare transfixed, up close with these vulnerable species. But another affordance of this Centre is that students can also realise that they are part of the continuum of human presence and interaction with the Bay. Presented with echoes of the past, students gain perspective on the adaptability of the Bay and its people as they change and adjust to natural and fabricated events. Importantly, they see that, as part of the continuum, they too are influencing this place in the present day in positive and negative ways as they go about their daily lives in and around the Bay.

Importantly, these young people come to know that they will continue to influence Moreton Bay in the future with every action and decision they make. It is our ability to know and understand this place both in the past and today, through the study of science, geography and history, that allows us to make educated choices about what our personal and societal legacy will be for Moreton Bay in the future. Further, it is by connecting to this place physically and emotionally, with our hearts as well as our minds that we can come to value the Bay and to embrace the need to care for and protect these waters through positive action as a "Champion for the Bay".

Notes

1 Belinda Daly, Eileen Mitchell and Tim Roe began the journey of pedagogical discovery for Moreton Bay EEC. The initial "Journeys across the Edge" concept began in conversations with Mark Cridland and Belinda Daly, who worked alongside the Moreton Bay team and the new principal, Dianne Aylward, to develop and embed a pedagogy that today underpins all planning, teaching and learning in our centre.
2 The "A Home for a Hermit Crab" program was originally developed by Glenda Crowther, MBEEC teacher, whose creativity encouraged a new way of thinking and working at Moreton Bay Environmental Education Centre. Her initial work has been refined over many years by Jill Praeger, Ralda Forzin and Cara Binney, and the essence of the program continues to be taught over 20 years later.

References

Barnes, R. S. K., & Hamylton, S. (2016). On the very edge: Faunal and functional responses to the interface between benthic seagrass and unvegetated sand assemblages. *Marine Ecology Progress Series, 553*, 33–48.

Connolly, R. M. (2009). Seagrass. A marine climate change impacts and adaptation report card for Australia. In E. Poloczanska, A. Hobday & A. Richardson (Eds.), *Report card of marine climate change for Australia* (pp. 1–14). Griffith University, QLD: National Climate Change Adaptation Research Facility.

EDGE. (2016). Retrieved from www.edgeofexistence.org

Moss, N. (2016). *Nicolamoss.* Retrieved from blogspot.com.au

Murcia, C. (1995). Edge effects in fragmented forests: Implications for conservation. *Tree, 10*(2), 58–62.

Neate-Clegg, M. H., Morshuis, E. C., & Banks-Leite, C. (2016). Edge effects in the avifaunal community of riparian rain-forest tracts in Tropical North Queensland. *Journal of Tropical Ecology, 32*(4), 280–289.

SEQ Catchments Ltd. (2013). *Flood impacts report 2013.* Retrieved from www.seqcatchments.com.au

Steele, J. G. (2015). *Aboriginal pathways: In Southeast Queensland and the Richmond River.* St Lucia, QLD: University of Queensland Press.

9 Place-responsive design for school settings

Ron Tooth and Peter Renshaw

Introduction

In this chapter we explore the question, How can a place-responsive pedagogy be designed in schools and regular classrooms based on the insights and practices documented by the Environmental Education Centres? We are acutely aware of the constraints that currently restrict teachers' capacity to work with students in place-responsive ways inside and outside the classroom (Lingard, Thompson, & Sellar, 2016). We noted in our introduction to this volume (Chapter 1) that the Centres, as they evolved their diverse pedagogies of place, benefitted enormously from being on the margins of the schooling system in Queensland. On the periphery they had the time and space to learn from extended professional engagement with each other. This exploratory professional space for innovation has largely evaporated in the present context of schooling where external accountability demands on teachers and principals are high (Lingard, Martino, & Rezai-Rashti, 2013). In addition, teachers are challenged by the sense of pessimism that arises from escalating ecological crises (Klein, 2015). There are no pristine natural environments in the Anthropocene Age where humans have caused mass extinctions of plant and animal species, polluted the oceans and altered the atmosphere to such a degree that ecosystems are now threatened across the whole planet (Hamilton, Gemenne, & Bonneuil, 2015). Students can be left feeling helpless and hopeless in the face of the rising tide of ecological crises (Kretz, 2013; McKinnon, 2014). How do we motivate students to be engaged and care rather than disengage and become sceptical or despondent (Kelsey & Armstrong, 2012; Ojala, 2012). This is why the work of the Centres is so important. They offer to teachers place-responsive pedagogies that have been shown to emotionally and aesthetically engage students and heighten their commitment to caring positively about the places around them. In the following sections we reflect on the key practices and insights distilled from the Centres, and we provide an example of one design process that worked effectively to transform the pedagogy used in a local school.

Designing for place-responsive teaching and learning

Storying

Storying is central to a place-responsive pedagogy. Rather than treating place as a backdrop for human activities and exploitation, storying of place situates humans in relation to the interests and values of the other living and non-living entities in place. Storying foregrounds place as the site of overlapping and unfinished stories that convey the perspectives and interests of different protagonists whether they are people, past and present, whether they are plants and animals, or whether they are the material features of the land itself that have aesthetic and ecological value. Storying is a relational process that reveals the interconnectedness of humans with the more-than-human world. In addition, storying of place can embrace the ways of knowing typical of scientists and poets and historians, as Margaret Somerville (2013) has proposed in her model of place pedagogy. She writes that "every knowledge framework, discipline and artistic modality has its own forms and genres of place stories" (Somerville, 2013, p. 12). This notion of storying invites teachers to consider how different strands of the curriculum can contribute to an integrated relationship to place. Pedagogies can be designed to engage students in different disciplinary blanket roles, for example, as an artist, or historian, or creative writer, or entomologist, or amphibian expert. Each lens provides one way of relating to place, and through scaffolded reflection on the affordances and limitations of different disciplinary lenses, students can begin to appreciate the complexity and interrelationships inherent in a place and the advantages of adopting multiple perspectives.

Connected teachers

Teachers' distinctive histories, knowledge and values are central in the design of place-responsive pedagogies. This is clear from considering the personal stories of the authors of the chapters in this volume. Each of the authors had developed a special knowledge and attachment to the places where they taught. They had a deep knowledge of the pedagogical affordances of their places, but it is important to realise that initially such affordances were not obvious. The authors recount how they learnt through experience to be acutely aware of nuanced possibilities inherent in each place for drawing out deep learning and responsiveness from students. So, place-responsive design is not merely a technical exercise of following a series of steps. It necessarily is mediated by the teachers' own sensitivity to place and commitments as a place-responsive educator. We propose, therefore, that one foundation of place-responsive design is that of the connected teacher. The notion of the connected teacher reimagines classroom teachers as inherently related to place, rather than simply passing through the place in a disinterested manner. Connected teachers have a commitment to growing their own ecological identity and their interest in local places, even if such places appear to be nondescript or ordinary. As noted in Chapter 4 place-responsive educators can see the extra in the ordinary.

Distinctive affordances of each place

As the authors of the chapters discovered through their extended professional engagement, each Centre offered a unique set of stories embedded in place. Each place held its own distinctive story but it required the expertise of the educators first to articulate the story and then design a place-responsive pedagogy that would engage students. By articulating these stories the educators could offer students unique opportunities for learning. Embedded in Karawatha (Chapter 2), for example, was primarily the story of Bernice Volz, whose actions and commitments as an environmental advocate provided a powerful way for students to relate to the ecology and history of this remarkable forest. Ron Tooth, as the primary designer of the pedagogy, had to research Bernice's advocacy as well as the features of Karawatha that made it so valuable and worth preserving. It is the authenticity of the story in place that seems so powerful to students and moves them to be so emotionally and fully engaged in the learning program. At Bunyaville (Chapter 4), the distinctive slow pedagogy of inquiry was made possible by the portal experience of suddenly exiting the fast-paced modern world and entering the calming and quiet space of the forest. The portal experience places students in a new world where extended inquiry and dwelling in the forest to experience it slowly are taken for granted. At Barambah (Chapter 5) it was the material tracks across the landscape that enabled students to understand the place through different modes of walking. Students engaged in learning through their whole bodies as they walked differently along creek beds or through thick undergrowth, or with effort up the hills. At Paluma (Chapter 6), a sense of the sacred is created by the timelessness of the rainforest sitting high in the clouds where light is refracted and reflected. In such a place, students shift easily to consider questions of spirituality and life's purpose. At Nudgee Beach (Chapter 7) time has a different rhythm from Paluma. Rather than the timelessness of the rainforest, each day at Nudgee Beach brings dramatic and constant change as the tides ebb and flow, and unpredictable coastal weather patterns require opportunistic pedagogy. Here students encounter endless change and unexpected moments of discovery when the tides reveal new secrets. At Moreton Bay (Chapter 8) the fragility, resilience and beauty of being on the edge is foregrounded. As the place where the city of Brisbane meets the Bay, it offers students multiple ways of understanding the edge – as a rich zone of life but also a place that is under threat from human activity and exploitation. Over time, these distinctive affordances were constructed by the Centre educators, as they learned what was possible to learn in each of their places. Each place held its own distinctive story but it required the expertise of the educators first to articulate the story and then design a place-responsive pedagogy that would engage students.

In summary, we propose (A) the process of storying, (B) the professional identity of the connected teacher and (C) foregrounding the distinctive affordances of specific places, as the foundations for a place-responsive pedagogy that can be designed in any school or site of learning. A number of the Centres described in this volume have worked closely with schools in collaborative projects where storying place, the connected teacher, and distinctive place affordances have been central for redesigning the school's curriculum and pedagogical practices. We turn now to describe the process used by Pullenvale Environmental Education Centre (PEEC) in these collaborative professional development projects. It provides a design template that might be useful to teachers considering change to a place-responsive approach to their everyday pedagogy.

Steps in place-responsive design

There are five main steps in the design process as outlined below. These steps are elaborated in describing a place-responsive curriculum called "following the figs" that was designed by PEEC staff in collaboration with a local city council and then trialled with a nearby school as part of a "sense of place project".

Identify the place

Deciding on the specific place for exploration and storying can be influenced both by local issues as well as the interests of teachers and students. Whatever place is chosen the design intent is to inspire children's sense of curiosity about the place and awaken their sense of agency. These places might include a school or community garden, a cluster of trees along the edge of a school oval, a nearby remnant of forest, a larger forest reserve or a remote wilderness or even a single tree within the school grounds.

Connect to the materiality of the place

A critical step in storying place is for the teachers to spend time connecting to the materiality of the place that has been chosen. This requires attentiveness to the affordances of place that will capture the interest of students. We have called these affordances "ecological hooks", that is, ordinary features of the environment that can be revealed as extraordinary when they are understood in terms of their complex inter-relationships with other features of the place. The purpose in identifying these "ecological hooks" is to create a grounding for the stories that amplifies the significance of the place and its features.

Choose a blanket role

Choosing the "blanket role" is important because this is what gives students a sense of purpose and meaning within the story as they find their own voice. For young children effective blanket roles seem to be those that mirror their curiosity and interest in play, for example, "nature detective" or "wildlife investigator". For older students effective blanket roles seem to be those where students can make a difference through their actions as part of a larger project with others, for example as "champion for the bay", or "environmental advocate", or "protector of the wetlands". It's important that the features of the blanket role are collaboratively developed with students during the storying process.

Create an engaging story linked to the place and to the blanket role

Nuanced stories of place can be based on real or fictional characters who have loved, protected or even exploited the land for different reasons. Specific sites or features located within the site (ecological hooks) are given heightened significance for the characters, and these are further elaborated within the story to engage students in episodes of inquiry or drama or thoughtfulness that expands their thinking and learning. The process of story creation evolves in response to the designers' changing experiences of a particular place until there is a sense that story and characters are complete. The goal is not to lay down any prescriptive image of the blanket role within the story but to present characters as being on their own journey of inquiry and meaning-making in the world.

Create a scripted and sequenced learning journey linked to place

Weaving the elements into a sequenced cumulative learning experience is a complex part of the design process. This sequence takes time to work out and is refined through discussion and reflection within the design team. When complete, the story of the place provides a scaffold to engage students over an extended period of time. This is what allows students to engage actively with the story and characters; participate in research, inquiry and attentiveness; step into (and out of) the story to influence the direction of events; dialogue with the characters in the story; and finally decide how they will take action to care for place.

The design process is not a neat orderly sequence but a complex interactive process

As the design team identifies the elements for students to engage with in the place, prompts in the form of ecological hooks are included in the story to ensure that this will happen. It's a matter of visiting and revisiting the place over and over the whole time the story is being written, adding new places and interactions into the story that then inform the developing excursion day script. The story and the experience of the place evolve together and are inextricably linked.

Applying the design process in a school and in a local parkland

In 2012 PEEC was commissioned by the Ipswich City Council to develop a story and excursion program for local school children that centred on a significant historical park in the city (Queens Park). A number of very old fig trees on the edge of the Park had been poisoned. These trees were treasures of the city and their deaths created waves of anger and outrage across the community. In addition after talking with archaeologists who had completed a detailed study of the park for the Indigenous custodians, the PEEC design team decided to include an Indigenous perspective within the program. Queens Park is culturally significant to the Indigenous people who were forcibly driven from the site in 1891 when the Park was gazetted. Indigenous people continue to meet and gather in the park. The program that was finally designed was called "Following the Figs."

A year later, in 2013, the principal of a local school (*referred to in this chapter as Sustain State School*) asked for assistance to address the high level of disengagement and cynicism amongst many students, especially in the last years of primary school. The teachers had been working hard to implement the new Australian curriculum yet students had little appreciation for the history and stories that made the school special. The principal explained that she wasn't looking for curriculum support but rather an alternative way of growing a strong culture of respect, care and appreciation in the school. She hoped that by adopting a place-responsive story pedagogy she could connect students with each other and their place. We named this project the Sense of Place Project. The two projects were eventually linked as part of an educational design project that resulted in unanticipated benefits for PEEC, the school and the local council. A further elaboration of each project and how the design process was applied by the PEEC design teams is provided below.

"Following the Figs"[1]

Through the design team's extended walks in Queens Park "ecological hooks" were identified and then used as a framework to create Cassie's story. The most interesting features of the park seemed to be ignored by most visitors. No one was present when the design team climbed the hill to the limestone ridge for the first time and sat under the giant fig. When they walked on the ridge under the canopies of the other figs they rarely saw anyone. Similarly, when they visited the half circle of twisted figs with their braches touching or sat in the circle of cypress trees watching people coming and going at the café, no one seemed interested in these special places. If they saw people walking through the grand avenue of figs they were usually on their way to the playground or café. The visitors didn't stop to look at the hand shape at the base of one large tree or the root at the base of another that looked like a heart. This idea of *two* parks, one obvious to most visitors and one hidden and neglected, later became central to the "Following the Figs" Program and had a profound effect on how the Sense of Place Project finally developed.

The designers wanted students to feel like they were making a difference in the world through their actions as part of a larger project, and so the blanket role was needed to embody this idea. "Story Tracker" was finally chosen as the blanket role because it captured the spirit of the Council's request for students to collect and share stories in their school and across the community. The idea grew from an interest in Aboriginal Tracking in Australia. The first recorded use of Aboriginal trackers was in 1834 in Western Australia when Mollydobbin and Mogo found a missing five-year-old boy in very rough country after ten hours of searching. In 1864, the Duff children had been lost for eight days in rough country and were found alive only after Aboriginal Trackers were brought in on the final day. The idea of tracking is an important feature of Aboriginal *songlines* which are sung as story maps that describe the key features of different places that communicate topography and special land forms through the pitch of the singer's voice. Experiences with Aboriginal people in the early years of PEEC were also influential. In 1982 I (Ron Tooth) walked in a forest with a group of Aboriginal friends. My two young sons were with me as we followed echidna tracks together along a sandy creek bank. We laughed and talked a lot that day and the vividness of the memory remains strong even today. Story Tracking, connecting to place through storying, seemed to capture exactly what the students were being asked to do as part of the "Following the Figs" project.

Cassie's story (see below) grew from the affordances of Queens Park and traces the adventures of two fictional characters: Cassie and Levi. They become best friends and together discover the secret world of Queens Park and its many hidden places. The specific features within the site (ecological hooks) were given heightened significance within the narrative by making them central to Cassie and Levi's lives. As part of the story Cassie and Levi create names for each key feature of the park to invest them with personal meaning and significance, for example, the Three Guards, Cassie's Fig, the Rock People, the Warriors, Cypress Sanctuary, the Avenue of Figs, the Hand and the Heart Root. The names were first created by the PEEC designers through prolonged engagement with the place and then woven into the story. Cassie's adventure begins with her running from a gang of bullies past the Three Guards up the hill to the giant fig tree where she finds sanctuary in its branches.

> Cassie couldn't remember the exact day when the bullying started. . . . She thought about the Aboriginal elder who had been invited to their classroom that day. . . . Cassie had never heard anyone talk about a place like that. She was so busy daydreaming she bumped straight into him (Grayson), smudging her melting ice cream right down the front of his shirt. "You idiot!" he screamed. . . . Cassie ran . . . passing three enormous trees growing closely together. . . . They seemed to steer her up a pathway . . . towards the high ridge. . . . Just ahead, an enormous fig seemed to beckon. . . . She climbed into the tree and sat down. . . . Overhead branches protected her from the afternoon sun, and a breeze blew across the park. Bliss!
>
> (Quote from Cassie's Story)

This is when she meets Levi. The story allows students to track Cassie and Levi over many weeks as they explore the park and spend hours on the limestone ridge with its twisting roots and imagine stories of fantastical creatures. Sometimes they sit in silence on the ridge and Cassie records her thoughts in her journal. Sometimes they meet in Cypress Sanctuary to watch people pass. This is where

Cassie finally confronts the bullies by refusing to hand over her journal full of precious stories and sketches. Each story moment in the excursion day is designed to provide opportunities for thoughtful reflection and inquiry where students are invited to think about why Cassie and Levi might have such a strong relationship with the park. A central device within the narrative is Cassie's recurring dream which continues to torment her with its haunting warnings and images of the heart root. The dream's hidden meaning about the possible poisoning of the trees eludes her. It's left to the students to find this out in the final moments of their excursion visit to Queens Park.

Weaving the "ecological hooks", the "story" and the "story tracker role" into a sequenced learning experience was a complex interactive process. The script included opportunities for students to use cameras to capture the fine detail of the limestone ridge, then write in their journals about their insights and feelings and create personal stories to share with others. To provide a powerful endpoint for this whole experience the heart root was chosen as the dramatic finale at the end of the excursion day when students would hear the truth about the poisoned trees and the meaning of Cassie's dream. When the draft excursions were piloted in the middle of 2013 the heart root moment at the end of the day was pivotal and brought students' emotions to a peak. "It's here. I didn't know it would be here" one boy called to his friends. Even though they all knew the story was fictional, it didn't seem to matter. The quote below from the leader's script describes this final moment which must be interpreted each time to allow the students to take control of the search.

> Let's follow the figs and discover the truth behind Cassie's dream. We're going to walk down to the "Avenue of Figs" . . . only on the roots and not touching the ground . . . "reading the roots" . . . . Walk slowly. . . . Can you see the hand? Come on down the Avenue of Figs. In Cassie's dream, as she passed by each of these trees they turned their backs. Once she reached this spot right here she felt that the giant fig tree on Cunningham's Knoll and her own fig up on the ridge were pleading and beckoning to her. She couldn't move. . . . Suddenly a strange heart shape appeared in the ground. Cassie and Levi found it. See. . . . It's here. Come here.
>
> ("Following the Figs" Script, 2013)

Foregrounding Cassie's story and the Story Tracker role gave the students even more control over their learning by encouraging them to speak freely about what they thought and felt on the day. This resulted in new levels of honesty and student voice that surprised everyone. The teachers extended this when they returned to school to continue the Sense of Place Project.

The Sense of Place Project[2]

When the Sense of Place Project began in 2013 in Sustain State School the PEEC team applied the same design process. They began with Cassie's Story, which the students loved, especially the fact that it was set in their own town and that many of the places mentioned were important to them. It prompted some of them to share their ideas about the significance of different places. They talked about the characters being real, like them, with the problems, strengths and qualities of kids living in their town. The fact that the characters lived in the same city and attended a local school allowed the students to re-imagine them as friends. They also loved the idea that they could become Story Trackers like Cassie and Levi and go on their own story hunting adventures. This also demonstrated that a pre-existing story can sometimes be used as long as the ideas it carries can be laid over or reinterpreted for a different place. This was an important insight because not all teachers have the skill or the time to create their own stories of place.

The PEEC design team walked the school grounds to identify "ecological hooks". They talked to teachers, students and support staff and listened for stories that might give them entry points for connecting students to the school in a fresh way. It's never just about deciding how a place will be used to support teaching and learning but also how educators inhabit that place and its stories and then model for students their own relationship to the place. A chance meeting with an Indigenous Teacher Aide confirmed that a number of fig trees in the school grounds had been planted years earlier in memory of some students who had been tragically killed. This was an important moment because everyone recognised the significance of this account for understanding the figs in this place. They epitomised why it was important to remember stories that had been forgotten, and why we should create new ones. It had already been decided that the line of large fig trees along the edge of the school oval would be an ideal meeting place for future activities and discussions outside the classroom. The story of the memorial Figs gave meaning to this decision. They were the ideal location for the workshops where students would explore the skills of Story Tracking.

The detailed learning sequence for the Sense of Place Project provided multiple opportunities for students to practice and refine the skill of attentiveness and grow their historical, botanical and ecological knowledge as Story Trackers. By making this role central, students became focussed on place as their primary concern, and they began expressing their own insights and views. Students' voices, agency and leadership began to emerge within their school. The Sense of Place Project was re-conceptualized as a holistic place-responsive experience where students could create and share their personal stories about the school and Queens Park as important environmental and cultural assets of the city. This fusion of ideas worked for both the school and the council.

Implementing the "Sense of Place" and "Following the Figs" projects

The PEEC team working in Sustain Sate School began the Sense of Place Project by first immersing students in drama activities linked to Cassie's Story. This helped to take them deeper into the story and to consider what they thought a successful Story Tracker might be like, how they might think, feel and behave. The qualities they identified were further developed through a series of workshops delivered by the PEEC team – *Attentiveness and Deep Listening in Nature, The Secret Life of Figs, Biodiversity Walks, Bush Foods and Indigenous Visons of the Land.* The success of these workshops depended on the teachers building a strong bond of trust with the students because initially some students were resistant to becoming involved. It was attentiveness that created opportunities for trust to grow.

> They were quite challenging children because (some) had come from some very difficult backgrounds, and they'd had a lot of adults do the wrong thing by them, so it took a long time for them to trust me. I noticed the biggest change when I took (the class) outside for the first time. I had chosen a tree after visiting the school many times. I chose this tree knowing I wanted the students to choose their own so they could connect with it as an ecological hook. I found it was through the attentiveness that I got to bond with the kids walking to and from the classroom, strangely enough, in those transitions when kids have a private conversation. Through the peace and quiet of attentiveness something in them just changed.
>
> (Personal communication, PEEC teacher who observed the first excursion)

The design team invited students to re-imagine their place like Cassie had done and to come with them on a journey of exploration and investigation into the school history and grounds, taking into account the figs planted in memory of the students who had died by giving special attention to the line of figs along the edge of the oval. These figs had been chosen as an ideal outdoor classroom because the students had responded so positively to them during the attentiveness sessions. A visiting botanist worked with the students and added to their understanding of why these trees were important and worthy of closer study.

> There were two sets of Figs in the school. One set were planted as a memorial for three children who died. The others the kids hooked into and loved because of the story of Cassie and Levi and the Figs of Queens Park. They wanted to get to know these Figs. Just like the relationship Cassie and Levi had. They got a kick out of climbing them because there' s not that freedom anymore so their teacher was very wise in allowing that to happen and of course she was safe about it and it opened up another element for them.
>
> (Personal communication, PEEC teacher who observed the first excursion)

As the workshops were implemented their teachers began to comment that the students were becoming more attuned to the fine details, patterns and changing moods of the figs and to the living creatures that visited them. Their view of the school grounds, and in some cases the school itself, began to change. They were invited to record their feelings and insights in personal journals, which became very important to them, even to the point that teachers and parents were commenting about their attachment. Students started to talk about their enthusiasm for the upcoming excursion to Queens Park where they would work as Story Trackers beyond the school as they followed in the footsteps of Cassie and Levi.

The excursions were enthusiastically received by the students and were a critical step in allowing them to fully engage with the Story Tracker role. The teachers credited this success to the highly skilled preparation at school by the PEEC teachers and to the enthusiasm and knowledge of the PEEC teacher who ran each of the excursions. Halfway through the first excursion she showed how responsive she was to the students by seamlessly incorporating a powerful meta-idea that had unexpectedly emerged during a discussion. The group had been quietly resting in the shade of Cypress Sanctuary watching people pass by when one boy commented that it was as if they were invisible and couldn't be seen. A rush of excitement moved through the group. Everyone became animated. The teacher grasped this moment. Maybe it was because they weren't Story Trackers and didn't have the skills to see the secret world of Cassie and Levi. Yes! This powerful idea of the "two parks" needed to be made more explicit and become the guiding idea on the day. The script was edited and this idea became central to all the excursions that followed.

> Something that not many people know is that there are actually two parks here overlaid one on top of the other – the Queens Park we all know and love and the "other", "secret" Queens Park that Cassie and Levi discovered. That is the Queens Park we want to discover today, the park where the stories lie, because you see the stories are here, waiting, you just need to find them!
>
> ("Following the Figs" Script, 2013)

What if there are two Sustain State Schools, just like in Queens Park, one obvious and the other hidden? Teachers talked to students about who would be best suited to find, uncover and record such hidden stories. As Story Trackers the students had an important role to play in finding the other Sustain State School. This idea transformed the Sense of Place Project. It was when all the previous work came together in a revitalized way and the students entered into the Sense of Place Project with a new enthusiasm and a much deeper commitment. Even those few students who had been hovering on the edge for weeks and were resistant became more involved and started to talk openly about why they wanted to become involved. A new level of honesty and trust between students and teachers emerged, mediated by the Story Tracking experience of place. Teachers reported that the students seemed calmer and more emotionally engaged when working as Story Trackers. From this point on the students searched for the lost stories of the Other Sustain State School as well stories as yet untold.

> They really hooked into the two levels of Queens Park and they loved that they had found that other dimension and they are beginning to find that here (at school) and I think there are heaps of stories here that haven't been tracked yet and there are heaps of opportunities.
>
> (Personal communication classroom teacher)

This whole two-year project culminated with celebrations, a film and an arts project shared with the school community. The students were clearly moved and expressed their experiences through presentations, displays, discussions, their personal journals and during individual interviews.

Reflecting on the legacy of this two-year project there are two key insights about place pedagogy in a school context. The first relates to the pivotal role played by a school leader. There are always difficulties associated with introducing innovation into a school, not the least being the many competing forces and pressures on the principal and teachers. In the case of Sustain State School the principal's positive mindset and support was critical, as was her decision not to force the change but to make teacher participation voluntary. This was a courageous choice that placed her in a vulnerable and risky position. The second insight relates to the necessity of quickly demonstrating to participating teachers how an innovation will benefit their students. Teachers are very pragmatic, and if they can't see how a new idea will be good for their students, they soon lose interest. What allowed the teachers at Sustain State School to persevere and move forward with confidence was the positive changes they saw in their students very early on. One teacher reported that something quite amazing was happening, especially with the reluctant learners, and this gave her the will to continue. This change motivated her to take on extra work and to make the difficult decision about what to keep and what to discard from her curriculum planning because she couldn't do everything.

Evidence of change

> There's been a transfer into the classroom, definitely . . . across the board.
> —Personal communication, Helen

At the end of the "Sense of Place" and "Following the Figs" projects, Helen, the lead classroom teacher, was interviewed and invited to reflect on changes that had occurred during and after the projects. In parallel, students from the participating classes were interviewed so that their perspectives and experiences could be considered.

Six different themes are elaborated below. The interviews revealed changes in students' peer relationships at school, their sense of themselves, and their engagement in learning at school. This suggests that place-responsive pedagogy can create a relational and connected way of learning that has longer-term effects on students' motivation to engage with the educational process.

A growing cohesion among students

The first area of change was in the growth of "cohesion among students". What intrigued Helen was the "buzz" that enlivened the whole class and created levels of engagement that continued for the whole life of the project. She'd been trying to improve relationships within the class and she was surprised by how success-fully this was being achieved through the application of the narrative pedagogy.

> The kids have changed and grown . . . it's been amazing. Class cohesion . . .
> has been something that has grown phenomenally. Kids have been working
> with kids that they would never have probably talked to within the class. . . .
> There's just been such a buzz of excitement over the whole project and
> I think that has been the impact.
>
> (Personal communication, Helen)

Helen's account is mirrored in the comments of the student below who seems genuinely surprised by what has happened to him. He is struck by the fact that he's no longer acting like he "usually" does but is now focusing on the talents of others rather than on what annoys him. Considering that he was known for his dismissive attitude to his classmates, this is a remarkable declaration.

> I have, instead of usually finding people weird, like he's gross and stuff
> I actually see things that they are good at and I usually become friends with
> them instead of thinking go away you are weird and everybody else thinks
> they are weird but actually I want to be as much of a friend as I can to them.
> Because I start to notice their talents . . . and I notice that there's nothing
> actually bad about them.
>
> (Year 7 Student)

An expanded vision of the self

A second major area of change was the way that students developed an expanded vision of themselves and their relationship to the wider world. This resonated with Helen's own values and beliefs about what good education should be. She wanted her students to think in more relational ways, to see themselves as valu-able with the power to bring about change in their own lives. This was particu-larly cogent for Helen because many of her students were from disadvantaged families where powerlessness was close to the surface. She longed for her students to discover their own agency and to see their own value and she was excited that the project was now helping her achieve this.

> I think that it's helping kids see that they are part of a whole huge picture
> of an ever changing planet and that's the super bit and that's how I would
> explain storythread to somebody else. . . . As helping kids see . . . that the
> world's not all about them . . . these days it's too much about them and not
> about how they fit into the bigger picture, and I think some of our kids hun-ger for power . . . some kids are fairly powerless because of circumstances and
> I think using storythread can help them see how valuable they are.
>
> (Personal communication, Helen)

In the words that follow this young boy expresses a similar idea. He acknowledges that the whole experience has allowed him to express his "true self" and move past just "acting cool" in order to gain friendship. You sense that he is surprised and even shocked by the simplicity of this idea. His view of himself has shifted and is now more relational.

> Yes. I have sort of expressed my true self in this experience because I used to . . . try to act all cool and stuff to get everybody to like me and that didn't always work out great and stuff and now because of this experience I have stopped acting all cool and acted how I would normally act at home around my friends and now I have gained even more friends.
>
> (Year 7 Student)

Creating curriculum knowledge connected to place

A third area of change was the shift in Helen's thinking about how to handle priorities in a crowded curriculum. She had been forced to curtail and even omit some curriculum areas due to limited time. This required negotiation with her principal who, while very supportive, was also constrained by systemic expectations and the push to measure and raise standards. The principal and the teacher took a significant risk in continuing with the project. but what kept them involved was the obvious positive impact on the students. This is what finally allowed the teacher to let go of her "planned science" lessons and replace them with this more embodied approach that hooked the students into science in a new way.

> We didn't finish some of the (planned) science . . . but there has been all the learning, the trees, and all the botany they've done and the classification they've loved, they've thrived on the scientific names of things. Instead of saying Fig they would say oh I'm going out to look at my Ficus Microcarpa which was just so important, they loved it. They've thrived on this science.
>
> (Helen, Personal communication)

In the following description a student contrasts the inactivity of sitting cramped on a seat inside a classroom with the activity and pleasure of being outside enjoying the breeze. It suggests that he has moved through a personal transition and even revelation that is allowing him to think very differently about school.

> The fact that it wasn't just inside it was also outside and we were moving around and we saw different things in real life not just on a board, . . . actually I was more interested and I was much more interested. A nice relaxed sort of feeling because you weren't just sitting down with a cramp in your back and there was a nice breeze going and you really felt like you could listen and participate easier because it was much more relaxing outside rather than inside.
>
> (Year 7 Student)

Another student identifies outdoor learning as a key factor that has allowed him to see the potential inside him that he'd never realized before.

> That there is more in me than I thought there ever was. To explore nature instead of sitting inside doing nothing, I liked going outside and doing more now.
>
> (Year 7 Student)

Growing character as engaged learners

The fourth area of change relates to the way students began to take on responsibility for their own learning. As Helen notes below, they began to work outside school hours to finish mandated work because they were so invested in the Story Tracker role and their place work with PEEC.

> To fit everything in . . . has been time consuming. I have really worked to get through all we had to get through [and] they have pitched in and really put their noses to the grind stone. They've worked in their own time . . . in lunch times. A couple of kids had a very big piece of English . . . those kids have worked lunch hour after lunch hour to get that finished . . . so character traits . . . I think this is very much about people more than it is about – say maths. The character development and the persistence in finishing off the task. I've seen that happen in child after child after child so that when we come back up to the room we are calm.
>
> (Helen, Personal communication)

The following student articulates how engagement happened for him. He demonstrates a remarkable level of meta-cognitive awareness as he links being involved in activities to levels of participation and enjoyment. This enables ideas to stay in his head rather than being "flushed out", which in his mind is what changed him.

> Because of the activities it has made me want to participate because they are enjoyable and once I participate and we start learning stuff I actually let that sink in and because it was an activity and it wasn't just sitting down learning and boring stuff it was actually enthusiastic and getting out there and because of that it has actually allowed me to keep it in my head rather than just let it flush out and . . . while it is in my head it actually changes me because of it staying in there.
>
> (Year 7 Student)

An expansive view of story that engages students beyond the "here and now"

A fifth area of change was the way that story was reframed in Helen's thinking as something more than just reading a narrative or telling a story. Helen had always loved using story to enliven her pedagogy, but after her involvement in the projects she realised that *storythread* places students into a "bigger narrative" where they became part of "living stories" that endure beyond the classroom.

> I love story, I love stories, my children love stories, I read to them religiously for fifteen minutes a day . . . and I think that strong sense of narrative . . . you have called storythread. It's the being part of a story and being part of a bigger narrative that's not just about someone telling a story, it's living the story and being part of that, part of that journey. It's you being imbedded in the story and how you can impact the story and can change the story by what you might say and what you might do and how you might think the way you might act and react to others.
>
> (Helen, Personal communication)

In the following comments we see a student's epiphany as they consider the idea that story is everywhere even in the most familiar and ordinary of objects and places.

> Basically everything, every single piece of grass to the biggest tree has its own story in, some kind of way and the plants as well and I guess the school buildings have a story as well.
>
> (Year 7 Student)

Creating voice and agency through the blanket role

A final area of change was in Helen's thinking about the efficacy and usefulness of the blanket role as a transformative teaching device. Early on she had been sceptical about the blanket role, but as students began to engage she changed her mind. The Story Tracker blanket role had given students a sense of their own agency as story weavers, and she found the impact on them "quite amazing".

> I think . . . helping them see that they are part of the whole process of being . . . part of the story and they are story weavers and story trackers who are part of weaving that whole tapestry of what life is going to be like on the planet in twenty years time. I really see that it's encouraging kids to take more of an interest in the actual world. . . . When I look at what the kids have created particularly in their writing it really does make my heart sing to see what they have been able to bring forward in terms of their writing. Absolutely amazing.
>
> (Helen, Personal communication)

Enthusiasm for the blanket role is evident in the following accounts from two students. The first foregrounds how the blanket role can inspire students to create personal knowledge through direct experience. The second highlights how the blanket role can support students in constructing a very personal vision of themselves as learners. The blanket role allows students to become active agents in constructing how they want to be and how they want to engage with the world around them.

> You should really try this, because it is a great opportunity to learn how to be a Story Tracker and a Story Tracker allows you to learn more and not only does it give you knowledge about stories but about . . . the names of trees and you pay more attention and you become a better student.
>
> (Year 7 Student)

> Everybody has the potential to be one and this opportunity allows the Story Tracker to become free and allows them to express their true self and improve their skills and be a much better Story Tracker in the future.
>
> (Year 7 Student)

Conclusion

In this chapter we have explored the question, How can a place-responsive pedagogy be designed in schools and regular classrooms based on the insights and practices documented by the Environmental Education Centres? We presented the place-responsive design steps used by Pullenvale Environmental Education Centre (PEEC) based on the three design principles of storying, connected teacher and distinctive affordances of place. The diverse place pedagogies presented in this book offer other lenses that can be used to implement the design process in different ways. The slow pedagogy of Bunyaville, for example, can be used to take learning to deeper levels of connection; the opportunistic pedagogy of Nudgee can be used to focus on the unexpected, personal and immediate; the walking-talking pedagogy of Barambah highlights how transitions between sites can be used to dialogue and develop relationships with each other and place; the sacred pedagogy of Paluma can be used to focus on the beauty and the aesthetics of life in any place; and the edge pedagogy of Moreton Bay highlights the importance of exploring edges where natural and human systems interact and where competing interests collide. Each of these lenses offers schools a way of thinking about place and provides an entry point for applying the design process.

Place-responsive pedagogy pushes against the grain of the current neo-liberal educational policy. The demands of a competitive and performance-oriented system of education and the escalating ecological crises can overwhelm even the most committed teachers. These constraints of performance pressure and despair about sustainability could have blocked the place-responsive pedagogy developed at Sustain State School. Overcrowded curriculum and performance pressures are the realities of contemporary schooling, and any reform agenda will have to face them. This is why the stories of change presented in this chapter offer hope because they show that when school leaders and committed teachers push ahead and take the risks then transformative change is possible. In this age of environmental degradation we can be left with a feeling of helplessness and despair. What we have presented in each of the chapters in this book are stories of hope where committed teachers have worked for many years to engage students emotionally and aesthetically with the living places around them.

Notes

1 The Design Team for "Following the Figs" was Madelaine Winstanley, Tonia Pickering and Ron Tooth. Madelaine Winstanley led the project, wrote all the resource materials and delivered the Queens Park excursions. Tonia Pickering authored Cassie's Story and collaborated with Madelaine in its editing.
2 The Design Team for the Sense of Place Project was Kate McGoldrick, Karl Fagermo, Daniel Rekdahl and Ron Tooth. Kate McGoldrick led the project and delivered story and attentiveness workshops. Karl Fagermo delivered ecological and attentiveness workshops with Daniel Rekdahl.

References

Hamilton, C., Gemenne, F., & Bonneuil, C. (Eds.) (2015). *The anthropocene and the global environmental crisis: Rethinking modernity in a new epoch.* London: Routledge.

Kelsey, E., & Armstrong, C. (2012). Finding hope in a world of environmental catastrophe. In A. Wals & P. Corcoran (Eds.), *Learning for sustainability in times of accelerating change* (pp. 187–200). Wageningen: Wageningen Academic Publishers.

Klein, N. (2015). *This changes everything: Capitalism vs. the climate.* New York: Simon and Schuster.

Kretz, L. (2013). Hope in environmental philosophy. *Journal of Agricultural and Environmental Ethics, 26*(5), 925–944.

Lingard, B., Martino, W., & Rezai-Rashti, G. (2013). Testing regimes, accountabilities and education policy: Commensurate global and national developments. *Journal of Education Policy, 28*(5), 539–556.

Lingard, R., Thompson, G., & Sellar, S. (2016). *National testing in schools: An Australian assessment.* London: Routledge.

McKinnon, C. (2014). Climate change: Against despair. *Ethics & the Environment, 19*(1), 31–48.

Ojala, M. (2012). Regulating worry, promoting hope: How do children, adolescents, and young adults cope with climate change? *International Journal of Environmental Science Education, 7,* 537–561.

Somerville, M. (2013). *Water in a dry place: Place-learning through art and story.* London: Routledge.

10 Environmental educators learning and theorizing place-responsive pedagogy

Robert B. Stevenson and Gregory A. Smith

Introduction

We are particularly pleased, owing to our different connections to the history and focus of this book, to have been invited to contribute this chapter of commentary on the previous chapters. As a seconded teacher and later a curriculum officer in the then Curriculum Branch of the Queensland Department of Education, the first author (Bob) was involved from 1975 in providing curriculum support to the first two Environmental Education Centres (EECs) in Queensland, as well as to schools through several EE curriculum and professional development projects. Thus, he is able to offer a historical perspective on the Centres from their formation. The second author (Greg) has a long history of writing and research on the practice of place- and community-based education using local knowledge, phenomena, and experience as the foundation for teaching and learning and connecting students more firmly to their own communities. As well, we both had the opportunity in the mid-1980s to work as educational researchers on different national projects for several years while undertaking PhDs at the University of Wisconsin-Madison. Our research experiences in these projects alerted us to the value of the kind of case studies and rich contextualized narratives in this volume for revealing the potential and challenges of innovative educational processes and the meanings attributed to them by the participating teachers and students. Like the educators in the previous chapters, we also share a deep commitment to engaging and preparing young people to participate in the shaping of a more sustainable and just society.

In this chapter we examine five features of the diverse pedagogies of place discussed in the preceding chapters. First, Bob traces the historical evolution of the professional development role of the EECs for visiting teachers and the professional learning contexts in which the pedagogical approaches of the Centre educators evolved. Next, Bob examines the influences that shaped the emergence of the place-responsive pedagogies and illuminates their distinctive characteristics by drawing on the concepts of pedagogical content knowledge and the professional, personal and political dimensions of teachers' work. Finally, informed by the literature on professional communities of practice, the significance is analyzed of a strong professional learning community among a core group of Centre educators/principals in shaping powerful learning about pedagogies of place. Following on, Greg turns to highlighting the book's diverse pedagogies and their contribution and potential to be transferable to other outdoor settings. These pedagogies and their contributions to the literature are also analysed by drawing on Gruenewald's (now Greenwood) (2003) concepts of decolonisation and reinhabitation in place-based environmental education. Greg then examines the similarities and differences between the processes of development, governance and pedagogical approaches to other international contexts (e.g., Great Lakes Stewardship Initiative). Finally, we jointly discuss how the pedagogies described might be used in schools and their local communities.

Historical evolution and focus of field study/ environmental education centers in Queensland

In Chapter 1 the editors describe the development, beginning in the mid-1970s, of a network of EECs (then called field study centres) by the Queensland Department of Education to enable schools to bring students for outdoor learning about (initially) the natural environment and human relationships with it. Besides the benefits for students, this network was also established in recognition of a need to demonstrate the value of field study areas for environmental teaching and learning and to encourage teachers to engage their students in outdoor environmental education. This need arose first from the obvious fact that school-based teachers spend far more time with students than the Centre educators. Second was the observation that many teachers lacked the confidence to engage their students in pedagogical activities outside the classroom, even within their immediate school grounds let alone in the local area and community surrounding the school. Thus, professional development of teachers was part of the rationale for the establishment of the Centres and seen as an important component of their function.

Professional learning opportunities for teachers about outdoor environmental pedagogy have included resource materials, formal experience-based workshops at Centres, informal observations and discussions as well as, more recently, collaborative curriculum planning with Centre educators. The initial two Centres established in 1975 were supported by a project, coordinated by the first author, which involved developing materials for primary/elementary teachers intending to take their classes to either of these Centres. The intent was twofold: (i) to integrate the Centre visit with the school-based curriculum and outdoor learning activities; and (ii) to complement and support the demonstration of approaches to outdoor nature-based learning observed by teachers when taking their class to the Centres.

Owing to the predominant use of these Centres by primary schools and an apparent greater demand from primary teachers for assistance in conducting field studies, the project focused exclusively on addressing primary teachers' needs. The selected approach was to develop teacher workshop kits for each centre that individual teachers could selectively work through in their own time and at their own pace. The materials included a series of introductory field study activities that could be undertaken in the biophysical environment of any school grounds or local park and designed for teachers lacking outdoor pedagogical skills and/ or confidence to develop their students' multi-sensory observational skills and basic ecological understandings. This approach was constructed to be consistent with the exploration of natural environments that was the focus of the first two Centres. Subsequently, a more diverse range of environments was identified for locating Centres, including human-modified rural agricultural and urban built environments, while secondary schools began participating in many Centres. More diverse approaches to teacher professional development also have been enacted.

The effort to integrate a Centre "destination excursion" or "environmental encounter" with learning at school through prior preparation pre- and post-visit activities has not only been continued but greatly expanded over the past four decades in scope, conceptualization and practice. Approaches vary, often by necessity of location. For example, in some Centres, particularly in urban or sub-urban areas where travel distances are not too demanding, teachers are required to attend an after-school interactive workshop before visiting with their students. Centre educators also conduct follow-up visits to schools to work collaboratively with teachers on furthering the development of students' understanding of concepts and ideas introduced during the excursion. For example, in some schools Pullenvale EEC has worked in partnership with teachers on curriculum plans in a mutual learning process of the best ways to support the development of students' understanding of their relationship to their local natural and human environment.

In sum, while maintaining a focus on a professional development role in assisting teachers, the EECs have evolved not only in the scope and variety of approaches to this task through pre- and post-school visit activities, but in their understanding and conception of teacher learning. In particular, their thinking and practice has moved beyond traditional knowledge dissemination forms to recognizing the powerful learning opportunities of working with (rather than on) teachers in school-embedded activities such as collaborative curriculum planning. At the same time, the EEC educators' own professional learning also has evolved through multiple influences to which our attention now turns.

Professional learning and evolution of diverse pedagogies of place

The Centres initially were staffed with teachers with some interest and/or expertise in outdoor learning or field studies. As the number of Centres rapidly increased, the need to further develop the environmental education and ecological systems knowledge and outdoor pedagogical skills of newly appointed staff was recognised. A five-week full-time induction program was developed and conducted by personnel in the Department for this purpose, although funding support was withdrawn after two years. Subsequently, besides later funding for a bi-annual professional meeting of Centre staff for a number of years, principals and teachers in the Centres were largely left to direct their own professional learning. The preceding chapters illustrate how successful they have been in this endeavour and discuss practices in keeping with literature that began emerging in the 1990s on teacher agency and learning that occurs in professional communities of practice (Cochran-Smith & Lytle, 1999) that we later examine.

It is informative first to examine the various influences that shaped the development of the sophisticated pedagogies of place detailed in this volume. Four major influences are evident. First, the autonomy and support they enjoyed from their employing policy authority, the State Department of Education. As noted in the editors' introduction to this volume (Chapter 1), the Centres, in developing their diverse pedagogies of place, "benefitted enormously from being on the margins of the schooling system in Queensland." During the first decade, two individuals within the unit that then was administratively responsible for the Centres, Jack Althaus and Lee Williams, played a prominent role in encouraging and supporting the educators at each Centre to experiment and develop their own teaching approaches that were appropriate to the unique environments surrounding their Centre and, of course, to the classes that came to experience and learn about these environments. This allowed a freedom to experiment without worrying about being held accountable if some methods did not work well. Norms of experimentation (and collaboration) have been identified as an important characteristic of successful schools (Little, 1982).

Second, in Chapter 1 the influence on the previous authors is described concerning the learning opportunities that arose from a series of visits to Australia from the early 1980s through the early 2000s by four prominent American environmental education educators and writers. Stapp, who visited several times from the early 1980s to 1995, was a key author of the broadened concept of environmental education and its emergence from the narrower concept of conservation education. The work of three of these visitors (Knapp and Van Matre during the 1990s and Thomashow in 2002) focused on the importance of direct experiences in nature, with Knapp advocating the notion of the power of silence and solitude in connecting to nature, while Van Matre emphasized not only knowledge of ecological systems but also the cultivation of an emotional attachment to the natural environment. Thomashow (1996) offered a broader and more sophisticated argument concerning the development of an ecological identity as a basis for accepting personal responsibility and working in the community for ecological ways of living. Each of these educators' ideas contributed to an emerging concern for a focus on the development of students' identity in relation to the natural environment.

A third phase of influence began with Ballantyne and Packer's (2008; 2009) research reports on the EECs which suggested that they were engaged in a so-called "fifth pedagogy" (beyond the four *Productive Pedagogies* framework of "intellectual quality", "connectedness", "social support" and "valuing diversity and active citizenship" described in Ch. 1). Described as "experience-based learning" and "teaching and learning through direct experience in authentic settings and places," this pedagogy was contrasted with classroom-based teaching and learning. This research apparently had two important influences on the Centres: first, it redefined them as important "centres of pedagogy," and more specifically, a pedagogies of place discourse emerged; second, as described in Chapter 1, it created recognition within the education bureaucracy of the significant contribution the Centres were making to student engagement and learning, which led to more staff and more resources for them.

The fourth phase, under the auspices of a subsequent Australian Research Council (ARC) Linkage research project, developed a more in-depth understanding of the EEC educators' pedagogy beyond the notion of a fifth pedagogy. Five key aspects of this fifth pedagogy were identified by Ballantyne and Packer (2008) as learning by doing, being in the environment, addressing authentic tasks, cultivating sensory engagement, and exploring local problems and issues. The focus and emphasis on these and other dimensions of pedagogies of place vary across the previous chapters. On the other hand, there are some common characteristics that reveal a conceptual and practical depth beyond the above descriptions of a fifth pedagogy.

The characteristics of the EEC's pedagogies of place: beyond a fifth pedagogy

Lee Shulman (1986) introduced the concept that teacher expertise demanded not only subject matter (content) knowledge and general knowledge of teaching or instructional methods (pedagogical knowledge), but also *pedagogical content* knowledge. "*In Shulman's view, pedagogical content knowledge is a form of practical knowledge that is used by teachers to guide their actions in highly contextualized classroom settings*" (Rowan et al., 2001, p. 2). He argued that this practical knowledge includes understanding "the complex ways teachers think about representing and formulating how particular content should be taught" (Shulman, 1986, p. 9). Central to pedagogical content knowledge is the manner in which teachers "transform" their subject matter knowledge to make it comprehensible or accessible to learners (Shulman, 1986). This transformation

> occurs as the teacher critically reflects on and interprets the subject matter; finds multiple ways to represent the information as analogies, metaphors, examples, problems, demonstrations, and/or classroom activities; adapts the material to students' developmental levels and abilities, gender, prior knowledge, and misconceptions (. . .); and finally tailors the material to those specific individual or groups of students to whom the information will be taught.
> (Cochran, DeRuiter & King, 1993, p. 264)

Shulman's model was later extended by Cochran, DeRuiter, and King (1993) to what they argued was more consistent with a constructivist perspective on teaching and learning. These authors described a model of pedagogical content knowledge that integrates two other forms of knowledge (besides content and pedagogical knowledge). One is teachers' knowledge of students' abilities, developmental levels, prior knowledge of concepts being taught, learning strategies and motivations (Cochran, 1997). The other component contributing to pedagogical content knowledge is "teachers' understanding of the social, political, cultural and physical environments in which students are asked to learn" (Cochran, 1997).

This second component, although referring to the broader contexts in which schooling is embedded, speaks to two key elements of EEC educators' pedagogical content knowledge that is illuminated in their narratives, namely their deep knowledge of the cultural and biophysical environments or places in which they work directly with students. Central to their pedagogical content knowledge is the manner in which these educators transform their intimate knowledge of place. As pointed out by the editors in Chapter 1, "place-responsive pedagogies require that educators have an intimate knowledge of the ecology and history of the place" (p. 10). This form of content knowledge is interrelated not only with pedagogical knowledge, captured by the description of a fifth pedagogy, but also importantly with pedagogical content knowledge that is identified in the completion of the above sentence: "this includes an acute awareness of the pedagogical affordances of specific sites within the Centre (forest or creek or tree or track)." Centre educators' descriptions of their interactions with visiting students reveal how such sites are skillfully employed. For example, at Bunyaville EEC, Noeleen Rowntree (Ch. 4) describes how they blend their understanding of systems thinking and its application to the complex patterns and connections among the parts of the forest, with a process of slow pedagogy and a (non-linear) experience-reflection-representation cycle to engage students in sharing, questioning and inquiring into their discoveries of specific inhabitants of the forest (e.g., a leaf or insect). This led to students' comments articulating "the parts as necessary to the functioning of the whole forest" (p. 78). Underpinning this pedagogical content knowledge that links together deep content and pedagogical knowledge is a view of place as a dynamic socially constructed site of "negotiation between related unfolding stories" (Ch. 1, p. 3).

The fifth pedagogy, as developed by Ballantyne and Packer (2006), does not situate experiential learning within teachers' knowledge frameworks. However, I would argue that the diverse pedagogies of place in this volume add an elaborated concept of pedagogical content knowledge to the literature in terms of outdoor experience-based environmental education teaching. That concept is a knowledge and understanding of "the unique affordances of particular places for learning about, in and for the environment" and as further elaborated by the editors, this knowledge involves the intersection of three dimensions of place:

1 the materiality of place itself, its unpredictability and its unique patterning of inanimate objects, natural features and animate beings;
2 the cultural meanings that have been storied into the place by Indigenous & non-Indigenous people, including the educators at each Centre; and
3 the agency of teachers, students & parents, whose purposes and goals selectively foreground and background what can be experienced and learned in place.

(Ch. 1, p. 4)

The editors' and some authors' discourse consistently refers to place-responsive pedagogy rather than the more common discourse in both the literature and practice of place-based pedagogy or education. When place-responsive is discussed in the literature it is often used interchangeably with place-based. However, in recent years some scholars have introduced an important distinction between the two concepts. Place-responsive pedagogy has been defined as "explicit teaching by-means-of-an-environment with the aim of understanding and improving human-environment relations" (Mannion, Fenwick, & Lynch, 2013, p. 803). From that perspective, the core process of working with teachers and students is both pedagogically and ontologically linked. According to Karrow and Fazio (2010), most conceptions of place-based education lack this ontological understanding and therefore can be distinguished from place-responsive education and pedagogy. On the other hand, Gruenewald/Greenwood's (2003) linking of critical pedagogy and place-based education is not only consistent with the above conception of place-responsive pedagogy but adds two specific and important concepts concerning human-environment relationships of decolonisation and reinhabitation (as discussed later in this chapter). Although not all authors refer to place-responsive pedagogy, the characterization of their pedagogy is consistent with Mannion's conceptualization of place-responsive.

The above definition of place-responsive pedagogy also relates to the concept of three dimensions of teachers' inquiry and pedagogy as embracing the professional, the personal and the political (Noffke, 1997). The professional dimension includes teachers' knowledge (content, pedagogical and pedagogical content); "*the personal dimension highlights feelings of self-awareness; and the political addresses democratic educational agendas for*" social change (Noffke, 1997, p. 322). As Noffke argued in the case for action research, the representations and "*manifestations of the professional, personal, and political dimensions in*" educators' "*work can provide a useful framework from which to view*" diverse place-responsive pedagogies in diverse places (Noffke, 1997, p. 321).

Most place-based education focuses only on the professional and/or personal dimensions of teachers' work, that is, the curriculum and pedagogical knowledge and skills and self-awareness for enacting such education. Yet the versions of place-responsive or experience-based pedagogy described in this volume "*have professional, personal, and political dimensions,* [although] *some are more fully articulated, emphasizing different things in different ways*" (Noffke, 1997) in different places. For example, pedagogy as advocacy (Ch. 2) is an explicitly political statement of the author's view of the ends of their EEC's work, as is the "Inspiring Champions for the Bay" approach at Moreton Bay EEC (Ch. 8) where students are encouraged to model their future behavior as adults on environmental champions of the past. At both Pullenvale and Nudgee Beach EECs students are introduced to the work of local environmental activists who have played significant roles in protecting land of ecological and cultural history values from development. Meanwhile, the pedagogy at other Centres, such as Bunyaville, Bururumbah and Paluma, is not explicitly political, but implicitly addresses the political through exposing students to alternative (to the dominant anthropocentric) world views and questioning and critiquing traditional understandings of culture, environment and consumption economics. As these examples indicate, the EEC educators in this volume describe teaching that reaches beyond the traditional realm of teachers' work into broader environmental and cultural issues.

The focus on local interests, collaboration with and within communities and across disciplines, and on the need for an ethic of care towards and action for environmental protection and improvement is a distinctive element of the EECs. The EEC educators also reveal a distinctive way of knowing about teaching and learning in the natural environment. The chapters identify a positioning of teachers as knowledge producers with linkages, as just argued, to social change. Rather than external actors developing or changing teachers through staff development, the focus at the EECs has been on their educators' agency and own production of knowledge and theorizing about teaching in and for place.

Finally, and most significantly, especially from the perspective of transferability to other settings, is the powerful learning that emerged from professional learning communities that were established over the years. This warrants a separate section to examine the concept, functioning and conditions of these communities.

The evolution of a professional learning community of practice

From the late 1970s through the 1980s there was a core group of Centre principals (then termed "officers-in-charge") who recognized they shared a common sense of purpose and passion, to the point of feeling part of a movement, "for raising consciousness amongst students and the community about ecological thinking and protection of the environment". This can be viewed as the beginning of the establishment of a strong professional community of practice (Lave & Wenger, 1991), an initial period that Ron Tooth described to me as one of a mainly "show and tell" approach whereby the members of this group regularly shared with each other what they were doing but also reflected individually and collectively on their practices. Within communities of practice, practice is developed and refined through the collaboration of "*groups of people who share a concern, a set of problems, or a passion about a topic, and who deepen their knowledge and expertise by interacting on an ongoing basis*" (Wenger et al., 2002, p. 4).

More recently, a core group of eight Centre teams elected to become involved in research on their pedagogical approaches. This demanded a commitment of time and money to an Australian Research Council (ARC) supported project to identify the contribution of the EECs to innovation in environmental education and review the development of their pedagogies of place. As also described above, this research identified a "fifth pedagogy" of experience-based learning as a central and unique contribution of the Centres (Ballantyne & Packer, 2008). The current project explored this pedagogy in more depth in six Centres, the outcome of which is documented in this volume.

Peter and Ron conducted: observations of the participants' teaching; probing in-depth interviews (up to three hours); as well as six workshops with the writing teams. The intent of these activities was to create a dialogue to help the authors tease out and articulate (both orally and in writing) the heart and soul of what they were doing. Observations, workshop discussions and informal dialogue functioned dialectically in a deeply reflective process, the kind of which the authors, with only one exception, had not previously experienced. These dialogues stimulated both analytical and creative thinking by the participants in conceptualizing their pedagogical practices in distinctive, even novel, ways. Critical to this process was the important leadership role of the editors in assisting the other authors in this book to conceptualize and narrate the stories of their pedagogies through a process of writing as knowledge-making that included many iterations of their emerging chapters. In that respect, this group represented a professional learning community in providing "the opportunity for professionals to learn new practices and to generate new knowledge" (Harris & Jones, 2010, p. 173).

The core group came to recognize that it was the Centre staff in their specific place that shaped their pedagogy. By contextualizing learning in dialogue with place, their chapters reveal that these EEC educators realized that they can foster students' development of relationships of care and stewardship for the places in which the students live and learn (Earthwise Centre, 2016). This arguably can lead to students accepting responsibility for actively participating and responding to sustainability issues in their local community.

What characterized this professional learning community of practice?

The core group developed a clear sense of having a collective identity with shared values and vision of what an EE Centre should be. This identity developed over many years of interactions and dialogue both informally among the members and in more formal settings with outsiders who contributed a range of different environmental education perspectives and expertise. As described in Ch. 1, a key event in cementing this identity was the public identification and departmental acceptance of the important contribution being made by EECs of a distinctive pedagogy of experience-place-based pedagogy. Subsequently, a core group of EEC educators engaged in reflective inquiry in an ongoing and systematic way, culminating in the deep further learning and knowledge generation represented in this volume.

Continuous learning actually became a group norm as evidenced by the shared belief from the beginning "that ideas should be continually refined in practice" (Ch. 1, p. 6) and recently by the decision of some of the contributors to this volume to set up a kind of book club which meets four times/year where they share and discuss their individual and group learning from books or journals on education and/or the environment. Further, there are now five other Centre teams interested in becoming part of the learning community and exploring place-responsive pedagogies through a planned follow-up professional learning project that builds on the insights presented in this volume.

In sum, the articulation of the diverse pedagogies presented in the preceding chapters represents the outcome of a lengthy process of reflective inquiry, deep learning about place and its pedagogical affordances for students, and intensive dialogue and debate among the educators at each EEC, along with community members with deep knowledge of the cultural history or ecological systems of their particular place. As the principal of Nudgee Beach EEC states in Ch. 7:

> The melding of cultural, ecological and historical knowledge of the staff with the ever changing and shifting nature of the natural systems that make Nudgee Beach a powerful context for learning, it is not something that just happened by accident, but is the result of many combined experiences, meetings and influences on[f] key individuals over many years.
>
> (Ch. 7, p. 144)

These characteristics of collective identity, collaborative and continuous learning, reflective inquiry, and dialogue are identified in the literature as associated with a strong professional community. This literature emphasizes the importance of reflective inquiry by the community of practice to address the challenges they face (Newmann, King, & Youngs, 2000; Snow-Gerono, 2005) and to build teachers' shared commitment and collaboration (King, 2002). In such communities this collaboration involves creating opportunities for "good conversation" or dialogue in which the focus is on questioning and learning and where, specifically, it is safe to ask questions, and uncertainty is not only valued but supported (Snow-Gerono, 2005). These descriptors aptly capture the characteristics of the EEC core community of practice as revealed in Chapter 1.

A review of the literature revealed that "professional learning community members operate as constructivist learners, making collegial decisions and planning self-generated learning . . . [as well as] consistently increasing their effectiveness through continuous learning" (Hord, 2009, p. 43). Hord (2009) also reviewed the literature on what are the conditions for success for a community of professionals to implement constructivist learning. These include:

A   *community membership* involving a sense of having become a unit rather than a collection of individuals;
B   *time and space for learning*, whereby there is an understanding of the need to adjust one's work schedule to enable time for learning, and to find space or opportunities to gain insight into colleagues' work and reflect on their own practices; and
C   *distributed leadership* which demands a willingness of group members to share power and authority.

These characteristics and conditions can serve as a useful set of reminders to communities of practice in reflecting on their purposes and processes. In doing so, relatively newly formed professional learning communities should keep in mind that the core members of the community of EEC educators that produced this volume have been together for nearly four decades and have had the freedom to essentially operate outside or on the margins of a bureaucracy. Nevertheless, the characteristics described and supported by the broader literature represent important aspirations for any professional learning community of educators and illustrate what can be achieved through collaboration, commitment and a focus on continuous learning.

Parallels to Greenwood's decolonization and reinhabitation

One of the central strengths of this volume lies in its description of a range of pedagogical approaches that have grown out of teachers' deep and extended relationships with particular places. What is presented here demonstrates the inventive creativity that can be tapped when teachers are encouraged to become curriculum creators attentive to the possibilities of their own locales. Educators in outdoor schools as well as other environmental learning organizations will find a wealth of possibilities worth adopting themselves; these chapters should serve, as well, as a source of inspiration to do something similar. The approaches furthermore offer insight into how it is possible for place-responsive educators to actualize David Greenwood's assertion that realizing the environmental and social benefits of this approach requires attending to the need both to reinhabit our home places as well as deconstruct or decolonize the forms of thinking and behaviour that have resulted in environmental destruction and human oppression. Reinhabitation involves the process of once more becoming thoughtful and active stewards of the land, something that fits easily within the vision most environmental educators share about the nature of their own work. The creation of school gardens, litter clean-ups, the adoption of green school activities like monitoring energy use, or involving students in the removal of invasive species all contribute to reinhabitation. Decolonization, however, involves the problematic naming and exploration of beliefs and behaviours commonly accepted in modern societies that contribute to serious social and environmental ills. For Greenwood, place-based or place-responsive educators must grapple with these issues, as well, even though doing so will almost certainly require stepping into territory that could be potentially controversial. What is impressive about the work of a number of the EECs described in this volume is the way they are addressing these related concerns.

Contributing to their ability to do so is the degree to which some of the Centres have drawn heavily on the presence or stories of Aboriginal groups who were the traditional owners of the land the Centres now occupy. More than in many other nations that have been built on a history of colonization, Australia has taken important steps to acknowledge the harm associated with the assumption that two centuries ago the continent was simply there for Europeans to take, regardless of the consequences to its original inhabitants. It is now common at public meetings and sporting events to include in opening ceremonies some recognition of local Aboriginal populations. The same is true in New Zealand. This has not altered the discrimination still meted out to these populations, but it is a start. Four of the seven EECs draw upon this emerging sensibility to introduce Australian children to the nature of colonization, the kinds of assumptions associated with land and human exploitation, and alternative visions or ways of being that point to more environmentally prudent and socially equitable ways of thinking and behaving. Such learning could potentially move the process of reconciliation and full inclusion of Aboriginal peoples forward by doing more than giving lip service to the sins of the past.

At the Barambah Environmental Education Centre (BEEC), faculty there admit that the land they occupy is contested territory. Cleared of its natural resources by European settlers, it had once been the home to Wakka Wakka and Gubbi Gubbi peoples. Elders and families of these tribal groups that still live in the vicinity regularly visit the BEEC and participate in its programs and events. Over the years, a number of Aboriginal artefacts have been found on the site, and students are acquainted with these during programs there. Students are taken on a walk to the Big Fig, for example, where they are invited to sit quietly and imagine how many people over the past 50,000 years have come to this spot where a stone ax was once found, and footholds cut into a large bunya tree to provide access to cones at its crown are still in evidence. Like Aboriginal children, they are encouraged to walk through the landscape with senses fully aware and then bring that awareness to the Clan Challenge during which they locate and eat bush food, learn about tool and fire making and construct an Aboriginal shelter. These experiences can be powerful for students and lead to a deeper regard both for Indigenous peoples but also Country, itself. One Year 10 student observed, "Up until now, I always knew that the land belongs rightfully to Aboriginal Peoples, but I never comprehended that they belong to it. The land is a life source and now I want to do everything I can to protect it for future generations to come – like the Elders have done for us". (Ch. 5, p. 111)

In the Centres at Bunyaville and Paluma, students are introduced not so much to survival practices of Australian Aborigines as to their ways of being with the land. At the Bunyaville Environmental Education Centre, students are introduced to "slow learning" and encouraged to look at the forest from multiple perspectives, not only as a natural resource. Drawing upon the insights of Aboriginal and Torres Strait Island elders, teachers at the Centre encourage students to become attentive and connect emotionally and cognitively with the forest. Rather than moving rapidly from one thing to the next while on walks with students, teachers take their time to allow young people to discover the extraordinary in the ordinary. "With slow time, learners can be immersed in inquiry to sense patterns, connection and relationships between the parts of the forest system and in reflection to make meaning of their learning" (pp. 107–108). At the higher altitude Centre at Paluma, educators draw on an Aboriginal orientation to the land called *dadirri* – a deep listening to Country. Although the Centre is from an institutional standpoint secular, it aims to impart to children "a sense of the sacredness of living systems and their inherent worth" (pp. 144–145). The attentiveness and deep listening associated with the practice of *dadirri* can result in significant shifts in young people's response to the natural world. At the outset of his visit to the Centre, one boy seemed minimally interested in the natural world, but after he engaged in the practice of *dadirri*,

M's attitudes changed from looking forward to socializing with his friends to looking back longingly at the rainforest; from a desire to have an adventure, to a fascination with a concern for protection of natural places. Through the sacred experience of walking through these clouds, something profound happened to M, something good, something that could make a positive change in the future if it happens to more students like M.

(Ch. 6, p. 135)

Although the approach to decolonization encountered in these Centres does not explicitly demonstrate the attention to power relationships and exploitation often associated with critical pedagogy, teachers are nevertheless acquainting students with ways of being in the world that stand in marked contrast to perspectives regularly found in the dominant, non-Indigenous society most of them come from. They are learning that the common sense understandings they bring to their experience of the world are not the only understandings, and that other perspectives may be more in line with what is needed to shape cultures that are socially just and ecologically sustainable.

This tension between different visions of how the land is viewed and used is explored in depth at the Pullenvale Environmental Education Centre (PEEC) and often illuminated by references to Aboriginal thinking and philosophy. There, educators have adopted a pedagogical process called Storythread that they in part attribute to working with Aboriginal educators across many years. The particular Storythread described in Chapter 3 immerses students in a narrative drawn from historical sources about the killing of tropical birds in the late 19th century for the fashion industry, and an effort to protect a creek that flows through the Centre and the land around it from this form of environmental degradation. At Pullenvale, students are asked to examine explicitly an approach to land use focused primarily on profit-making rather than preservation. The title of the drama into which students become improvisational partners is "Hoodwinked," in itself an invitation to look more carefully at contrasting perspectives regarding land use. By drawing students into stories grounded in local issues, using artefacts (like a 19th-century collection of preserved birds that have since become extinct), inviting them to engage in "deep attentive and reflective listening" and giving them a chance to participate in the drama themselves, teachers create a set of experiences that can lead to a shift in ethical sensibilities and sense of agency. One boy observed, for example, that what he encountered at PEEC:

changed me because I care about things more and I like to go out into the garden now and then and just go water some flowers and stuff like that and like look after my garden.

(Ch.3, p. 63)

At some EECs, teachers focus more on Greenwood's concept of reinhabitation than decolonization, especially as this term relates to population groups that have themselves been colonized. During the Karawatha program students are acquainted with the work of a local activist named Bernice Volz whose efforts were largely responsible for the preservation of land that would have otherwise become a housing estate. Students walk into the forest at the centre and learn about Bernice's work. At the same time, they are encouraged to adopt the deep attentiveness captured by the Aboriginal term *dadirri*. They are invited to use cameras to create images that they believe represent the perspectives of different animals and to sit very still and see what animals approach them. Teachers do not tell students that they, as well, should become environmental advocates or activists, but they hope that "emotionally charged experiences and reflections" (p. 43) will impact their relationships with the natural world and willingness to speak up for places in need of protection as they grow into adulthood in the same way Bernice spoke up for the Karawatha forest. It is through such activities that natural spaces once degraded or threatened with degradation will be restored, a central aspect of reinhabitation.

The centre at Nudgee Beach does something similar by recounting the story of another environmental activist, Anne Beasley, who played a major role in preserving a beach close to the Brisbane Airport. In addition to being introduced to the constantly shifting reality of the beach and ocean at this site, students hear stories of the different people who have been in relationship with this land from the traditional Aboriginal owners to European settlers and the changes they wrought to more recent stories of people like Anne Beasley who sought to protect the beach and bay. Through these overlapping stories, students are able to gain a more complex understanding of issues tied into land use and its protection and preservation and develop a more finely tuned critical perspective about these issues. The aim of activities at the Nudgee Beach Environmental Education is to

> engender in them an appreciation of place that motivates them to care and consider how their own actions might have positive and negative impacts. Our motto, "empowering keepers of the wetlands", captures our ultimate goal but our approach is built around the primacy of experience and a heightened sensitivity to the ever-changing nature of the environment.
>
> (Ch. 7, p. 152)

Reinhabitation requires exactly this kind of willingness to be a keeper of the land sensitive to environmental changes and their implications for appropriate human responses.

Teachers at the Moreton Bay Environmental Education Centre have devised yet another way to alert students to the importance of reinhabitation. There, young people are introduced to "Champions for the Bay" from the past and present and then encouraged to become those champions in the future. As part of this process, students are asked to adopt different roles associated with preserving and restoring natural environments including junior archeologist, marine scientist, history detective, or ornithologist. With these roles in mind, students then participate in the Centre's different programs that include becoming shipwrecked ex-convicts at nearby Fort Lytton or water quality scientists on the Centre's catamaran as it ventures into the bay. As at other Centres, teachers emphasize the importance of interconnection and recognizing that damage to one element of an ecosystem will affect other elements. The experience of being a thoughtful steward is impressed upon children through the snake-line where they must walk exactly in the footsteps of the person in front of them to avoid crushing shelled creatures that live on the beach. At the end of their day at Moreton Bay, students sign a pledge to protect it.

Through simulations, role plays, direct experiences of the natural world, conversations with local activists, and opportunities for reflection, young people who visit these EECs are in subtle ways introduced to understandings that can contribute to decolonization and reinhabitation. Tooth and Renshaw argue that processes like these avoid what Bakhtin called an "authoritative discourse" that cannot be questioned and that views the perspective of the teacher as superior to that of students. Instead, students are presented with experiences that can lead them to question previously unexamined assumptions and adopt ways of interacting with the world that encourage the care and attention needed to move our societies in the direction of cultural and ecological sustainability.

Comparisons to different processes of development and governance

One of the challenges faced by place-based or place-responsive educators is tied to the question of innovation dissemination. In the early 2000s, Jack Chin, a program officer at the San Francisco-based Tides Foundation, took it upon himself to educate the philanthropic community in the Bay Area about place-based education. One of the people he hoped to persuade was Marshall (Mike) Smith, who after serving as an Assistant Secretary of Education in the Clinton Administration was asked to oversee educational grant making at the Hewlett Foundation. Smith discounted place-based education because he saw no way to bring it to scale, no way for it to quickly stimulate improved education outcomes in ways that would gain the support of either policymakers or large funders.

In some respects, Smith's judgment about bringing place-based education to scale is on target. Effective place-based approaches – like those described in this volume – cannot be mass produced in the manner of national standards and the high-stakes tests that accompany them. Place-based education is by its nature local rather than universal and dependent on the creativity and commitment of individual teachers or teams of teachers rather than multinational publishing houses with their eyes on the production of textbooks with the greatest market appeal. But finding some way to in fact disseminate place-based approaches seems imperative, especially in a period where the need for a citizenry with the critical capacity to differentiate socially just and life-enhancing policies and practices from those that are not could not be greater. It is in this regard that the evolution of Queensland's EECs is promising and could potentially serve as a model for program development and innovation dissemination in other parts of the world.

In contrast to the centrally imposed educational innovations that have dominated schools in the United States and elsewhere for nearly three decades, the curricular and instructional practices encountered in the EECs grew out of the efforts of teachers responding to the unique affordances presented by their own places. These educators were trusted enough to make good decisions that held the promise of achieving the state's desire to nurture environmentally informed and concerned citizens. These educators, however, were not operating in isolation but instead were members of a state-wide collaborative team that had articulated a common vision that undergirded their dispersed efforts. Not only this, but they also met with one another on a regular basis to share their experiments and seek one another's advice. Throughout this process, the relationships they developed engendered a responsibility to the group that contributed to a self-enforced accountability very different from the kind of fidelity now demanded of teachers forced to implement one new curriculum or another. That so many of the contributors to this book have been in their positions for two or more decades speaks to the way this kind of work environment supports longevity and the enactment of what can only be described as a calling. They are the kinds of teachers most parents hope their children will encounter at some point in their educational career.

Interestingly, this model of innovation development and dissemination is not unique to Australia. Starting in 2007, the Great Lakes Stewardship Initiative (GLSI) in Michigan (United States) has been doing something similar. Enjoined by its sponsoring organization, the Great Lakes Fisheries Trust, to prepare Michigan's youth to become citizen stewards, it adopted environmentally focused place-based educational approaches to accomplish this end. The GLSI divided Michigan into nine hubs and invited interested organizations - from universities to community foundations to educational service districts – to take on the task of developing local teachers in their region to partner with agencies, businesses, and other organizations to engage students in projects that benefited their communities and the natural environment. Aside from aligning their activities with that broad vision, staff in each of the hubs – from very urban centres like Detroit to very rural locations like Michigan's Upper Peninsula – were encouraged to identify local assets, resources, and needs around which they could organize their activities.

At least once each year, educators from the hubs gather at a state-wide conference during which they can share what they are doing and learn from one another. Staff from the different hubs meet more frequently. Each of the regions sponsors smaller gatherings during which relationships are built and good ideas shared, just as happened with the educators in Queensland's EECs. Over the nine years the GLSI has been in existence, over 1,500 teachers in 283 schools have worked with more than 80,000 students.

In Michigan, place-based education is indeed being brought to scale but in a manner that trusts teachers and students to make good decisions and that encourages them to use their own creativity and intelligence to respond appropriately to local possibilities and needs. What is being shared, in this instance, is not so much a curriculum or a specific educational method but a different perspective about what educators can be and can accomplish. That the GLSI has been able to make this process work in the era of No Child Left Behind and Race to the Top suggests that in even unfavorable institutional environments a change process that builds on a teacher's and a community's strengths may be worth pursuing by environmental and sustainability educators elsewhere. Although neither the EECs nor the Great Lakes Stewardship Initiative are likely to result in the rapid dissemination of place-based or place-responsive educational practices, both have demonstrated the capacity to develop and extend these approaches to a growing number of schools and teachers.

The relevance of pedagogies of place to schools

One of the primary strengths of the EECs is tied to their ability to provide students with intense, short-term learning experiences in primarily outdoor settings where they encounter opportunities to engage with the natural world as well as issues that tend to be substantially different from what occurs in most conventional classrooms. As presented in the preceding chapters, children's imaginations and social/ecological consciousness are seemingly touched in powerful ways that can lead to shifts in awareness as well as their sense of responsibility and self-efficacy. This volume, at least anecdotally, speaks to the impact these experiences have on some students. The challenge is that the brief amount of time teachers at the Centres have with students forces them to use activities that are primarily imaginative in nature (i.e., simulations, role plays, or dramatic presentations) or so different from what students typically encounter in school that they seem removed from the real-life experiences students encounter in their own communities. Even the observational or data collecting activities presented to children at the Centres are only rarely incorporated in most school curricula. The result is that learning encountered at the Centres seems so divorced from typical school experiences that their potential impact may be unnecessarily circumscribed.

The EEC educators have not only recognized this important concern but have worked in different ways over the years to try to address this issue through pre- and post-school visit activities. Pullenvale EEC educators, for example, work in partnership with teachers on/with their school's curriculum plans to determine the best ways to support the development of students' understanding of their relationship to their local natural and human environment. They also assist teachers in enriching their pedagogy to include place-responsive pedagogies by taking students into unique places in their local context to inquire, be reflective, and gain insight into their own ecological identity.

Ron Tooth, as principal of Pullenvale EEC, describes in the previous chapter his work with the whole school leadership team at one school with the Centre becoming in essence an extended campus of the school. The central question posed to the leadership team was: How can the school best use Centre staff to help teachers use their unique places to foster their students' identity development? The principal wanted to use a bushland area by the school as one of these places. Thus, the destination excursion and place-based site for environmental and identity learning became the local area, in addition to the Centre. Most importantly, as described in Chapter 1, EEC educators view the programs provided by the Centres as "a point of entry for leveraging positive change towards sustainable practices and values within the whole school community" (p. 10).

As described in Chapter 7, one school principal who recognized that students' deep understandings developed over time decided to send students out of the city into a natural environment over an extended period every two weeks. This enabled the Nudgee Beach EEC to work with students in depth and facilitate their reported transition *"from regarding the environment of Nudgee Beach as alien to being at ease and interested in its diverse life"* (Ch. 7, p. 146). In Term 4 the Centre staff worked in the school to consolidate the students' scientific and values learning from their experiences at the beach environment and to help them create innovative presentations to the whole school community of their year's study.

We offer some suggestions on how EEC educators might further extend their engagement with schools while acknowledging that these ideas may have already been implemented but couldn't be included in their chapters. Teachers who encounter the advantages of engaging students in citizen science activities at Moreton Bay, for example, could be supported to find relevant projects in their own locales. Those who see the benefits of acquainting children with the work of environmental advocates could seek to discover similar advocates for environmental or social justice causes in their own communities. Students could interview them and publish articles or oral histories on school websites or local newspapers or create a blog on which their writings could be freely distributed and archived.

Teachers might also incorporate long-term research projects about environmental or sustainability issues of local concern that are presented at public symposiums. Students at the Aka'ula School on Molokai in Hawaii have been doing projects like these for the past 20 years. Similar attention could be directed to the experience of lower income or discriminated groups in students' home communities. At the Young Achievers Math and Science Pilot School in Boston, second grade students investigated, among other things, the experience of homeless people and the impact of diesel exhaust on neighbourhood asthma rates and shared what they learned on a broadcast of a radio talk show hosted by one of their grandfathers. Teachers could also speak with the staff of local natural resources agencies like watershed councils and find ways to engage their students in water quality monitoring activities and data collection, something that is now happening in numerous communities.

Finally, there is no reason that language arts as well as biology teachers could not incorporate the observational and reflection activities that can be so effective at tapping into children's curiosity and often readiness to experience a sense of connectedness to nature if simply introduced to this possibility and given the time to cultivate it. Nearby parks and even cemeteries have served this purpose for a variety of schools, and if such facilities are not available, sections of a school ground can be landscaped with native plant, vegetable, butterfly, or flower gardens to provide a resource for this kind of regular and sustained rather than infrequent activity.

In these ways, experiences that at the EECs are exceptional could become common and in becoming so have even more long-lasting and significant impacts on students' acquisition of skills associated with protecting and advocating for the environment as well as their willingness to become engaged in such activities. Something like this has been happening in conjunction with the Great Lakes Stewardship Initiative where students in Detroit collect abandoned tires or weatherize draughty houses or in rural communities build bioswales[1], participate in beach clean-ups, or monitor invasive animal species like zebra mussels or rusty crawfish with underwater robots they have built themselves. Such experiences give students the opportunity to take direct responsibility for addressing issues or problems that are of local concern, empowering them to become actors within the context of their own communities rather than merely passive observers. The simulations they participate in and the narratives they hear at the EECs could then serve to alert both themselves and their teachers to these expansive possibilities.

It's useful to remember, as well, the kinds of learning experiences that can take place outside the regular curriculum. After-school clubs can provide a setting to explore these possibilities freed from the constraints of standards and tests. A number of years ago in Wausau, Wisconsin, two upper elementary school teachers started a club called the You Can Do It League. Drawing on models from a national program in the U.S. of the same name, they worked with sixth graders after school to identify community problems they wanted to address. One of these involved finding ways to encourage the city and county to build a bike path between parks on the Fox River that were connected by only a county road on which cars travelled at over 50 miles per hour. As students investigated this issue, they learned that adult decision-makers had earlier attempted to construct this bike path but failed because of their inability to persuade some property owners along the proposed route to grant the easements needed to complete the project. When students approached the same property owners, however, the owners granted the easements and the path was built. This project demonstrates exactly the kind of problem solving, advocacy and action demonstrated by the individuals honoured by some of the Centres. In addition, access to the bike path gave children growing up in this community the opportunity to have experiences in nature that could reinforce lessons about interconnectedness and care like those encountered at the Centres. The EECs could serve as the inspiration for similar projects and ideally provide venues at which teachers and potential agency partners could gather on a regular basis to consider potential projects students in nearby regions could adopt.

Conclusion

Historically, the EE Centres in Queensland were organised to be centrally administered yet emphasize the unique or special characteristics of each Centre's location and the implications for development of distinct pedagogical approaches appropriate for their unique settings. Now over 40 years since the founding of this network of Centres throughout this large and diverse state, the various pedagogies of place developed by educators in several of these Centres have been documented in the preceding chapters. The authors have contributed to pedagogical theorizing, addressing not only the means to environmental education but also the ends and expanding the concept of pedagogical content knowledge in outdoor environmental education. They also have provided vignettes of their teaching with visiting students and extracts from interviews with children to use for "further reflection, theorizing, and subsequent actions" (Noffke, 1997, p. 323). This theorizing, research and practice occurred in a long-serving professional learning community of practice, supported by two funded research projects.

In contrast to dominant conceptions of teacher learning as either acquiring formal knowledge generated in universities or developing practical knowledge from teachers' reflections on practice, Cochran-Smith and Lytle (1999) argue for a third conception whereby "teachers learn when they generate local knowledge of practice by working within the contexts of inquiry communities to theorize and construct their work and to connect it to larger social, cultural, and political issues" (p. 250). If environmental is added to the list of issues, then this succinctly captures the professional learning and practice of the community of environmental educators in this volume.

Note

1 Bioswales are landscape elements designed to concentrate or remove silt and pollution from surface runoff water. They consist of a drainage course with gently sloped sides and filled with vegetation and/or compost.

References

Ballantyne, R., & Packer, J. (2008). Learning for sustainability: The role and impact of Outdoor and Environmental Education Centres. St Lucia: School of Tourism, University of Queensland.

Ballantyne, R., & Packer, J. (2009). Introducing a fifth pedagogy: Experience-based strategies for facilitating learning in natural environments. *Environmental Education Research*, 15(2), 243–262.

Cochran, K. F. (1997). Pedagogical content knowledge: Teachers' integration of subject matter, pedagogy, students, and learning environments. *Research Matters – to the Science Teacher*, NARST Publications, No. 9702. Retrieved from www.narst. org/publications/research/pck.cfm

Cochran, K. F., DeRuiter, J. A., & King, R. A. (1993). Pedagogical content knowledge: An integrative model for teacher preparation. *Journal of Teacher Education*, 44(4), 263–271.

Cochran-Smith, M., & Lytle, S. (1999). Relationships of knowledge and practice: Teacher learning in communities. *Review of Research in Education*, 24(1), 249–305.

Earthwise Centre. (2016). Vision, *Mission & Principles*. Retrieved from http:// educationforsustainability.info/about/vision-mission-principles/

Gruenewald, D. A. (2003). The best of both worlds: A critical pedagogy of place. *Educational Researcher*, 32(4), 3–12.

Harris, A., & Jones, M. (2010). Professional learning communities and system improvement. *Improving Schools*, 13(2), 172–181.

Hord, S. (2009). Professional learning communities. *Journal of Staff Development*, 30(1), 40–43.

Karrow, D., & Fazio, X. (2010). Viewpoint: NatureWatch, schools and environmental education practice. *Canadian Journal of Science, Mathematics and Technology Education, 10*(2), 160–172.

King, M. B. (2002). Professional development to promote schoolwide inquiry. *Teaching and Teacher Education, 18*(3), 243–257.

Lave, J. & Wenger, E. (1991). *Situated Learning: Legitimate Peripheral Participation*. Cambridge university press.

Little, J. W. (1982). Norms of collegiality and experimentation: Workplace conditions of school success. *American Educational Research Journal, 19*(3), 325–340.

Mannion, G., Fenwick, A., & Lynch, J. (2013). Place-responsive pedagogy: Learning from teachers' experiences of excursions in nature. *Environmental Education Research, 19*(6), 792–809.

Newmann, F. M., King, M. B., & Youngs, P. (2000). Professional development that addresses school capacity: Lessons from urban elementary schools. *American Journal of Education, 108*(4), 259–299.

Noffke, S. (1997). Professional, personal, and political dimensions of action research. *Review of Research in Education, 22*, 305–343.

Rowan, B., Schilling, S. G., Ball, D. L., & Miller, R. (2001). *Measuring teachers' pedagogical content knowledge in surveys: An exploratory study*. Ann Harbor: Consortium for Policy Research in Education.

Shulman, L. S. (1986). Those who understand: Knowledge growth in teaching. *Educational Researcher, 15*(2), 4–31.

Snow-Gerono, J. L. (2005). Professional development in a culture of inquiry: PDS teachers identify the benefits of professional learning communities. *Teaching and Teacher Education, 21*(3): 241-256.

Thomashow, M. (1996). Ecological identity: Becoming a reflective environmentalist. Cambridge, MA: MIT Press.

Wenger, E. (2000). Communities of practice and social learning systems. *Organization, 7*(2), 225–246.

Wenger, E., McDermott, R., & Snyder, W. (2002). *Cultivating communities of practice*. Cambridge, MA: Harvard Business School Press.

Index

For Product Safety Concerns and Information please contact our EU
representative GPSR@taylorandfrancis.com
Taylor & Francis Verlag GmbH, Kaufingerstraße 24, 80331 München, Germany

www.ingramcontent.com/pod-product-compliance
Ingram Content Group UK Ltd.
Pitfield, Milton Keynes, MK11 3LW, UK
UKHW021613240425
457818UK00018B/533